First Edition

Common Core
Support Coach

TARGET ► Reading Comprehension 8

Common Core Support Coach, Target: Reading Comprehension, First Edition, Grade 8
T231NA   ISBN-13: 978-1-62362-010-3
Cover Design: Q2A/Bill Smith   **Cover Illustration:** Scott Balmer

Triumph Learning® 136 Madison Avenue, 7th Floor, New York, NY 10016

Contents

Fiction

Nonfiction

Common Core
State Standards

RI.8.1, RI.8.10, L.8.4.c,
L.8.4.d, L.8.5.b, RH.6-8.1,
RH.6-8.2, RH.6-8.9

Tools

Graphic Organizers and Close Reading Worksheets

Fiction

Fiction is any story made up by an author. Fiction includes many genres, like mystery, historical fiction, and science fiction. The story you are about to read belongs to the science fiction genre because it takes place in the future and includes imagined technologies, such as regular space travel between planets. What genre would you expect to read if this picture were a part of the story? How do you know?

Skills Focus

Across the Stars, Part I

Sequence | Plot Elements

Across the Stars, Part II

Make Predictions

Differences in Points of View

Practice the Skill

Sequence is the order of events in a story. The author of a fictional work puts events into a specific order to create meaning. For instance, an author might begin a story in the middle of the action, tell what led up to that moment, and then go on to tell the rest of the story. This is a common storytelling form. Starting in the middle creates a sense of excitement and grabs your interest. Later, when you unravel all the events that make up the plot, you can infer the order in which events would have actually taken place. Then you can analyze why the author might have switched the order of things around.

The clues for determining sequence within a text are words like *before*, *after*, *next*, and *then*. These words can help you put events into the proper order so you can better understand the plot.

Try It Read the following paragraph.

> Elena turned her bicycle over, balancing it on its handlebars and rear fender. Next, she worked the flat tip of a screwdriver between the tire and the steel rim, eventually popping enough of the rubber tire out so that she could pull out the inner tube. She then held the tube in a tub of water. Finally, she squeezed the tube and located the stream of bubbles that revealed where the hole in her tube was.

Discuss Think about sequence. Which words in the paragraph above tell you the order in which Elena is performing these actions? Underline the words you identify. What does the sequence of events tell you about what Elena is doing here?

As you read, complete the Sequence Chart on page 281.

Practice the Skill

Plot is the series of incidents that propels the action in a story. A well-written plot is one that keeps the reader engaged, eager to turn the page to see what happens next. Each of the following plot elements helps to move the story from its introduction, through its conflict, and finally to its resolution.

- **Exposition:** the story's beginning, where the characters and setting are introduced
- **Rising action:** the point where the story's main problem or conflict is introduced
- **Climax:** the turning point, which may involve great physical danger or strong emotions for the main characters
- **Falling action:** the point at which the story begins to wind down
- **Resolution:** the story's end, where conflicts are resolved and loose ends are tied up

Dialogue is another element that helps move a story along. Characters often reveal their reactions to plot events through their dialogue. These reactions can help you determine which plot events the author considers most significant.

Try It Read the following scene.

> Rico knew that if his article wasn't submitted in the next half hour, Candace would break the story first. If she did, she'd probably win entrance to the Summer Geniuses Program, which he'd been working toward all year.
>
> As Rico wrote furiously, he thought of his brother's advice, but he just couldn't bring himself to take it. Even though he'd gotten to the scene of the accident long before Candace, who had broken the rules by crossing the police tape, he was dead set on following the rules. The clock's hands clicked louder and louder. His fingers raced over the laptop's keys. He'd show everyone how a genius operates under pressure.

Discuss What is the conflict? What details support your ideas? Circle the phrases that refer to the larger story this scene is likely a part of.

As you read, record your answers to questions about plot on the Close Reading Worksheet on page 282.

Purpose for Reading

Read along with your teacher. Each time, read for a different purpose.

First Read	Focus on the sequence of events.
Second Read	Focus on plot elements.
Third Read	Focus on evaluating the story critically.

ACROSS THE STARS, PART I

CHAPTER 1
A Sense of Mission

Underline four things Captain Diaz does in this part of the story. Write the actions on the **Sequence Chart**.

How do Captain Diaz's actions propel the plot?

1   The ship's computers woke Edgardo Diaz first. Groggy from months of **cryogenic** sleep, the captain of the *Pegasus* slid into the ship's pilot seat and punched a button on the control panel. The universe spread out before him, a black velvet blanket studded with diamonds. He cleared his eyes, focusing on an object in the middle of the star field—a planet getting larger by the second. He'd have to "defrost" the rest of the crew soon, but for the moment, Captain Diaz gazed out across the stars, pondering the mission ahead.

2   A signal had indicated there was life on Pleiades 19, or they wouldn't have ventured 140 light-years[1] from Earth. Each of the *Pegasus*'s six crew members had been hand-selected to make contact with whatever life there was.

3   Captain Diaz woke the Karpelys first. Adel and her husband Paulus were in their midsixties—not the best candidates for space travel, one might think, yet their skills were vital. Paulus was an engineer and Adel a psychiatrist, whose presence Captain Diaz found calming whenever he addressed his crew.

4   Standing at the head of the table, Captain Diaz took in the freshly showered faces: Holly Matson, his second in command, bleary-eyed but excited; Raquel Shapira, a protective arm around her eleven-year-old son, Victor. They were a team, experts in the elite field of speculative archaeology, and Victor had a particular genius for deciphering random patterns.

[1]**light-year** the distance light can travel in a year. Light travels 186,000 miles every second.

5   "Our mission is critical, since Earth is in crisis—we need new technologies and new ideas if our world is to survive. As you know, our scientists detected radio signals from this planet twenty years ago, and we believe those signals were an invitation from alien beings, who, if they still exist, may well represent the last best hope for humanity."

6   Captain Diaz pressed a button, and Pleiades 19 came up on the view screen, a blue-green marble streaked with veins of jade green.

7   "It looks good enough to eat," Victor said, gazing at the shining sphere.

8   Most of the crew laughed, but Adel scowled, warning them, "We don't know if we'll find intelligent life, since even if the signal was real, that civilization could have collapsed by the time we get there. The universe is so massive that even at the speed of light, it takes a long time for a signal to travel across it—it's actually been hundreds of years since they made the broadcast."

9   "We have to hope," said Holly, her words trailing off.

10   "Even if we don't find a living civilization," Raquel added, "whatever they left behind could be useful."

11   "Hope aside, it's time to get to work," the captain said.

12   After the briefing, Captain Diaz and Paulus headed for the launch bay, where Paulus, the ship's masterful engineer, began tinkering with the expedition's robotic vehicle. Big as a truck, it was built of subrobots in a variety of sizes that could detach and function on their own. The machine's technical name was AR860, but everyone called it Artie. Like a mobile factory, Artie would build the devices and structures they'd need as they explored the planet.

13   "It's time to switch him on," said Paulus, and tiny lights glittered to life on the robot's control panel.

14   "Greetings, Captain Diaz," a warm human voice said with a slight southern accent, "I assume we've achieved orbital status."

List the main events in paragraphs 6–13 in the correct order on the **Sequence Chart.**

How does the dialogue on this page set up the rest of the story?

Why does Captain Diaz make the point about the importance of the team's mission?

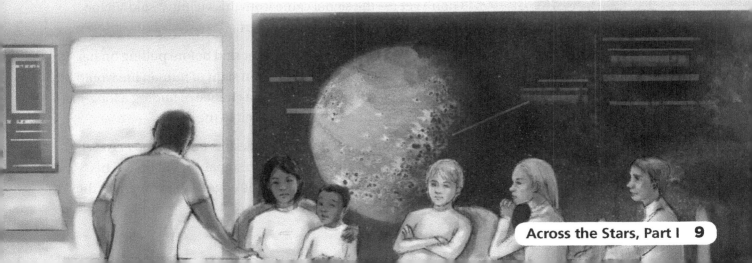

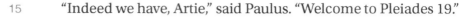

Circle textual evidence that hints at Victor's conflict.

What is the main role Raquel plays in the plot?

15   "Indeed we have, Artie," said Paulus. "Welcome to Pleiades 19."

16   After the captain's briefing, Raquel and Victor returned to their tiny cabin. Victor sat on the bed, shoulders slumped. "They think I shouldn't have come, that I'm just a kid," he muttered.

17   "Not the ones who know, Victor, and that's who you have to listen to," Raquel said quietly. "Remember when you deciphered your first glyph? You were only seven then. How is this any different?" She was trying to reassure her son, but so far she hadn't succeeded. "The way your mind works, Victor, is a gift—but you have to believe in it."

18   Victor rubbed the back of his head, as if he were stroking the brain that had put him in this position, light-years from home, with all the responsibilities of a grown-up.

19   "Come on—your job's simple compared to mine," Raquel laughed, adding, "since I have to actually find the stuff, while all you have to do is read the label!"

20   Victor smiled weakly and said, "We're a team, right?"

CHAPTER 2
Touchdown

21   The landing was rough, but it wasn't Holly's fault—she was forced to dodge boulders that hadn't shown up on the scanner. When the *Pegasus* finally came to a stop, everyone was OK—though a trench stretching like a wound extended for half a mile in their wake.

22   "Looks like we're here," someone muttered.

23   "Artie's on his way in," said Captain Diaz, glancing at a monitor.

24   Victor and his mother watched through a portal as the robot landed near them in a towering pillar of jade-green dust, then wasted no time assembling small robots that headed out in all directions, questing for signs of life.

25   "I don't get it—the signal came from this vicinity," said Victor, looking out the porthole at empty desert.

26   "If you landed on Earth," his mother said before pulling on her helmet, "your chances of landing within sight of human life would be **infinitesimal**. You'd have just as good a chance of finding a long-lost shipwreck the first time you ever jumped in the ocean."

27   Victor and Raquel put on their spacesuits and left the *Pegasus*, headed toward the location of the radio signal. As Victor and his mother hiked toward a distant ridge, the edge of the vast crater they'd

landed in, they chatted over their helmets' closed-circuit radios that allowed them to communicate.

28   "Just keep in mind, this signal could mean anything" Raquel said. "Remember those shapes you saw in the jungle that turned out to be a Mayan temple, in Mexico?"

29   Victor held his silence—he was concentrating hard, ignoring the tiny robots that scuttled nearby, analyzing soil for traces of life.

30   Trekking through the wide crater to the ridge took hours. They paused just short of the ridge's knife edge, and the little robots, unable to negotiate the ascent, fanned out across the soft green plain behind them and waited.

31   Victor scrambled up the crater's lip to the top of the ridge.

32   *Cities are like writing*, he told himself, gazing out over another plain beyond—whether modern and alive or ancient and dead, they were scribbles on a planet's surface. The green plain beyond was studded with gargantuan stones, like the ones they'd dodged coming in. The atmosphere was clear, the air motionless—immaculate viewing conditions—so he cranked the magnification on his helmet's visor.

33   *Nothing but randomness*, he thought, but then his radio squawked.

34   "We've got something here, Blue Team," Artie drawled, addressing Victor and his mom. "Right in your neck of the woods, approximately 50 miles from where you're standing now. It's 48.7 miles precisely, to the north and west."

35   Victor followed the coordinates, amplifying his visor's magnification to maximum. On the distant horizon, he could see a dark object moving fast—one of Artie's explorer robots, kicking up a rooster tail of dust the color of fresh grass or **verdigris** as it plunged between a pair of boulders.

36   Only they weren't boulders.

Find three important events on this page. Write them in the order they happen on the **Sequence Chart**.

How does Artie see something Victor doesn't notice at first?

CHAPTER 3
Ancient Days

Victor notices that the boulders are far too regular to be natural. Why is this important to the plot?

37   Victor willed his heart to simmer down. The "boulders" were far too regular to be natural. He saw hundreds of them, all sitting upright, casting elongated shadows in the afternoon light. They were all about twenty feet tall and seemed to have been **hewn** by machine—or superb craftspeople. The rows of boulders stretched for miles, beyond the horizon.

38   Artie showed up with the rest of the crew, having converted into rover form and gathered them all up just minutes after Raquel's call. Victor and Raquel climbed aboard with the rest. Everyone was excited—except for Adel, who remained her usual skeptical self, though as the team's morale officer, she had the courtesy to hide it. Finding a path Artie could negotiate to the standing stones proved difficult—the land was crisscrossed with dry riverbeds that carved deep gullies into the surface. But soon they found one that led toward the boulders, and Holly accelerated, speeding fast along the river bottom.

Synthesize

Based on the plot so far and the talents of the characters, what will likely be true about the stone blocks? Cite textual evidence from the story to support your ideas.

39   "Riverbeds are a good sign," Raquel explained, "because the more water, the better the chance for civilization."

40   "But what if they're all dry?" Victor asked. "Doesn't that mean the inhabitants are long gone?"

41   "Earth has plenty of dry riverbeds, Victor," said Captain Diaz, "and anyway, the stones are situated pretty much exactly where the radio signal came from in the first place."

42   The rover bucked hard as Artie skipped across ancient mud ripples. Victor was thinking, *a 140-year-old radio signal, twenty years to plan the expedition, then 140 years for us to get here—will anyone still be here after three hundred years?*

Vocabulary: Context Clues

When you come across a word that stumps you, often just reading ahead or looking back a sentence or two will give you a clue to its meaning. These clues in the surrounding text are called context clues. **Context clues** are words or phrases near an unknown word that help you determine the unknown word's meaning.

Try It Read the opening paragraph of "Across the Stars."

The ship's computers woke Edgardo Diaz first. Groggy from months of **cryogenic** sleep, the captain of the *Pegasus* slid into the ship's pilot seat and punched a button on the control panel. The universe spread out before him, a black velvet blanket studded with diamonds. He cleared his eyes, focusing on an object in the middle of the star field—a planet getting larger by the second. He'd have to "defrost" the rest of the crew soon, but for the moment, Captain Diaz gazed out across the stars, pondering the mission ahead.

If you don't know what the word *cryogenic* means, read the other words in the paragraph. Underline the words that help you figure out the meaning of *cryogenic*.

Discuss **Brainstorm definitions of the word *cryogenic*.**

The following are some difficult words found in "Across the Stars." Find the words in the story. Underline the context clues that help you understand what each word means. Write a definition of each word and use it in a sentence.

1. **infinitesimal,** p. 10 _____

_____

2. **verdigris,** p. 11 _____

_____

3. **hewn,** p. 12 _____

_____

Practice the Skill

When you make **predictions**, you consider what has happened so far in the story and make a forecast about what might happen next. You think carefully about the text and decide what seems likely based on what you know about life in general, about fiction stories, and about the specific story's plot.

A good prediction takes everything into account—what the text hints might happen, the things characters say and do and what they think about the future, and what you already know about how plots usually work. You can test the accuracy of your predictions by seeing if something you guessed beforehand happens in the story.

Try It Read the following opening to a story.

Back from the Brink

Sylvia grabbed the last of the D cell batteries. Her hands were too full. She had to set down the album of photographs she wanted but didn't need. Out in the driveway, her daughter Marcy leaned on the horn, annoyed that she was missing another soccer game because of weather. The water was coming fast, and all Marcy could think of were the soccer fields. Grabbing the batteries, Sylvia ran to the car.

As she drove, Sylvia could barely handle looking back and seeing the wind tearing through the trees and the water at the end of their street creeping toward their neighbors' houses.

Discuss **What do you predict will happen next in the story? Underline details that helped you make your prediction.**

As you read, complete the Make Predictions Chart on page 283.

Practice the Skill

Point of view is a term that can describe how the author, the characters, and you, the reader, view the events of a story. For example, a character might express bravery in the face of danger, while you are afraid of what might happen to the character. Or the author might describe how dangerous an experience is, but the character reveals only how brave and strong he feels. These two differing points of view can create suspense in a story.

Differing points of view can create a number of effects, such as suspense, humor, irony, and tension. For example, **dramatic irony** occurs when you know something that the characters do not know. For example, you might know that a character is about to learn devastating news, while the character thinks she's having a lovely day.

Try It Read the next scene from "Back from the Brink."

> When Sylvia and Marcy arrived at Sylvia's brother Jerome's house, Marcy was still sulking. Jerome and Sylvia were staring silently at the TV as images of flooded neighborhoods flashed across the screen. Sylvia wondered how high the water was on their street and when she'd be able to return to see it. Meanwhile, all Marcy could think about was when she'd be able to play soccer again. She didn't care about the flooding or what the reporters were saying on the news. Even at her uncle Jerome's house, she couldn't practice, because it was still raining.

Discuss How do Marcy's and Sylvia's points of view differ? Circle details that show what each character is thinking. As a reader, what is your point of view about what is happening?

As you read, consider how the story makes you feel—your own point of view. Do you find yourself siding with particular characters? Do you think your point of view coincides with that of any character?

> As you read, record your answers to questions about point of view on the Close Reading Worksheet on page 284.

Purpose for Reading
Read along with your teacher. Each time, read for a different purpose.

First Read   Focus on making predictions.

Second Read   Focus on differences in points of view.

Third Read   Focus on evaluating the story critically.

ACROSS THE STARS, PART II

CHAPTER 4
A Clue

What facts from the story support a prediction that the stones are not natural? Write the facts on the **Make Predictions Chart**.

Circle textual evidence that shows Victor is nervous about the mission.

1   By the time they got to the location from which the radio signal had been transmitted, night had fallen.

2   "Let's circle the wagons, people," Captain Diaz announced with authority, "and tomorrow morning, we'll see what we've got here."

3   It wasn't the **cramped** quarters of the rover that kept Victor awake that night, it was whether or not the stones had writing on them and, if they did, whether he could decipher it. The whole weight of the mission had fallen upon his small shoulders. What if he came up short?

4   The pearly green of dawn took some getting used to—the light from Sirius, the nearest star, flowed around the crew members like ripples in a placid lake as they emerged from the rover and suited up for exploration. As the mission archaeologist, Raquel took command, ordering teams to fan out in a pattern based on the stones' layout.

5   Victor tried to calm his thumping heart. The mustard-yellow blocks of stone now showed themselves to be all different shapes—some were L-shaped, while others were curving, serpentine walls the length of a city block—and the only thing they had in common was their machine-made appearance and their twenty-foot height.

6   Raquel and Victor paused before one of the stones, examining its deeply worn and pitted surface—had it been scoured by wind?

7   "Our research showed they get major sandstorms around this time of year," Raquel explained, "and that's why the sky's green instead of blue—dust dissipates into the atmosphere."

8   As they focused on the divots in the stone, a voice suddenly broke over the radio.

9   "All teams, this is Holly—I think I have something here." She gave her position and then added, "I think I need Victor."

10   When Raquel and Victor reached them, Holly and Paulus's smiles shone behind their helmet visors. The worn surface of the stone they'd found was shrouded in carvings—shallow grooves and finger-size divots covered the stone from top to bottom and on all four sides.

11   "They're so . . . primitive," Adel croaked, dismissing the stones.

12   "Is it writing, Victor?" Paulus asked.

13   Victor shrugged before replying, "I have to investigate it, Paulus, and that takes time."

14   Victor continued to gaze at the carvings, lost in thought. After a minute, he spoke again. "Actually, team, I suspect there may be no intelligence here. I don't see anything approaching a pattern. But like I said," he added, "I'll need some time."

15   The discouraged crew members made their way back to the rover, where in the rover's workroom, Victor and Raquel pored over the images they had taken of the stones. Tension filled the air as, once in a while, crew members dropped by to watch the boy poised over the strange, erratic markings.

16   A few more samples of the squiggles had been found, one of them on a stone that had broken down completely. The shattered rock exposed clearly what they all suspected—the standing stones were solid, not structures or some alien form of data storage or machines.

17   Everything came down to the writing, and Victor just couldn't figure it out.

What do you predict Victor will find in the stone carvings? Record your prediction and the textual evidence that supports it on the **Make Predictions Chart.**

How do most of the crew members feel about the mission so far? Describe your point of view on the mission at this point in the story.

Across the Stars, Part II   17

Now that you've read the story, what's an example of dramatic irony that occurs when Adel says she thinks she sees a pattern? What do you know that she doesn't? What effect does this have?

Why do Captain Diaz and Paulus think they might stay for months? What do you hope to find? Cite textual evidence to support your ideas.

18   "Mom, I just don't get it," Victor said, as Raquel sat down next to him. "I know that an alien culture might have patterns different from ours, or they might not even have patterns like we know them—but even *that* is a pattern. And there's nothing here." He looked up at his mother. "I mean, like, *nothing.*"

19   "I think you should talk to Adel," Raquel urged her son.

CHAPTER 5
The Writing on the Wall

20   "Sometimes the best thing you can do is not to think at all," Adel advised Victor as they were sitting in the room she shared with her husband, Paulus. They were alone—Paulus was outside helping Captain Diaz work on a more permanent **dwelling**. The mission might well take months, and they would be more comfortable in something that better resembled a **home**. As Diaz had put it, if aliens had landed on Earth, how much time would they spend exploring the great pyramids in Egypt before they stumbled on Cairo, where they'd find people and civilization?

21   "Yes, Adel, I do that—I blank my mind and look at the figures again. If something has a meaning, I may not know exactly what it says, but I see the patterns almost right away—this just looks like gobbledegook."

22   Adel peered at the screen between them and conjectured, "Some of these do seem to repeat, Victor, like the little squiggles—I mean, I know I'm the skeptical one, but I do believe I see something."

23   "Think about a seashore, Adel," Victor said, "where you see patterns—repeated shapes, like scalloped sand when the tide goes out. Nature leaves patterns, but they're random—honestly, that's what this is, just random."

24   "But you can't be sure, Victor," Holly said, coming through the door, adding, "I mean, I know you're a smart kid, but what else could this be?"

25   Suddenly Paulus poked his head in and interrupted, "Wait a minute . . . something about seashores . . . I'm an engineer, so bear with me, because I think in terms of machines. You see rocks on the shore all the time that are scarred with divots just like these," he thought aloud, then peered up at everyone, his face a puzzle. "They're made by worms called piddocks."

26   Of course! The natural explanation suddenly lifted the weight from Victor's shoulders, relieving pressure so intense, he felt himself almost

rising up from the rover's metal deck. The need to squeeze meaning out of squiggles that held none had vanished.

27   The lifting sensation gave him an idea, so Victor visited Captain Diaz alone in his cabin, where he summoned the nerve to say, "I have a request, sir." He could hardly keep the excitement out of his voice, but he needed to be taken seriously.

28   "Calling me *sir* now, eh?" Captain Diaz smiled broadly and asked, "So, what's your big request?"

29   Victor explained what he needed, and Captain Diaz grunted his approval. A couple of hours later, Artie had built what Victor asked for.

30   "It's good for about five hundred feet up, not much altitude after that," Artie said. Beneath the robot's bulk lay its latest creation, a hovercraft custom-made for Victor.

31   "Tell me you're not going up in that," his mother said as the crew gathered around.

32   "Artie made it, Mom, so it's plenty safe," Victor asserted.

33   Victor climbed in and saw that the controls were clearly marked, and the crew crouched against the blast of dust as the hovercraft lurched skyward.

34   Peering out from his perch, Victor saw it right away. The sun's low angle let him read the stones as clearly as a book, because that was what they were—the stones *themselves* were writing.

35   Deciphering the writing took only a few hours—Victor found the stones' code easier to crack than Mayan glyphs—and when he was done, the crew assembled in his cabin to hear Victor read the alien words aloud.

Now that you know the stones themselves are writing, what do you predict will happen next? Write what you think in the **Make Predictions Chart.**

How does your point of view change because of Victor's newfound excitement? What effect does this have on the story?

The story ends with a cliff-hanger. What do you think will happen next? Record your prediction and the reasons you made it on the **Make Predictions Chart**.

Why doesn't the narrator ever reveal what kind of danger Earth is in?

Connect

How do the talents of each team member help them work together to succeed in the mission? Cite textual evidence to support your answer.

36   *Traveler, we salute you, for you have crossed the halls of space, and you have mastered science and language. We trust you come in peace. We dwell below now. Where this message ends, we can be found.*

37   The crew was all stunned, none more than Adel, who said humbly, "I know I've always doubted. I guess that's been my job—the voice of reason—but I never doubted *you*, Victor." Her eyes wrinkled into the warmest smile Victor had ever seen as she added, "and I never will."

38   While they waited all afternoon for Artie to fashion itself into a digging machine, Captain Diaz and Paulus took careful measurements near the stone Victor said was the last in the message.

39   Artie began to dig at the spot Paulus decided was the right one. Suddenly Artie came flying out of the hole, and the robot barely had time to curl into a ball before it hit the ground with an impressive thud. Following immediately behind it, a vast, shining steel column plowed up through the sand, a small door appearing in its flank like a miniature elevator as green dust flew everywhere.

40   Victor shuddered—not with fear but joy, for the message had spoken of peace and trust, and now he felt both.

41   His mother rested her hand on Victor's shoulder, Captain Diaz straightened himself and brushed the sand from his suit, the Karpelys hugged, and Holly smoothed back her hair.

42   The door slid open.

Vocabulary: Distinguish between Denotation and Connotation

Denotation and **connotation** are two varieties of meaning that a word can have. Denotation is the literal, dictionary meaning of a word. Connotation refers to the feeling or idea that a word expresses. Words with similar denotations can have positive, negative, or neutral connotations. Think about the words *stingy* and *thrifty*. Both words refer to someone who doesn't spend a lot of money, but a *stingy* person is thought of more negatively than is a *thrifty* person.

Try It Read these sentences.

"Anna finally won a race," Donnie grumbled.

"Anna finally won a race," Chuck cheered.

"Anna finally won a race," Jenny said.

Discuss **Which verb at the end of a sentence has a positive connotation? Circle it. Which has a negative connotation? Box it. Which has a neutral connotation? Underline it.**

The following are words from "Across the Stars" that have definite connotations. Find the words in the story. Write whether each word has a positive, negative, or neutral connotation. Then explain why that connotation fits the sentence in "Across the Stars."

1. **cramped,** p. 16 _____

   _____

2. **dwelling,** p. 18 _____

   _____

3. **home,** p. 18 _____

   _____

Respond to Text: Point of View

In "Across the Stars," each character has a distinct point of view. As a reader, you may also have had your own point of view about the events and the characters' actions.

Try It Think about the points of view suggested by different characters in the story.

 Discuss **What do Captain Diaz's thoughts as he first looks out at Pleiades 19 reveal about his point of view regarding what will happen on the planet? What is Victor's main concern, and what is his mother's? How is Adel's point of view expressed? Is your point of view similar to that of any of the characters? If not, how does it differ?**

On Your Own Write a paragraph that describes the differences in points of view of the characters and you as a reader in "Across the Stars." What effect do these differences create in the story? Include details from the story to support your response. Use the next page to help you plan your response. Then write your paragraph on a separate piece of paper.

Checklist for a Good Response

A good paragraph

✔ describes the points of view of the characters.

✔ describes your own point of view as a reader.

✔ identifies the effect created from the differences in point of view.

✔ includes details from the text to support your conclusions.

✔ shows your understanding of what you have read.

✔ includes a topic sentence, supporting ideas, and a concluding statement.

Comparing My Point of View and the Characters'

1. **Topic Sentence** Include this information in your first sentence:

   The differences in point of view in "Across the Stars" create

   _____

2. **Detail Sentences** In each row, compare or contrast the point of view of two or more characters (including the narrator) and note how that similarity or difference creates an effect in the story. Use your own point of view in one row. Use this chart to organize your ideas.

Characters' Points of View	How the Point of View Creates

3. **Concluding Sentence** Your final sentence should restate your conclusions with a new twist.

   _____

   _____

On a separate sheet of paper, write your paragraph.

Read on Your Own

Read the story independently three times, using the skills you have learned. Then answer the Comprehension Check questions.

First Read — Practice the first-read skills you learned in this lesson.

Second Read — Practice the second-read skills you learned in this lesson.

Third Read — Think critically about the ideas in the selection.

The History of Disaster

Make Predictions Think about how the narrator's father's knowledge of old objects from daily life will be of use in the family's current situation.

Plot Elements What incident propels the plot here? Underline the first reference to it.

Critical Thinking Think about why the storm and America's past are so closely related.

1   When I say my sister and I were critical of dad, you have to understand we didn't mean anything so mundane or silly as his parenting style or his approach to household economics. No, Elyse's and my feelings ran deeper than that—and I think our mother shared them. I'd bet you would, too. Because the truth is, we found what he does for a hobby boring, and what he does is study and collect antiques. He does not just collect old furniture and knickknacks, either, but casts them as "objects in daily life that create their own historiological significance" or something like that.

2   As I said: boring and of very little use—until Hurricane Zane.

3   Obviously it was a record year, since named storms usually peter out before they get far down the alphabetical list of names. The farthest along I could remember was Tony. This year we added Uma, Vincent, Wendy, Xavier, Yolanda, and now Zane, roaring toward our house on the New Jersey Shore like the clichéd freight train.

4   Except this was real, so the fact that it sounded like an actual train wasn't amusing—it was terrifying. Fortunately, while Dad is boring, he's smart, too, and we rode out the storm in style. However, we wound up with a house that, while intact in every other way, was missing a key utility: electricity.

5   My sister has a tendency to look on the bright side that I do not share. All she talked about was playing board games by candlelight. All I could imagine was having to bathe with the water so close to ice, it seemed to flow slower out of the faucet.

6   But to this problem, there was a solution—one drawn from America's not-too-distant past.

7   Dad introduced us to the concept of boiling water in vast quantities.

8   Long ago he'd bought a giant pot that we thought was just good for cooking lobsters. As it happened, it worked extra well as an all-purpose hot water reservoir. We still had gas, so with the stove on low, we could keep this **cistern**—as Dad called it—constantly on simmer. Just dip in a big brass ladle Dad had also collected. Then fill a can and get clean or make a cup of tea or some instant oatmeal.

9   You may ask how we carried all this hot water safely from place to place in the dark. That was, I have to admit, one of Dad's greatest strokes. When he emerged from the cellar carrying a pair of railroad-style hurricane lamps, each **glowing** like a separate sun, he exclaimed, "Let there be light!"

10   Mom and Elyse clapped their hands, and truth be told, I was (happy) to settle down to games of chess and checkers and backgammon, warmed by a roaring fire and illuminated by the tangerine glow of oil lamps and candles. With its crackling pinesap and candles and oil stove smells, the air conjured winter holidays and summer camp all at once. You could focus on playing a game because, well, other than windblown branches tapping the windows, there wasn't a whole lot else to contemplate.

Make Predictions Think about how the narrator will feel about his father by the end of the story.

Differences in Points of View How does the narrator's point of view about playing games change? Circle the details that indicate the change. Some details have been circled for you.

Critical Thinking Think about three ways in which Dad uses his prior knowledge to create a pleasant environment for his family.

Sequence Think about the sequence of events involved in turning the dinghy into a sailboat, especially the order in which they modify it.

Differences in Points of View Think about how Dad's point of view about the loss of power seems to differ from that of the narrator.

11 Over the five days of the power outage, my dad resurrected other historical treasures of daily life. As a family, we were way beyond joking about this. Each new gambit was a winner. Toasting cheese in the fireplace on homemade spits made from metal hangers went back, Dad said, "At least two hundred years, maybe more . . . maybe to the Stone Age."

12 We made shadow puppets on the walls in the flickering firelight, with Dad showing us enough traditional ones that we could make up a dozen more. We made things like flying saucers and cartoon characters.

13 There was outdoor fun to be had, too. The little marsh behind our house had flooded into a rather large lake. We already had an old dinghy, and Dad and I spent a whole afternoon rigging a sail for it. We used a ten-foot length of PVC for a mast and some plastic sheeting that had blown into our yard for a sail. Getting the rigging tight was the hardest part, but once we got it in place—using no electric tools at all, of course—it was a proud-looking vessel.

14 Dad said it's traditional to name vessels after women, so we called it the USS *Elyse*, which gave my sister a swelled head for about a day. But then we went on an expedition to claim new territories.

15   As we sailed past the darkened houses in our neighborhood, it struck me how sad they seemed. Here and there we saw a tendril of smoke coming out of a chimney, but for the most part, the homes just looked cold and empty. Or even worse, they had generators roaring in their garages, which seemed like cheating somehow. The residents were missing out on getting forced to do things differently.

16   Our days were full to bursting. As I steered the USS *Elyse* along the shore of our unexplored lake, I had a bigger appetite than I'd ever remembered. Our days were full, our nights were eventful—and we all slept hard.

17   Life without electricity is work, for sure, but it's the kind of work that shows a reward right away and makes your blood pump, just as rowing all the way back up the lake did. The air was chilly, but the work warmed my sister and me just fine. Dad said there was a way to sail into the wind, but we couldn't figure it out. Maybe we'd learn that the next day, if the wind wasn't too strong. Meanwhile Elyse and I each rowed an oar, cutting the work in half as we shouted out loud the things we wanted to eat when we got home. The neighbors must have thought we were nuts, but we didn't care.

18   We wanted toasted cheese.

Differences in Points of View Now that you've read the story once, think about an example of dramatic irony that occurs when the narrator says, "Maybe we'd learn that the next day."

Plot Elements What action drives the plot on this page? <u>Underline</u> the first reference to it.

Sequence Think about the sequence of events in this story.

Critical Thinking Think about the antiques that Dad has around the house and how the family views them before and after the storm.

19   By the third or fourth day, Dad's tips on how to take sponge baths were invaluable. We were as grateful for everyone else's baths as we were for our own. During the day, I joined Dad in scavenging the beach for things we could use that night. We didn't just look for firewood but for colored sea glass to fit into holes in a tin can for a decorative lantern.

20   Funny, but the stories that went with these objects were not boring to hear at all. When you're going through it, a sponge bath is pretty dramatic stuff—the air's cold, the water's super hot—but the result feels great. Your skin tingles. Reading a good book by the flicker of lamplight actually felt thrilling.

21   When the lights came on before we had a chance to try out the lantern we made, my heart fell a little. I don't know which of us was the first to tell Dad his hobby was no longer, in fact, boring. But I'll never forget his response: "Once you know the story behind anything, it's never boring again."

22   I think he got that right.

✅ Comprehension Check

1. How does the father's point of view shape the action of the story? Cite textual evidence to support your answer.

_____

_____

2. Read paragraph 8 on page 25 that contains the word _cistern_.

   Circle the words that help you understand the meaning of the word _cistern_. Then use _cistern_ in a new sentence that demonstrates its meaning.

_____

_____

3. Describe the sequence of events that leads to the narrator appreciating his father's interests.

_____

_____

_____

4. What plot element drives the narrator to feel that his family gained something positive from the storm that other people didn't?

_____

_____

5. What was important about the children rowing by themselves and inventing more shadow puppets after their father showed them how?

_____

_____

_____

6. Read this sentence from the story.

   When he emerged from the cellar carrying a pair of railroad-style hurricane lamps, each glowing like a separate sun, he exclaimed, "Let there be light!"

   Explain whether the word *glowing* has a negative, neutral, or positive connotation.

_____

7. Predict what the family might do and feel if another storm knocked the power out. Use details from the story to support your prediction.

_____

_____

_____

8. Why did his father's hobby of studying and collecting antiques become less boring to the narrator? Cite textual evidence to support your answer.

_____

_____

Lesson 2
Traditional Literature

Traditional literature includes stories we know as myths, folktales, fairy tales, fables, and legends—stories that originated long ago as oral tales and were passed down from person to person, then were later recorded in writing. These stories reflect the cultures in which they've been told. They express a comment about life, explain an event in the natural world, or give a lesson about behavior. This photo shows the constellation Orion. Early peoples from different parts of the world had various stories to explain the significance of this pattern of stars in the sky. Are there any constellations you can identify in the night sky? Do you know any stories about them?

Skills Focus

The Turnip

Draw Inferences   Analyze Theme

Thunderbird / The Power of Rain

Ask and Answer Questions   Setting

Practice the Skill

First Read Draw Inferences

Authors don't always express ideas directly. Often, they use literary techniques to help readers determine what it is they want to say. Authors may describe what a character does, for example, but allow readers to interpret those actions to determine what the character is like.

To **draw inferences** means to decide what the author implies but does not state directly. Drawing inferences requires that you use the facts and details in the text as well as your prior knowledge and experiences to understand ideas that the author intends to convey but does not state directly.

Try It Read the following paragraph.

Andrea looked at the runners lined up at the starting line. Some were stretching; others were jogging in place. Andrea felt sure that they had taken the time to train for this event, and in fact, may have even been training for months. Andrea had made the decision to enter the race at the last minute. She had never run more than a mile in her life, but she had no time to worry about that. She had only heard about the race a few hours earlier, and she had hurried downtown to the race headquarters and gotten in line. When Andrea got an idea in her head, she acted on it quickly and thought about it later.

Discuss **What kind of person is Andrea? How do you know? Underline the clues in the text that help you make inferences about her character.**

As you read, complete the Inference Chart on page 285.

Practice the Skill

Analyze Theme

The **theme** of the story is the central message the author wants to convey. The theme might be a lesson the author wants to teach, but it can also be a general observation about life. The theme in any work of fiction is revealed through its plot, setting, and character development. In traditional literature, the theme is usually more obvious than it is in contemporary fiction and can often be expressed as a comment about life. Fables, for instance, usually have morals that explicity state the theme.

Theme and topic are not the same. Think back to the example paragraph on the previous page. The topic of the story is a girl who on a whim decides to enter a race. The theme, however, might be that it is important to plan and prepare for things ahead of time.

Try It Read the following paragraph.

> The tree stood tall and proud at the edge of the forest, as it always had, marking the path that would lead the woodcutter back home. When he looked at that magnificent trunk, he thought of the wood it would provide for his people. It would provide enough wood to rebuild the homes in his village that had been damaged by the storm. The woodcutter weighed his decision, and he considered his duty to help the villagers. Then, in a moment of sadness, he lifted his ax.

Discuss **What is the topic of the story? What is the theme? Circle the words that tell you the woodcutter's predicament. Draw a box around words that describe the tree.**

As you read, record your answers to questions about theme on the Close Reading Worksheet on page 286.

Purpose for Reading
Read along with your teacher. Each time, read for a different purpose.

First Read   Focus on drawing inferences.

Second Read   Focus on analyzing the theme.

Third Read   Focus on thinking critically about the story.

The Turnip

Circle traits that describe the two main characters. What theme might be developing, based on what you know about the characters so far?

How might the merchant feel about his hardworking brother? Cite textual evidence to support your ideas.

1   Long, long ago in a kingdom far away, there lived two brothers who were as different in mind and deed as any two brothers could be. They had grown up together, and as children, they had vowed to stay together always. But one brother was diligent about work and amiable toward his fellow man, while the other brother was indolent and hostile, so as they grew up, their differences drove them apart.

2   The amiable and hardworking brother made enough money to buy a small plot of land, on which he built a comfortable home and farmed his field for a living. But hard times had come to the kingdom, and no matter how diligently the man worked, he had only just enough to feed himself and nothing to sell at market. He never complained, however, because he had enough food to survive and enough land to keep him busy. He was industrious by nature, and he placed far more value on contentment than on riches.

3   The indolent and hostile brother derived little contentment from anything other than scheming ways to get rich and swindle others out of their fortunes. He moved to the city and became a successful merchant. The people who knew him well knew that he was dishonest, and they were aware that he made his money through unscrupulous methods. Nevertheless, he soon made enough money to buy a large chunk of land and enough servants to work it, and he worked his servants long and hard so that he could enjoy the fruits of their labor.

4   When the merchant brother saw how his industrious brother was struggling, he felt superior. To show his brother how much richer he was, he sent some of his servants to help in the industrious brother's fields. The brother with the small farm had noticed the way his rich brother treated his servants and said no to the offer of help.

5   As time passed, a long drought devastated much of the kingdom, and farmers fell upon harder and harder times. The hardworking brother persevered. He worked to improve his farming **techniques** so that his land would yield more crops. When his crops died, he planted more. When they died as well, he planted turnips. Turnips, he knew, grew under the ground, where they would be protected from the scorching sun and would have a better chance of surviving.

6   Every day the industrious brother worked hard to nurture his turnips, and soon he was rewarded for his efforts when the first signs of green turnip tops sprouted. He began to dig up his harvest, but he left one of the turnips in the ground for good luck. Each day it grew bigger and bigger. In time, it grew as large as a pumpkin. Soon it was as large as a rooster. When it had grown to be as large and heavy as the farmer could manage, he dug it up, hoisted it onto a cart, and tied the cart to his donkey. Then he rode on the donkey to the royal palace to take the turnip to the king.

7   "Your majesty," said the kind farmer, "I have been blessed with a fruitful harvest. I have plenty of turnips to eat, and it would be selfish to keep more than I need. This turnip is large enough to feed many others in the kingdom. Please accept this gift, and distribute it as you see fit."

8   The king was touched by the man's generosity, and he wanted to reward his kindness. He gave the man a pile of gold, a magnificent house, and a much larger plot of land. The man planted the land and worked hard to grow enough food to feed any villagers in need. He had no use for the gold, however, so he buried it in the yard.

9   "Someday, I may need it," he said.

Why does the farmer refuse the merchant's help? Underline textual evidence that supports your answer. Record your inference and support on the **Inference Chart**.

Why does the farmer have no use for the gold? Underline textual evidence that supports your answer. Record your inference and support on the **Inference Chart**.

Why does the king consider gold and land a fitting reward for the farmer? Cite textual evidence that supports your answer.

Why does the merchant plot revenge against his brother? Underline the details in the story that support your inference. Record your answers on the **Inference Chart**.

What theme about the relationship between wealth and happiness is the author developing?

10   Before long, everyone in the kingdom knew that the poor farmer had become the recipient of the king's gift and had more than he could ever hope for. His brother the merchant was beside himself with anger and decided that the only way to best his brother was to take a gift to the king that was much grander than the turnip.

11   The indolent and jealous merchant had plenty of gold to give the king, but he was hardly predisposed to part with his possessions. Still, he took a few coins from his stash and tied them in a bag. Then, just as his brother had done, he rode his donkey to the king's palace and presented his gift. The king appeared touched by the merchant's gift, as he had been touched by the gift of the hardworking brother, and he saw fit to bestow the merchant with a reward that was much more precious than gold.

12   "The most fitting reward I can think of is the fruits of the labor of a man who gave most generously when he had nothing," said the king.

13   He gave the selfish brother the giant turnip. The merchant turned red with anger and fell speechless in his rage and despair.

14   The merchant spent the following weeks plotting revenge against his brother. He had heard that this brother had buried his gold, and he planned to steal his brother's wealth and get rid of his rival for good. The selfish man took more gold coins from his stash, and he paid the village thieves to assist him.

15   "Go to my brother's farm tonight after dark and kidnap him," he told the thieves, "and then take him deep into the forest, tie him up in a bag, secure the bag tightly, and hang it from a tree."

16   The selfish man was sure that with his brother disabled and tied up in a tree, he would have plenty of time to dig up the gold—and then he would have plenty of time to move from the city and take over his brother's farm. The wicked merchant continued plotting and gloating until the sun set below the horizon and darkness fell over the land.

17   When it was dark and all good people were asleep, the thieves carried out the merchant's orders. They kidnapped the kindly farmer, took him to the forest, tied him up in a bag, and hung it from a tree. When the thieves reported to the merchant that his brother had been **captured**, he ordered them to carry out the rest of his evil plan.

18   "Go to my brother's farm and find and dig up that gold, but don't do it yet," he admonished them. "Wait until I give you the orders, because there is something else I have to take care of first. Stay right here, and wait for my return."

19   As eager as the merchant was to find the gold and take over the farm, he wanted to make absolutely sure that the thieves had done their job. He ordered the servant he trusted the most to go into the forest and look for his brother, though he paid him only one copper penny in return for his labors.

20   The servant did what his master instructed. He walked deep into the forest, and in the thickest, darkest part, he saw a very large bag hanging from a tree.

21   In the bag, the farmer came to with a start, having heard the servant's footsteps. He knew those were not the footsteps of his brother, who had a much harsher and heavier gait.

22   "Is someone there?" he cried out. "Oh, what a lucky day it is for you!"

Underline the textual evidence that supports the idea that the merchant is lazy and cheap.

Why doesn't the merchant order the thieves to kill his brother?

Why does the farmer consider the servant worthy of the gold? Write your answer on the **Inference Chart**.

What is the theme of the story? Cite textual evidence that supports your answer. ✎➡

23   The servant stopped in his tracks, bewildered. "I am here," he said hesitantly, "and I could use all the luck that I can get."

24   "Then this is certainly your lucky day, indeed," said the farmer from inside the bag. "For I have accidentally but fortunately stumbled upon the bag of wisdom, and as long as I stay in here, I know everything there is to know."

25   Now, the servant had no reason to trust the man, but he had nothing to lose by trusting him either. If he were privy to the wisdom of the world, he could escape his life of **servitude** and move on to build a life for himself. He would know how to help others in need, he would know how to solve all the world's problems, and he would know what to do to help people like the merchant see the error of their ways.

26   "Oh, please, kind sir," said the servant, "won't you let me sit in the bag of wisdom? Oh, it makes my head spin to think of the things I could do to help others if I had all the wisdom in the world."

27   "Well"—the farmer hesitated—"I suppose you could sit in the bag for a while—as long as you promise to let me back in when I return, but you'll have to cut me down from the tree and let me out first."

28   The servant jumped at the farmer's offer. He took a knife from his pocket, cut the rope, and let the farmer out of the bag.

29   The farmer tied the servant up in the bag. "I promise I'll be back in one hour," he told the servant, and he ran home to dig up his gold. He was as good as his word. He went home and dug up the gold, then brought it back to the forest and gave it to the servant. In that one instant, the merchant's servant became the richest man in the kingdom. The merchant was sent to prison. And the farmer—well, he simply went back to his farm and carried on.

Interpret

What is the purpose of the farmer's telling the servant about the bag of wisdom? Cite textual evidence that supports your answer. ✎➡

Vocabulary: Greek and Latin Roots

Many words in English have a Greek or Latin root. A **root** is the main part of a word that carries its core meaning. Knowing the meanings of these roots can help you determine the meanings of many words you do not recognize. Though a word can be composed of parts, such as the root, a prefix, and a suffix, the root carries the main meaning.

Try It Read this sentence from the selection.

If he were privy to the wisdom of the world, he could escape his life of **servitude** and move on to build a life for himself.

> Discuss **The word *servitude* contains the root *serv*. This root comes from the Latin word *servus*, which means "slave." Based on the context of the selection and your knowledge of this root, what does *servitude* mean?**

Read the sentence from the selection that contains each word. Based on the context of the sentence and the meaning of the root given, write a definition of the word. Then write a new sentence using the word.

1. **techniques**, p. 35: The Greek root *tech* means "craft or skill." _____

_____

_____

2. **captured**, p. 37: The Latin root *capt* means "to seize." _____

_____

_____

Practice the Skill

First Read **Ask and Answer Questions**

Asking and answering questions while reading can help you make sure you understand what is going on in a text. You can begin by asking questions that news writers refer to as "the five Ws." The five Ws are questions that begin with *who*, *what*, *where*, *when*, and *why*.

While reading, it's important to ask yourself questions about the characters, the plot, and the setting. If you can't answer questions about these elements, reread the paragraphs. If you still are unsure about what is happening, read on, because your question might be answered later in the selection.

Try It Read the following story.

The Tortoise and the Hare

Everyone knows that a hare can run faster than a tortoise, and no one knew that better than Hare himself. Hare was quite proud of that fact, too, and he took to boasting about it quite shamelessly.

"I'll prove to you that I am faster," said Hare to Tortoise. "Race me," he said, and Tortoise agreed.

Tortoise and Hare left the starting line at the same time. Hare darted off and, in a flash, he had disappeared around the bend. He was about a mile from the finish line when he decided to stop for a nap.

"This is ridiculous," said Hare. "I'm tired. I'll still beat that old Tortoise even if I sleep for a while."

He fell fast asleep. When he awoke, Tortoise was slowly but surely crossing the finish line. He had beaten Hare by a mile!

Discuss **Whom is the story about? What happens at the end? Where does Hare take a nap? When does Tortoise take the lead? Why does Tortoise win the race? Underline the answers to these questions in the story.**

As you read, record your answers about asking and answering questions on the Close Reading Worksheet on page 287.

Practice the Skill

The **setting** of a story is where and when the action takes place. It includes the geographic location and the physical scenery that helps define that location. Setting includes the historical period in which the story takes place.

Setting also includes the cultural and social environment in which a story takes place. These affect the characters and plot. For example, a character in a story that takes place in colonial times might face very different problems than a character in a story that takes place in the present day. However, each story might convey a similar theme, or message about life.

Setting can also be affected by circumstances. For instance, if a village is poverty-stricken, it would affect the plot of a story set there.

Try It Read the following paragraph.

> Henry and David were not friends, but they saw each other every day on the track at their middle school. They were both preparing to try out for the track team, and they both prided themselves on their speed. They decided to have a race to determine who was the fastest. Each called all his friends to come and watch the race because each was certain that he would win. On the day of the race, it rained hard and turned the field into mud. David failed to show up for the race, so Henry was declared the winner.

Discuss **What words does the author use to describe the setting? How many elements of setting can you identify? Circle the words that describe the setting. What is the main difference between the setting of this paragraph and the setting of "The Tortoise and the Hare"?**

As you read, complete the Setting Chart on page 288.

Purpose for Reading

Read along with your teacher. Each time, read for a different purpose.

First Read — Focus on asking and answering questions.

Second Read — Focus on words the author uses to describe setting.

Third Read — Focus on thinking critically about the stories.

Thunderbird

Underline the details that describe what the main characters want to find and why.

Circle the words that describe the brothers' village and the mountain they find. Write them on the **Setting Chart.**

1   Long, long ago, when the world was new, two brothers from a northern tribe set out to find the origin of thunder. One day in the dead of winter, the brothers left their family and their village and set out farther north to find the source of the rejuvenating thunderstorms that would bring about seasonal change. For far too long the deadly winter wind had held an icy grip on the villages, and the people suffered. The young boys were brave and strong and felt they had no choice but to set out on a long and treacherous journey to find thunder and bring it back to their people.

2   For weeks the brothers walked through frosty villages and across frozen streams, until finally they came to a mountain enshrouded in clouds, silhouetted against the black sky, and surrounded by a halo of light. The boys walked toward the mountain, and as they did, the mountain opened, and in the next instant, it slammed shut. Some **mysterious** force within this magnificent landform opened and shut the mountain repeatedly, and the brothers, awestruck by this show of power, felt compelled to enter.

3   For a long time the boys stood in silence, their eyes focused on a cleft in the mountain, as if attempting to summon up courage from the powers inside. If they wanted to enter, they had only a split second to jump through the cleft in the rock when it opened before the force would slam the mountain shut again. Finally, fueled by some mysterious energy, the first boy jumped through the cleft and landed safely on the other side of the mountain. His brother jumped in next, but the mountain slammed shut and engulfed him, and he did not come out on the other side.

4   The first boy, overcome with sorrow over the loss of his brother, found himself thrust into a world of eternal summer, alone beyond the clouds, where the sun shone brightly and everything was in bloom. He walked along bubbling streams and across fields lush with berries and flowers, and he allowed the bright golden sun to warm his cold heart. At last, he came to what appeared to be a clearing in the woods, and as he approached the clearing, he heard voices. He tucked himself behind a large tree, where he watched and listened.

5   A group of boys was sitting in a circle, chanting. The boys looked much like the boys from his own village, and the young boy squinted through the bushes and watched them intently. Before too long, one of them spoke. "Come," he said to the others. "Now it is time for us to go."

6   The boys went into their wigwams. In just a few minutes, they emerged wearing wings that were large and **unwieldy**, and the boys appeared to struggle to support them. Then, in seconds, they took off and were airborne. The boys steadily gained control of their wings as they rose swiftly into the air, and soon they were flying and soaring gracefully in the sky. They flew off together.

7   The first brother continued watching until they disappeared. Cautiously, he stepped out from behind the tree and walked across the clearing toward the wigwams. An elderly gentlemen came out of the biggest one, and he greeted the boy and inquired as to his business there.

Underline details that explain where both boys end up after jumping into the mountain.

How is the setting different on the other side of the mountain than in the village? Record your answers on the **Setting Chart**.

What does the mountain represent?

What does the elderly gentleman explain to the boy?

Underline the text that explains Thunderbird's responsibility.

Circle details that explain how the tribe's weather will change as a result of Thunderbird's coming.

Draw a box around the details that show how the messenger's feelings have changed.

8   The boy explained that he had come with his brother in search of thunder and that his brother had been trapped in the mountain when he tried to jump through the cleft. The old man smiled kindly, as if he held the wisdom of the world in his hands, and touched the boy's arm. The old man told the boy that while inside the mountain, his brother had become the Thunderbird, that he had been entrusted with the honor of renewing the earth each year with rejuvenating rains. The old man told the young boy that the boys he had just seen were thunderbirds themselves, and that his brother had been chosen to lead them.

9   "The thunderbirds are young boys, like your brother, who have been chosen to serve the mountain," the old man explained. "We are not to question the ways of the mountain," he admonished. "We are to accept them, and that you shall. Your brother is now Thunderbird. And you, my son, are his messenger. You will tell your people to watch the skies for the flash of Thunderbird's eyes in the darkness. Tell them to listen to the thunderous roars and know that he is flapping his wings."

10   "I will tell them, and we will watch for Thunderbird," said the boy. "We will watch for the return of my brother."

11   Suddenly and without warning, the boy's sadness disappeared. He felt comforted by the knowledge that his brother had become guardian of the change of the seasons, and he felt honored to be the chosen messenger who would bring this news to his people. From that day forward, the people have known that Thunderbird will always protect them by ensuring that the seasons come and go as they always have, that the cleansing rains will come in the spring, and that summer renews the land.

The Power of Rain

1   Everyone in the village knew about Mudjadji, the rain queen of the Lovedu who lived deep within the Drakensberg Mountains and who had the power to control the clouds, the thunder, the lightning, and the rain. No one Savannah knew had actually met this mysterious rain queen, but Savannah accepted the queen's power as fully as she accepted the existence of the rain itself. Of course, in the Zimbabwean community where Savannah and her family had made their home, the rain tested that belief. It was dry as a bone most of the year—something Savannah had a hard time getting used to. She had grown up in the United States, in Seattle, Washington, where it rained much of the time. In this part of Africa, however, the rains were stubborn. The land depended on them, but for extended periods of time, they refused to **materialize**, and come November of each year, the people in the villages suffered. This year, Savannah vowed to make the journey to the Drakensberg Mountains for the annual rainmaking ceremony, which was presided over by Mudjadji herself. Savannah had confidence that the ceremony would ensure the return of the rain—and besides, ever since she had come to Africa, she had wanted to take part in this fascinating and mysterious tradition.

2   Savannah had already lived in the African village for several years by the time she decided to attend the rainmaking ceremony. Her life in the United States had been drastically different from her life here. Savannah's family had come to Zimbabwe with a volunteer group to build orphanages and medical clinics, and Savannah's parents had fallen in love with the village she had now come to call home. On their last trip, they had made the decision to stay for a while.

Underline the textual evidence that explains why Savannah lives in Zimbabwe.

What does the author explain about the setting of Savannah's village? Write your answer on the **Setting Chart.**

Why is Savannah so interested in attending the rainmaking ceremony?

What does Savannah enjoy about Abaju?

Record details on the **Setting Chart** that describe what the culture is like in Savannah's village.

3   Savannah still remembers the sense of belonging she felt when she first arrived in the village and the people there reached out to her. She fell in love with these people and their beliefs and traditions, and she proudly adopted the people, the village, and the land as her own. Savannah had especially fallen in love with the stories of Mudjadji, the queen of the Lovedu, who commanded the clouds and held the secret of rain. It was Abaju, the village weaver, who told Savannah about Mudjadji.

4   "She is a strong woman who has been entrusted with tremendous powers," Abaju explained. "Mudjadji comes from a long line of female monarchs who have ruled the Lovedu for centuries, and the people respect her greatly." Savannah could understand the idea of respecting a monarch, but she couldn't picture this mysterious rain queen. The only image that popped into her head was of a fairy tale queen in a red velvet robe sitting on a throne next to a king. *What would a rain queen look like?* she wondered.

5   Savannah sat in the same spot on the ground in front of Abaju's hut now as she had when she first heard the story of Mudjadji. Abaju sat on her woven chair outside the door, where she could weave and keep her eye on the villagers. "I keep my eyes and ears open," she had told Savannah long ago, "and I see things, I hear things." Now, once again, Savannah sat and listened to Abaju. Abaju had wonderful stories, and she had told them so often, she could recite them like poetry—which was exactly why Savannah begged her to tell them over and over, again and again.

6   "Mudjadji has no army and no palace," Abaju explained, "but she has as much power as if she ruled an empire with a powerful military. Tradition says that she consults with a rain doctor and owns a secret charm. She is descended from the great king Mambo, who lived here, in what is now southern Zimbabwe," Abaju continued. "He lived in a city made of stone that held the secret rain charm, and he kept the secret hidden for many years so that he alone had control of its power."

7   Savannah looked at the parched lands around her and then looked down at the dust that swirled around Abaju's cracked, gray feet.

8   "Then one day, so they say, Mambo's daughter stole the rain charm," Abaju continued.

9   "She fled south with the charm and founded the Lovedu tribe. Because she could control the rain, she became the first of the Lovedu rain queens; she became the first to be called Mudjadji. But she became known to her people as 'She Who Does Not Fight' because she was a peacemaker among her people. She was highly respected among the neighboring chiefs; even the great Shaka Zulu admired her."

Why doesn't Abaju want to tell Savannah that Mudjadji lives like a modern woman?

10   Savannah remembered reading about Shaka Zulu in history class; Mudjadji was starting to seem more like a real person. Savannah was determined to meet Mudjadji and find out what this rainmaking business was all about.

Circle details that describe Mudjadji's home. Think about how the description helps explain her appeal. Write your answers on the Setting Chart.

11   "I'm going to go to that ceremony," she told Abaju. "I can see the Drakensberg Mountains from here. Surely there's a bus I can take, isn't there? Do they let just anyone attend the rain ceremony? Do you think the queen would let me meet her—if she knew I really believed in her power?"

12   "I'm not sure about that," said Abaju, "because I don't know anyone who's ever actually seen her." Abaju did not want to tell Savannah that the rain queen was simply a modern woman and that Savannah would not be able to pick her out among a crowd of village women shopping in the square. So instead, she told Savannah that the Drakensberg Mountains were a long way away and that Mudjadji lived in the deepest part of them, in an area that was surrounded in mist. She told Savannah that whatever happened in those mountains today remained as secret as it had ever been and that the power of the ceremony lived strongest in the people's hearts. Abaju knew that the woman Savannah imagined was as mysterious as the legends made her out to be, and Abaju had no intention of destroying the magic.

13   "It is my belief that no one has seen Mudjadji," Abaju said with conviction, "not for a long, long time. The ceremony of legend may or may not still take place, but the people know the queen is there when they see the smoke billowing above her mountains. The people know that she holds ceremony with a rain doctor and that they burn secret medicines that release black smoke. They know that the smoke transforms the clouds and makes them heavy with water; they hear the thunderclouds burst over the mountains, and they feel the rain pour down on their land."

What does Savannah learn about the power of rain from the Lovedu rainmaking ceremony?

(Circle) details that explain how life in Zimbabwe differs from life in Seattle.

14   "So, the people farm the land," Abaju continued, and out of the corner of her eye she watched Savannah. "They farm the land for food and shelter, for clothes and tools, for cooking vessels and medicine. The Lovedu are a peaceful people who rely on no one but themselves. They take care of their people. And they have a treasured tradition that holds them together."

15   Savannah was a smart girl, and she was beginning to get the picture. She also realized why her parents had been so set on staying in the village. When the family had first come to build the orphanage, Savannah had felt like a stranger in a strange land. She was happy to be able to help, but she had felt no connection to these people, this village, this land, or these traditions. Savannah's life was back in the States, and no one she knew there lived in a hut or told ancient legends or talked about the rain in any way other than to complain that it had ruined the activities they had planned for the day.

16   Savannah looked up and smiled at Abaju, who smiled back, her face cracked with age and wisdom. "You know the secret of the rain yourself, now, don't you?" Abaju asked. Savannah looked at the sky and saw the beginnings of dark, heavy rain clouds forming in the distance. "Now you know the tradition that gives the Lovedu people hope," Abaju said.

17   So, it was from Abaju the weaver that Savannah learned about tradition and hope. It was from Abaju the storyteller that she learned about a culture that, suddenly, Savannah felt very much a part of. A few months later, a reporter from the United States came in search of Mudjadji to gather information for an article he was writing on African rainmaking. The reporter talked to Abaju, and she told him about the Lovedu rain ceremony. Savannah read the article, and thought how, sadly, the reporter had missed the point.

18   He talked about heat as a **destructive** force in southern Zimbabwe and about the importance of rain to these agricultural people. What he failed to explain or to understand, however, was the power of tradition. That's what Mudjadji's story was all about—and that's why Savannah came to love every part of the legend. Every year in October, the people approach the queen with gifts. They shower her with gifts; they dance for her. And every year without fail, the seasons turn, and the life-giving rains begin to fall on the earth. None of Savannah's friends or family in Seattle had a queen that could make the rains fall, but Savannah did— it was part of her culture now. It made her different from the girl she had been in Seattle, and every day Savannah spent in the village, she felt a little bit more a part of Zimbabwe.

Analyze

Why do the people believe in Mudjadji's power? Cite textual evidence to support your ideas.

Vocabulary: Greek and Latin Affixes

Affixes are word parts that come either before or after a root word and help readers determine the word's meaning. A **prefix** comes at the beginning of a root word. A **suffix** comes at the end of a root word. Like roots, affixes can be derived from Greek or Latin.

Try It Read this sentence from "Thunderbird."

Some **mysterious** force within this magnificent landform opened and shut the mountain repeatedly, and the brothers, awestruck by this show of power, found themselves compelled to enter.

> Discuss   **The word *mysterious* contains the Latin suffix *-ious*, meaning "full of" or "having the quality of." Based on this, what does *mysterious* mean?**

Read the sentence from the selection that contains each of these words. Based on the context of the sentence and the meaning of the prefix or suffix given, write a definition of the word. Then write a new sentence using the word.

1. **unwieldy,** p. 43: The Latin prefix *un-* means "not." _____

   _____

   _____

2. **materialize,** p. 45: The Greek suffix *-ize* means "to become like." _____

   _____

   _____

3. **destructive,** p. 48: The Latin suffix *-ive* means "to perform an action."

   _____

   _____

Respond to Text: Compare a Modern and a Traditional Tale

"Thunderbird" and "The Power of Rain" are both fictional stories. "Thunderbird" is a traditional tale, while "The Power of Rain" is an example of modern fiction. You can compare and contrast traditional and modern stories by examining how they deal with elements such as theme, types of characters, or patterns of events.

Try It Both stories are about how the changing seasons and rain can bring renewal. Each story tells about a culture that has its own way of explaining how and why the rains come. What is the same and what is different about each story? Which one is more believable?

> **Discuss** **How is the modern telling similar to the traditional story? How is it different?**

On Your Own Compare and contrast the modern story "The Power of Rain" with the traditional story "Thunderbird." Compare the pattern of events from each story that tells why and how the rains come. Use textual evidence from each story to support your response. Use the chart on the next page to help you write your response, and then write your paragraph on a separate piece of paper.

Checklist for a Good Response

A good paragraph

✔ compares the modern telling with the traditional tale.

✔ compares the pattern of events from each story.

✔ cites textual evidence from the story to support ideas.

✔ includes a topic sentence, supporting details, and a concluding sentence.

My Comparison of the Stories

1. **Topic Sentence** Include this information in your topic sentence:

    "Thunderbird" and "The Power of Rain" have a similar pattern of events

    that describe _____

2. **Detail Sentences** Compare and contrast the patterns of events in the
    two stories.

	"Thunderbird"	**"The Power of Rain"**
How does each story explain how the rains come?		
What are the major differences between the two stories?		
How is the pattern of events in the two stories similar?		

3. **Concluding Sentence** Your concluding sentence should summarize the
    similarities and differences between the patterns of events.

    _____

    _____

On a separate piece of paper, write your paragraph.

The Three Wishes

Draw Inferences
Why are the villagers so hesitant to change? Underline details that support your inference. Some details have been underlined for you.

Critical Thinking
Think about the contrast between how hard the villagers work and yet how passive they are in relation to their environment.

1   A long time ago in a village near the edge of a forest, there lived a poor woodcutter and his wife. The couple had been born in the village, their parents had been born in the village, their grandparents had been born in the village, and *their* grandparents had been born in the village. For as far back as anyone could remember, the village had always been the same.

2   Nothing changed in the village because no one had ever thought of changing anything. The people who lived there were common folk, and they were brought up to accept their lot in life and make the best of what they were given. Each family in the village had a modest hut that provided little more than shelter from the elements, and they had enough food to survive and not much more. There was a river full of fish, but the fish were too clever to be caught. There was a forest full of animals, but the animals were too clever to be hunted. The only food to be had was what the villagers grew themselves.

3   The poor woodcutter and his wife never thought of leaving the village to make a better life for themselves. No one in the village had ever left, and no one ever would. Even if they had, they likely would have starved before they got anywhere worth going to, as there was nothing around for miles and miles—or at least the villagers didn't think there was. No one had ever left, so no one knew for sure. But the people in the village accepted things as they were and never thought to question ideas that had been proven true through the test of time. They worked hard to make ends meet, and their children would work hard to make ends meet, and their children's children would work hard to make ends meet. That was simply the way things were.

4   The woodcutter and his wife had no children, so they had no one to care for but themselves. As a result, they had grown bitter and selfish, though they continued to long for a child. While the other villagers worked hard and shared the little food they grew with their neighbors, the woodcutter and his wife kept everything they had to themselves. Granted, they had little to share in the first place, but they did have a small area of land with good, rich soil. Had they exerted one iota of effort to farm that land and give the plants the tender care they needed to grow and thrive, they would have had more than enough food to keep themselves alive and healthy. But the woodcutter and his wife had grown lazy as well as bitter and selfish, and they were horrible **procrastinators**.

5   One could surmise that they recognized the error of their ways because they spent most of their time blaming each other. Instead of tilling the soil, they argued about whose turn it was to till it, and instead of planting the field, they argued about whose turn it was to plant it. They never argued about whose turn it was to reap the harvest, however, because there was nothing to reap. Instead of making their little home comfortable, they blamed each other for how bleak and inhospitable their hut was. Despite the fact that the woodcutter and his wife never expended the energy necessary to help themselves or anyone else, the other villagers could not bear to see them suffer and gave them enough food to keep them alive.

6   Now, wise men would say that souls as selfish and unkind as the woodcutter and his wife should never be bestowed with the blessing of children, but the couple wanted them nevertheless. Years went by, however, and the couple remained childless.

Ask and Answer Questions Where do the woodcutter and his wife live? How do they spend their time? Circle the details that answer the questions.

Setting One part of the setting described is the fertile plot of land the man and woman own. Think about how what they do with this land shows their natures.

Analyze Theme Think about how the emphasis on the couple's wanting children is contributing to the development of the theme.

Draw Inferences
Why is the visitor described as mysterious? Think about how the woodcutter and his wife would probably describe her.

Analyze Theme Think about how unusual it is for someone to come to the door of the couple's hut.

7   Years went by, and the couple continued to argue and blame each other for having no blessings bestowed on them. They continued to blame each other for having no children and no food, for the poverty of their lives, and for their drab, cheerless home. The villagers continued to help them because nothing changed in the village, nothing had ever changed, and nothing would ever change. No one ever came to the village, and no one ever left.

8   Now, wise men would say that things happen when we least expect them, and wise men would say that everything happens for a reason, too. One day, a mysterious woman wandered out of the woods and into the village. She was old, the air was freezing cold, and she was wrapped in only a thin shawl. When she arrived in the village, she walked to the first hut she came upon and knocked weakly on the door. The hut happened to belong to the woodcutter and his wife.

9   For a while, neither the woodcutter nor his wife responded to the knock, and the old woman remained for what seemed like hours outside in the freezing cold. She could hear the man and his wife arguing about who would answer the door. The old woman knocked and knocked until it finally opened, and there stood the woodcutter and his wife. They both gave the intruder an angry look.

10   "Please, gentle people," the woman said to the couple, "I have walked a long way and am freezing out here on this cold day. Would you be so kind as to let me warm myself by your fire for a spell before I go on my way?"

11   For a minute, the couple simply stared at her. Then for some reason, the woodcutter took pity on the old woman. Perhaps he saw that she was old and ill-prepared for the weather, or perhaps he was simply so exhausted from arguing with his wife that he welcomed the company of a stranger. Whatever it was, he invited the woman inside, gave her a warm blanket, and made her a bed by the fire.

Setting Think about how the hut seems different to the visitor than it does to the woodcutter and his wife.

12   "Oh, thank you, kind sir," the old woman said to the woodcutter. "Thank you, good lady," the old woman said to the woodcutter's wife.

13   "Perhaps she can be of some use," the woodcutter said as he watched the old woman sleeping.

14   "You fool," the woodcutter's wife responded. "The woman is old and too weak to work. How can she possibly be of any use to us? She can stay the night and no longer."

15   The woodcutter and his wife continued to argue through the night about the stranger who, due to the woodcutter's moment of weakness, slept safe and warm by the fire. The next morning, the woman woke early, rested and **rejuvenated**, and she smiled sweetly at her hosts.

16   "You have shown me such kindness, sweet couple," she said. "I shall now grant you three wishes. You may wish for anything your heart desires. But think carefully before you speak them aloud, for the minute you make a wish, it shall be granted."

17   Then in an instant, the woman disappeared right before their eyes.

18   Now the woodcutter and his wife were foolish, but they recognized magic when they saw it. And far be it from them to snub magic when it came knocking at their door. The woodcutter and his wife were ecstatic and began thinking about all they could wish for.

Ask and Answer Questions What happens after the old woman leaves? (Circle) the details that answer the question.

Setting Think about why most of the action takes place inside the hut.

Critical Thinking Think about how things would be different between the woodcutter and his wife had they not wasted their wishes.

19   The woodcutter's wife wanted a child more than anything. "A child will come when we are prepared to care for it," the woodcutter insisted. "What we need now is gold and riches, a magnificent mansion to live in, and servants to work in the fields."

20   The woodcutter and his wife argued for hours. They argued throughout the day and into the night. By morning, their fire had gone out, and the woodcutter felt weak from hunger.

21   "I wish I had a big, juicy sausage," he said aloud, his mouth watering at the thought of it, and then, in an instant, a big, juicy sausage appeared in front of him. The man quickly began to devour it without stopping to think what he had done.

22   "You fool!" cried the wife. "You've wasted one of our wishes, and for what? A measly sausage! I wish that sausage were attached to your nose!"

23   Then in an instant, what was left of the sausage jumped off the table and stuck tight to the woodcutter's nose. He pulled and pulled at it but to no avail—the sausage wouldn't budge.

24   "Our second wish—gone!" the woodcutter blurted out to his wife in anger. "You get this sausage off my nose right now!"

25   The woodcutter's wife refused to help him, so the woodcutter had to help himself—he could hardly spend the rest of his life with a sausage attached to his nose. "I wish the sausage would disappear," he said aloud.

26   In an instant, the sausage was gone.

27   The couple had used their three wishes, and they were miserable. They always had been miserable and they always would be—because nothing ever changed in the village. Nothing ever changed at all.

✅ Comprehension Check

1. Why does the author introduce the visitor?

    _____

    _____

    _____

2. Identify the theme of the selection. Write your response as a complete sentence.

    _____

    _____

    _____

3. Why does the woodcutter take pity on the old woman?

    _____

    _____

    _____

4. How does the setting contribute to the overall feeling of the story?

    _____

    _____

    _____

5. What message does the author convey about fortune by contrasting the actions of the visitor with those of her hosts?

_____

_____

6. This story was told a long time ago and in many different forms. What makes this tale significant today?

_____

_____

7. Read this sentence from the selection.

   But the woodcutter and his wife had grown lazy as well as bitter and selfish, and they were horrible procrastinators.

   The Latin word *crastinus* means "of tomorrow," the Latin prefix *pro-* means "forward," and the Latin suffix *-ate* makes a noun a verb. The suffix *-or* means "one who." Based on the meanings of the root, prefixes, and suffixes, write a definition for the word *procrastinators*.

   _____

8. Read this sentence from the selection.

   The next morning, the woman woke early, rested and rejuvenated, and she smiled sweetly at her hosts.

   The Latin root *juv* means "young." Based on the meaning of the root and the context of the sentence, write a definition for the word *rejuvenated*.

   _____

   _____

Lesson 3
Drama

Drama refers to stories that are meant to be performed onstage. Dramas, or plays, are made up of acts and scenes, and the stories are told mainly through the characters' dialogue. Dramas can be short, as in one-act plays, or long, with many acts that contain multiple scenes. What do you think is the topic of the play being performed in the photo?

Skills Focus

The Setup, Scene 1

Summarize   Dramatic Structure

The Setup, Scenes 2 and 3

Compare and Contrast   Characterization

Practice the Skill

Summarize

To **summarize** means to capture the main ideas of a selection without giving too many details. Think of the way you might tell a friend the plot of a movie. You would note how the movie begins, who the main characters are, where and when it takes place, what crucial events happen in the middle, and then how it ends. Most likely, you would leave out a character's choice of clothing or your opinion about how the movie ended. A summary should contain only the most essential ideas and leave out your opinion.

Try It Read the drama below.

KING: (*speaking to his court*) As you know, I have promised twenty gold pieces to anyone telling a story so unbelievable, there is no way it could be true. (*to his guard*) Summon the first storyteller!

STORYTELLER 1: Sire, on the other side of the world lives an animal with the features of a bird, a reptile, and a mammal.

KING: Stop! That's just a duck-billed platypus. Take this man away!

(*Storyteller 2 is brought in.*)

STORYTELLER 2: My great-great-grandfather was so unlucky, he was hit by lightning a thousand times!

KING: Stop! That's not necessarily a tall story. It *might* have happened. Take this man away!

STORYTELLER 2: (*in a low, warning whisper, so only the king can hear*) That's a bad idea, your highness. There's a mob of angry peasants out there, claiming you are stealing their money. They mean you great harm.

KING: (*laughing idiotically*) Congratulations. There is no way that story could be true. Here is your gold.

> **Discuss** Circle the name of the character this drama is mostly about. Underline what this character wants. Box the most important events in the drama. Double underline what happens at the end of the drama. Now, summarize the drama.

As you read, complete the Summary Chart on page 289.

Practice the Skill

Second Read **Dramatic Structure**

Dramas are organized into one or more acts, and each **act** is made up of one or more scenes. **Scenes** often change when the setting or the characters onstage change. Dramas are mostly made up of dialogue, but there are **stage directions** that tell the actors what to do and how to say their lines. Characters speak to one another onstage, and the stage directions give information about the setting and how the characters move or speak. In an **aside**, a character speaks dialogue that he or she wants the audience, but not the other characters, to hear.

Like stories, dramas have a plot structure that includes conflict, rising action, climax or turning point, falling action, and resolution. The acts and scenes help the story move along by switching settings and having characters move on and off the stage.

Try It Read the drama below.

SETTING: *In scenes 1 and 2, Lita and her friends have gone to an abandoned house to explore. Lita gets separated from her friends.*

Scene 3

SETTING: *A dark room full of broken furniture in the abandoned house. Lita tries to feel her way around and hears a sound.*

LITA: (*scared*) Wh-who's there?

(*sound of breathing*)

LITA: (*annoyed*) Ha-ha-ha. Very funny, you guys. I can heeeear you.

> Discuss ⟩ **Look closely at the setting and stage directions. Which details and directions tell you how the character is feeling? Which simply tells the actor what to do? How are both kinds of directions helpful to performing the drama?**

As you read, record your answers to questions about dramatic structure on the Close Reading Worksheet on page 290. ✏️➡

Purpose for Reading

Read along with your teacher. Each time, read for a different purpose.

First Read	Focus on summarizing.
Second Read	Focus on dramatic structure.
Third Read	Focus on evaluating the play critically.

THE Setup, SCENE 1

A one-act play

CAST OF CHARACTERS

AMBER, a thirteen-year-old girl

MRS. TWILLER, mother of Amber

THE PRODUCER, Jack

THE ASSISTANT, Josh

DR. LORETTA, a psychologist

EX–BEST FRIEND, former best friend of Amber

AUNT CHLOE, sister of Mrs. Twiller; aunt of Amber

Scene 1

What does the setting tell you about scene 1 and the characters involved?

What differences do you see between the producer and his assistant? Underline an example of how each character behaves.

SETTING: *The scene takes place on the set of* You're Not My Mother, *a reality TV show where a mother and daughter trade places for a week. The set looks like an ordinary living room but is surrounded by cameras, lights, and harried-looking people rushing around wearing headsets. As the play opens, Amber and Mrs. Twiller sit stiffly on a couch, while the producer and the assistant mill around.*

1 THE PRODUCER: (*clapping for attention impatiently*) OK, people, take five—and I mean *five*! (*to the assistant*) I'm losing it, Josh.

2 THE ASSISTANT: Jack. Jack. Calm.

3 THE PRODUCER: I *cannot* work with these people . . . I'm a professional . . . I have standards!

4   THE ASSISTANT: (*nodding sympathetically*) I hear you, Jack—wherever did you find these folks?

5   THE PRODUCER: (*sighing theatrically*) On the crosstown bus. They were sitting next to me, having an argument, when the kid says something like, "You just don't understand what it's like to be me," and the mom says, "Oh, I understand all right—and you're still not going." So I think, *Bingo!* and give them my card—they seemed so perfect!

6   THE ASSISTANT: I don't know, Jack—at this rate, the show won't survive another episode, much less another full season.

7   THE PRODUCER: (*clapping for attention impatiently*) OK, people—showtime! Back on the set!

8   THE ASSISTANT: (*mimicking the producer*) *Ladies!*

9   THE PRODUCER: (*to Mrs. Twiller, with exaggerated patience*) Now, Mrs. Twiller, I need you to repeat what you said before the **break**, only this time make it more—*natural*. More like—

10   THE ASSISTANT: (*interrupting*) Reality. More like reality.

11   MRS. TWILLER: Well, it's a *reality* show, isn't it—isn't that funny?

12   THE PRODUCER: (*sighing*) Please Mrs. T., just tell us what happened this week when you traded places with thirteen-year-old Amber, what you learned, what insights you got, how your perception of her changed.

13   MRS. TWILLER: (*speaking to the camera*) My perception? Yes. Well. I used to think my daughter had it too easy, but after standing in her shoes, I've done a complete one-eighty. I can't believe how well she manages everything—school, homework, chores. I couldn't do half as good a job . . . and to top it off, she has so many friends!

How did Mrs. Twiller and her daughter end up on the show? Write this important detail on the **Summary Chart.**

Circle details in the stage directions that indicate the producer is not happy with the Twillers.

Describe the exchange between Mrs. Twiller and Dr. Loretta. Record these details on the **Summary Chart.**

In line 24, why does the producer speak in an aside? ✎⟹

What tells you that Dr. Loretta is more interested in how she appears on TV than in giving good advice? Underline details that show this.

14   MRS. TWILLER: (*continuing*) I mean, she's got best friends, next–best friends, almost friends, soon-to-be friends, ex-friends, ex–best friends . . . It makes your head spin!

15   THE PRODUCER: (*excitedly*) *Ex*–best friends, you say?

16   MRS. TWILLER: Well, sure. Like this one girl in her class, Felicity—

17   AMBER: Mom! Private!

18   THE PRODUCER: (*trying to rile Amber up*) Wow. Wow. Amber, does your mom do that a lot—broadcast details of your personal life all over town? I'd say your mom has boundary **issues**, Amber, but let's bring in an expert to weigh in. Dr. Loretta?

(*Dr. Loretta **appears** and sits primly and properly on a chair opposite Mrs. Twiller and Amber.*)

19   THE PRODUCER: Dr. Loretta, you've been listening to this backstage. In your professional opinion, does Mrs. Twiller have boundary issues? Yes or no?

20   DR. LORETTA: Without knowing the situation? Yes, Mrs. Twitter—

21   MRS. TWILLER: *Twiller.* Mrs. Twiller, not Twitter—*Twiller.*

22   DR. LORETTA: (*waving a hand dismissively*) Twiller, right, what I said.

23   MRS. TWILLER: No, dear, I distinctly heard you say "Mrs. Twitter."

24   THE PRODUCER: (*aside to Dr. Loretta, apologetically*) Sorry, Janet, we'll clean this up in postproduction—let's just get on with the diagnosis, OK?

25   DR. LORETTA: (*turning to smile broadly at the camera*) Mrs. *Twiller* is obviously suffering from acute parental personality dysfunction disorder—commonly known as APPDD—with a tendency toward double-blind countertransference.[1]

[1] The "disorders" that Dr. Loretta suggests here and later are made up and are meant to mock TV therapists, some of whom offer diagnoses not commonly accepted by the mainstream medical community.

26 THE PRODUCER: Whoa, Nelly! What a mouthful!

27 DR. LORETTA: (*winks at the camera, then becomes overly serious*) Yes. Acute parental personality dysfunction is a serious condition, affecting more than 67 percent of all mothers of teenage girls. When you combine it with arrested projection deficit syndrome, you've got a perfect storm. Basically, Mrs. Twiller's situation is hopeless.

28 THE PRODUCER: Sheesh. Sure sounds like it. Thank you, Dr. Loretta, for your always valuable insights. But before you go, the name of your newest book?

29 DR. LORETTA: It's called *Motherhood/Otherhood*, and it'll be available in paperback just in time for the holidays—and 10 percent off your order if you mention this show! Ciao!

    (*exit Dr. Loretta*)

30 MRS. TWILLER: May I say something here? I know Dr. Loretta is qualified and all, but I'm not sure I understand—

31 THE PRODUCER: Well, of *course* you don't understand! You're not a *certified psychotherapist,* are you? Well, *are* you?

32 MRS. TWILLER: No, but I'm far from ignorant when it comes to—

33 THE PRODUCER: Now, now, Mrs. Twiller, mustn't be so defensive! I'm sure your daughter doesn't think you're *ignorant*. Not really. Not so that you'd notice, anyway. Right, Amber?

34 AMBER: What are you saying? That my mother's *ignorant*?

Summarize the exchange between the producer and Mrs. Twiller. Write your summary on the **Summary Chart.**

How is the language used by Dr. Loretta different from the language used by the other characters? What does this show about her character?

What does Amber say about her experience trading places with her mother? Write these details on the **Summary Chart**.

In terms of dramatic structure, this is the play's turning point. What happens at the end of scene 1 that brings the action to a very tense point? What has the producer done to make this happen?

Analyze

Think about how the producer tries to create drama and think about Dr. Loretta's lines. How has the author been poking fun at reality TV shows? Support your viewpoint with examples from the text.

35 THE PRODUCER: Amber, Amber, Amber. Let me put it this way: This week, when you traded places with your mom, what did you find out about her that you didn't know before?

36 AMBER: Um . . . That she works hard?

37 THE PRODUCER: What else?

38 AMBER: (*cheerfully, smiling at her mom*) Well, I used to wish I was my mom until I spent some time in her shoes. I never realized how much she does—working in an office all day, then shopping, cooking, cleaning, helping me with homework . . . Whew! After a week of being her, I definitely appreciate her more.

39 THE PRODUCER: (*needling*) Hmmm. Cooking, cleaning, shopping . . . Your mom sounds like a real drudge.

40 AMBER: She's not a drudge. She's great! We're friends!

41 THE PRODUCER: *Friends?* Doesn't she have her *own* friends? (*to Mrs. Twiller*) What are you, some kind of loser, Mrs. T.? You must be a great embarrassment to your daughter.

42 MRS. TWILLER: (*getting angry*) *Excuse me?*

43 AMBER: Of course she's not—I'm very proud of my mom.

44 THE PRODUCER: Oh, come on, Amber, you can tell me the truth! If your mom is an embarrassment, maybe she should know.

45 AMBER: But she's not an embarrassment—I already told you that.

46 THE PRODUCER: Whoa, whoa there, little lady! Is that *attitude* I hear? Where does *that* come from? (*to Mrs. Twiller*) Your daughter insists she got her bad attitude from you. Does that make you happy?

47 MRS. TWILLER: No! *No!*

48 THE PRODUCER: (*to Amber*) Hear that, Amber? She's *not happy!* And it's all your fault! How can you live with that?

49 AMBER: With what? What are you talking about? You're making me angry!

50 THE PRODUCER: (*shaking his head*) Mrs. Twiller, I'm afraid your daughter is a very, very angry girl.

(*enter the assistant, who whispers to the producer*)

51 THE PRODUCER: (*to the assistant*) She's *here*? Bring her in, man, bring her in! *OK, KIDS, BREAK FOR LUNCH!*

Vocabulary: Multiple-Meaning Words

Multiple-meaning words have more than one meaning. These words may have different pronunciations and might be different parts of speech. When looking up such a word in a dictionary, look for the meaning that makes the most sense in context. Use context clues to help you. Try substituting the dictionary meaning for the word in the text. If it makes sense, you know you've got the right definition.

Try It Read this section of dialogue from *The Setup*.

> DR. LORETTA: It's called *Motherhood/Otherhood*, and it'll be available in paperback just in time for the holidays—and 10 percent off your order if you mention this show! Ciao!

Look at this dictionary entry for the word *order*.

or·der ('ȯr-dər) *noun.* **1:** a command to do something; **2:** the way in which things are arranged; position in a series; **3:** clean, neat, or proper condition; **4:** the items purchased or sold

Discuss **Which meaning of *order* is used in this sentence? Why?**

Read the sentences in the drama that contain the following words. Look up each word in a dictionary and decide which meaning is being used in the sentence. Write it down. Then write a new sentence using the meaning you decided on.

1. **break,** p. 63 _____

_____

2. **issues,** p. 64 _____

_____

3. **appears,** p. 64 _____

_____

Practice the Skill

To **compare** means to find out how two or more things are alike. To **contrast** means to find out how two or more things are different. Compare and contrast refers to a way of looking at parts of a text and thinking about how they are similar and different.

When reading dramatic literature, you might compare and contrast the settings of different scenes, how characters react to events, and how characters think about one another.

Try It Read the following excerpt from a drama.

> ERMA: (*excitedly*) Let's run over to Clark's Candy after school today. I want to see if they have anything new.
>
> HORACE: (*yawning*) No, we went there yesterday. I'm bored with everything we do.
>
> ERMA: Well, we haven't been to the playground in a few weeks. Let's go there and play. I heard the swings are finally fixed.
>
> HORACE: No, not there, either. Besides, we're too old to be playing on swings.
>
> ERMA: I got it! (*She runs to the window, pointing.*) The arcade! We can try a new video game. (*Erma is jumping excitedly.*)
>
> HORACE: Ugh, no! (*He shakes his head and walks away, annoyed.*)

Discuss **Underline two details that show Erma's emotions. How does Horace feel differently? Why might it be important to have two characters who think very differently in a story?**

As you read, complete the Compare and Contrast Web on page 291.

Practice the Skill

Characterization is the way an author reveals a character's personality. In dramatic literature, a playwright usually does not give you direct information about the characters. You must make inferences about the characters based on what they say and do and how other characters react to what they say and do. As with real people, listening to two characters talk to each other can reveal a lot about who they are and what their relationship is.

Try It Read the following scene from a play based on the Greek myth of Echo and Narcissus. The dialogue is between Hera, wife of the god Zeus, and Echo, a mountain nymph.

Scene 2

ECHO: You have sent for me, goddess?

HERA: (*in a rage*) Vile mountain nymph! You've tricked me!

ECHO: What are you talking about? I don't understand!

HERA: Do I really need to spell it out? You deliberately distracted me so that your little friends could get away in time. As if you didn't know.

ECHO: Please, Hera. They weren't doing any harm. Zeus has no interest in them. Why, anyone can see how devoted he is to you! You're all he talks about!

HERA: (*shaking her fists*) Don't insult my intelligence! No one deceives the queen of Mount Olympus! *No one!* I'll fix it so nobody will ever talk to you again. From now on, you'll be doomed to repeat the last thing you hear. Now be gone!

ECHO: Now be gone!

Discuss **What do you learn about the characters from this scene? How do Hera's words reveal what kind of character she is?**

> As you read, record your answers to questions about characterization on the Close Reading Worksheet on page 292.

The Setup, SCENES 2 and 3

Scene 2

What conflicts are escalating between the characters in this scene?

In what way does the girls' behavior contrast with the producer's expectations? Cite textual evidence to support your ideas.

SETTING: *Same as scene 1.*

(*Enter the ex-best friend. She and Amber stare at each other for an uncomfortable moment. The mood is tense. Suddenly they both break into wide grins; they hug.*)

1   AMBER: How cool is this, right? We're actually on TV!

2   EX–BEST FRIEND: Totally cool!

3   AMBER: And so amazing to see you, Felicity!

4   EX–BEST FRIEND: Taking Spanish with me this year?

5   THE PRODUCER: (*head in hands*) *Out!* Get her *out*, Josh . . . I thought they were enemies. In case you haven't heard, *the definition of enemies is that they hate each other! Sheesh!*

6   THE ASSISTANT: (*confused, frustrated*) Sorry, Jack. This Amber and her mother, they're cut from a different cloth—I mean, I've never even heard of the kind of cloth they're cut from. So, what now?

7   THE PRODUCER: I've got one more trick up my sleeve—that sister Mrs. Twiller hasn't spoken to in forever. You made all the arrangements for that, right?

8   THE ASSISTANT: Yeah. Should work. They haven't seen each other in about ten years—something about an inheritance.

9   THE PRODUCER: Sounds promising. She prepped yet?

10   THE ASSISTANT: Uh-huh. I am sure this one will create the drama we're looking for. As a matter of fact, that's her right there.

   (enter Aunt Chloe)

11   AUNT CHLOE: Hello? Where can I find—(*looks around and sees Mrs. Twiller*) Oh, Esther, my dear sister, there you are!

12   MRS. TWILLER: Amber, look! It's my sister Chloe who moved to New Zealand when you were three! Hi, Chloe! (*Aunt Chloe and Mrs. Twiller embrace.*)

13   AUNT CHLOE: Oh, Essie! I've missed you—what a naughty girl you are for not writing more and not coming to visit me in forever! (*focusing on Amber*) This couldn't be teensy-weensy little Amber—she's certainly turned out to be a fine young lady!

14   THE ASSISTANT: (*shaking his head in disbelief*) No. No. No.

15   THE PRODUCER: (*furious*) Why, oh, why are these people so unbelievably, ridiculously, impossibly boring?

16   THE ASSISTANT: Time to fire them, boss?

17   THE PRODUCER: (*mumbling, exhausted*) Yeah. Whatever. We'll get them to sign a **waiver** canceling the contract, hand them a check, and everyone goes home. Well, everyone except me. I'll be here all night, going through my files, finding a replacement . . . if it takes all night and into tomorrow.

Underline text that shows how Mrs. Twiller's reaction to seeing her sister differs from what the producer expected.

How has the producer's attitude changed at the end of scene 2? Circle dialogue and stage directions that support your answer.

Scene 3

Record details on the **Compare and Contrast Web** that show how the producer and the assistant are different.

In scene 3, how does the producer change when it comes to dealing with Mrs. Twiller?

SETTING: *An office on a high floor in the same building. Seated at a conference table are the producer and the assistant on one side, looking anxious, and Mrs. Twiller and Amber on the other, looking somewhat confused.*

18 THE PRODUCER: (*to Mrs. Twiller as he reaches into his desk drawer and extracts an envelope*) Let's make this short and sweet, just settle up and call it a day—it's more than ample, according to the terms of the contract.

19 THE ASSISTANT: (*nods vigorously*) Generous, even.

20 THE PRODUCER: Josh, please.

21 THE ASSISTANT: Sorry.

22 THE PRODUCER: (*sounding exhausted and holding out the envelope*) Just take the check, Mrs. Twiller . . . the least we could do to show our appreciation for the very, *very* exemplary work you and your lovely daughter did on the show—and, incidentally, could you sign this teensy legal thing? It's nothing really; you just waive your rights to the show, including the words *you're*, *not*, *my*, and *mother*. (*shrugs*) Standard.

23 MRS. TWILLER: (*looking surprised*) A check? Money! Well, I don't believe it—do you believe it, Amber?

24 AMBER: (*in disbelief*) No, Mom.

25 MRS. TWILLER: It's just that—well, we didn't expect to get *paid* for this, for television, of all things!

26 THE PRODUCER: (*trying to hustle them out*) Is that a fact? . . . Well, life can be unpredictable sometimes . . . **serendipity** reigns supreme and all that—here's your check.

27 MRS. TWILLER: (*Pushing the envelope back toward the producer, she waves them away.*) Absolutely not. Under no circumstances.

28 THE PRODUCER: (*skeptically*) Not take the check? *Not take the check?* My dear Mrs. Twitter—

29 MRS. TWILLER: Twiller.

30 THE PRODUCER: Twiller. If it's not enough money, Mrs. *Twiller*, I'm sure we could get our lawyers to **arbitrate** a new—

31 MRS. TWILLER: No, that's all right—we don't have any need for that money.

32 THE PRODUCER: But I haven't even told you the amount!

33 MRS. TWILLER: It really doesn't matter. If it's a lot, then I'm sure there are people who could really use it, and if it's only a little bit—well, then go and buy yourself something to eat. You look famished—when's the last time you had a proper meal? (*to Amber*) As a matter of fact, Amber, dear, do you still have that apple from lunch?

(*Amber forages in her backpack, finds the apple, happily hands it over to the producer who, thoroughly bewildered, takes it as Amber and Mrs. Twiller turn to go.*)

Record details on the **Compare and Contrast Web** that show how the producer and Mrs. Twiller are different.

How does the playwright convey the idea that Mrs. Twiller is a humble and caring person?

What new information about Mrs. Twiller's character adds to the contrast between her and the producer? Record your ideas on the **Compare and Contrast Web**.

34   THE PRODUCER: Before you go, Mrs. Twiller, can I ask you a question—a couple of questions? Mrs. Twiller, why are you and your daughter so *nice*? What makes you different? Why aren't you like the others? What's your secret?

35   MRS. TWILLER: Oh, there's really no secret to speak of; we keep busy is all. There's always so much to do. Amber has her schoolwork and her friends and her hockey and her chess club.

36   AMBER: Well, you work and go to night school. And don't forget the community garden and your book group and the animal shelter.

37   MRS. TWILLER: (*laughs*) I don't suppose I'd get a single *thing* done if we had a TV around the house!

38   THE PRODUCER: No TV?

39   MRS. TWILLER: Nope. We like it that way—more time for each other. Anyway, come, Amber, time to go home.

40   THE PRODUCER: You . . . don't . . . have . . . a . . . TV . . .

(*exit Amber and Mrs. Twiller*)

(*The producer is in a trance; then, slowly, almost without noticing he's doing it, he picks up his phone.*)

Analyze

How do the producer's interests seem different at the end of the play? Cite textual evidence to support your ideas.

41   THE PRODUCER: Gladys? Jack. Look, Gladys, can you get me a list of all the reputable charities in this area? . . . I said *reputable* . . . Good idea, hurricane relief . . . and could you cancel all my appointments until next Wednesday? Yeah, I thought I'd take some time off, go back home, see the folks, that kind of thing . . . I'm sure Josh can cover for me . . .

Vocabulary: Consult a Dictionary

A **dictionary** lists words in alphabetical order. It provides you with information about a word, including its pronunciation, syllabication (or how the word's syllables are divided), part of speech, and meaning. In cases of a word with more than one meaning, each meaning is given, along with its part of speech.

Try It Read this sentence from *The Setup*.

THE PRODUCER: . . . Look, Gladys, can you get me a list of all the reputable charities in this area? . . . I said *reputable* . . .

If you look up *reputable* in a dictionary, you might find this entry:

rep·u·ta·ble ('re-pyə-tə-bəl) *adjective.* known to be honest, reliable, or respectable

Note that the word is divided into four syllables and that the stress is on the first syllable. Note also that the word is an adjective.

| Discuss | **How does the entry show the different syllables of the word?**

In a dictionary, look up the following words from *The Setup*. Write the pronunciation and part of speech for each word and then write an original sentence using the word.

1. **waiver,** p. 71 _____

_____

2. **serendipity,** p. 73 _____

_____

3. **arbitrate,** p. 73 _____

_____

Respond to Text: Compare and Contrast Characters

In *The Setup*, there are both major and minor characters. The major characters are the focus of the play and carry most of the action. Various minor characters make appearances as well: Dr. Loretta, the ex–best friend, Mrs. Twiller's long-lost sister. These people are not main characters, but they help move the plot along and bring out the personalities of the main characters. By comparing and contrasting all the characters, you can better understand the play.

Try It Think about what you learned about how to compare and contrast characters.

 Discuss **What are some similarities between the characters in this play? What are some differences? Base your answer on the characters' dialogue and their actions.**

On Your Own Write a paragraph in which you compare and contrast the characters in the play. Which characters are similar and which are different? Make sure your answer is supported by sound reasoning and evidence from the text. Use the next page to help you plan your response. Then write your paragraph on a separate sheet of paper.

Checklist for a Good Response

A good paragraph

✔ compares and contrasts all the characters in the play.

✔ explains the reasoning behind your ideas.

✔ includes evidence from the text.

✔ shows your understanding of the play.

✔ includes a topic sentence, supporting details, and a concluding statement.

My Comparison of the Characters

1. **Topic Sentence** Include this information in your first sentence:

   Based on what I read in *The Setup*, some characters are similar because

   _____ ,

   and some are different because _____

   _____ .

2. **Explain Your Answer** The sentences of your paragraph should provide details that explain your answer. Use this chart to organize your ideas.

Character Qualities	Similarities	Differences
values		
attitudes toward fame and money		

3. **Concluding Sentence** Your final sentence should restate your conclusions with a new twist.

   _____

   _____

   _____

On a separate sheet of paper, write your paragraph.

Read on Your Own

Read the drama independently three times, using the skills you have learned. Then answer the Comprehension Check questions.

First Read   Practice the first-read skills you learned in this lesson.

Second Read   Practice the second-read skills you learned in this lesson.

Third Read   Think critically about the drama.

Animal Shelter

a play in one act

CAST OF CHARACTERS

MARGARET, animal shelter director

KINGSTON, dog

Summarize Circle the sentence that indicates the main event so far.

SETTING: *Margaret's office at the animal shelter. Margaret is sitting at her desk; Kingston is sitting on the floor facing her, looking nervous but vaguely hopeful. Margaret is interviewing Kingston, who has just arrived at the shelter.*

1   MARGARET: (*clicks her pen,* <u>*all business*</u>) And you are a . . .

2   KINGSTON: Dog. *D-O-G.*

3   MARGARET: Breed?

4   KINGSTON: Mutt. I think my father was a—

5   MARGARET: Name, please.

Characterization <u>Underline</u> details that show what each character is like. The first detail has been underlined for you.

6   KINGSTON: (*fidgeting with his paws*) Kingston. I was named Kingston when I was rescued—I don't know exactly why.

7   MARGARET: (*She stops writing for a second and looks annoyed at Kingston, who is trembling.*) You don't know exactly why you were rescued or you don't know exactly why you were named Kingston?

8   KINGSTON: (*looking across the room and then at Margaret's pen poised over the paper*) Both, I guess.

9   MARGARET: Hmm. (*She writes something down.*) Any fears? Thunder? Lightning?

(*Kingston says something inaudible.*)

10 MARGARET: Look here, Kingsley (*looks at her chart*) uhh . . . Kingston. I'm totally backed up with work. At this rate, I'll be here all night. Can't you just answer the question? Speak up, speak up.

11 KINGSTON: I said I suffer from severe anxiety. Sorry.

12 MARGARET: Hmm. Well, you're honest at least.

13 KINGSTON: Most dogs are. For instance, when we're hungry, we can't say we're *not* hungry. Do you see?

14 MARGARET: I think so. Age?

15 KINGSTON: Can't say. I feel young, but with these gray hairs, no new tricks in a year or two, anyway—well, now that I think about it, I'd say I'm probably quite old.

16 MARGARET: Short answers, please. Now, health issues?

17 KINGSTON: I've had kennel cough, ringworm, fleas . . . (*His voice **trails off** as he thinks of all the ailments he's had.*) Nothing serious, no severe or acute illness, nothing I can think of that would exclude me from—

18 MARGARET: Are you—completely trained?

19 KINGSTON: Madam, please.

(*Margaret writes for a long, long time while Kingston tries, unsuccessfully, to look over her shoulder.*)

20 MARGARET: (*looking up*) So, Kingston, what kind of work do you do? Do you herd sheep?

21 KINGSTON: No, ma'am.

22 MARGARET: Guard?

23 KINGSTON: (*sheepishly*) No, ma'am.

24 MARGARET: How about tricks? Can you roll over, play dead, jump through hoops, walk on your hind legs?

25 KINGSTON: Hardly. (*Kingston jumps onto a chair and faces Margaret.*)

26 MARGARET: (*irritated*) Well, are you good at *anything*?

27 KINGSTON: Does sleeping count?

28 MARGARET: You must be good at something. (*Kingston shrugs.*) Oh, come on now, Kingston, everyone is good at something . . . Take me—I happen to be a marvelous cook.

Dramatic Structure
Think about how the stage directions help you understand more about what Kingston is feeling.

Critical Thinking Think about why the answers to questions about Kingston's talents might matter.

Summarize Summarize what has happened so far in this play.

Characterization Think about how the playwright develops the characters in this play.

29 KINGSTON: (*brightening*) Really? What's your specialty? (*Kingston straightens up and appears less nervous now that he's becoming less of the focus.*)

30 MARGARET: Oh, this and that. Last night . . . hmm . . . fried chicken.

31 KINGSTON: I bet your family appreciated it—assuming there were mashed potatoes, gravy, maybe some green beans on the side . . .

32 MARGARET: (*in a quieter, less confident voice*) Actually, to be quite honest, I have no family . . . I live alone . . . It's a **solitary** life.

33 KINGSTON: Hmm. (*pause*) Any pets?

34 MARGARET: I had a guppy once.

35 KINGSTON: Any *real* pets?

36 MARGARET: (*She puts down her clipboard and begins to reminisce.*) When I was little, I wanted a real pet. But I wasn't allowed to have one. My parents said that because pets die, I was better off not having one.

37 KINGSTON: Excuse me, but by the same token you could say, I'm not going to the party because I may not have a good time; I'm not getting on a plane because it could crash; I'm not crossing the street because I could get run over; I'm not going to apply for a job because I might not get it . . .

38 MARGARET: I know where you're going with this, Kingston.

39 KINGSTON: (*on a roll*) . . . I'm not picking up the phone because I don't know who's on the other end; I'm not talking to anyone because I don't know what they're going to say; I'm not starting a relationship because the person may disappoint me . . .

40 MARGARET: (*icily*) I *said* I get your point.

41 KINGSTON: Now where were we?

42 MARGARET: I was saying how I've always wanted a real pet. Like—

43 KINGSTON: A dog. That's it, isn't it? Well, I'll be. You've always wanted a dog.

44 MARGARET: No! No! I'm away all day! Dogs need to be walked! They need exercise! It wouldn't be fair to the dog!

45 KINGSTON: Of course not. Have to be fair to the dog, naturally. *Unless* . . .

46 MARGARET: Unless?

47 KINGSTON: Unless, of course, the dog is, you know—old . . . and sleeps all day . . . and *adores* food.

48 MARGARET: You, for instance?

49 KINGSTON: Why, yes! Now that you mention it.

50 MARGARET: (*considering this*) Would you like to come home with *me*, Kingston?

51 KINGSTON: I'm not sure . . . I hardly know a thing about you . . . First off, what's your name?

52 MARGARET: I was born Alice, but I'm called Margaret—I don't know exactly why.

53 KINGSTON: You don't know exactly why you were born Alice, or you don't know exactly why you're called Margaret?

54 MARGARET: Both, I guess.

55 KINGSTON: Health?

56 MARGARET: Well, I've had bronchitis, conjunctivitis, tonsillitis; earache, eyestrain, stomachache; athlete's foot, runner's knee, tennis elbow . . .

57 KINGSTON: Whoa! Too much information!

58 MARGARET: Sorry. I was trying to be thorough. I get nervous when I'm put on the spot.

59 KINGSTON: I understand completely.

60 MARGARET: It's a condition. There's a name for it.

61 KINGSTON: Anxiety?

62 MARGARET: Yes, that's it.

63 KINGSTON: At least you're honest.

64 MARGARET: Yes. I try to be. For instance, I can't say I'm not hungry when I am. Do you see?

Summarize Box
dialogue on this page that reveals information you would exclude from a summary of the drama.

Compare and Contrast
How do similarities and differences between the characters come out as the interview changes?

65 KINGSTON: Rent or own?

66 MARGARET: (*nervously*) Well, right now I rent, but if you look at it the right way, you might say my position is improving, at least enough to—

67 KINGSTON: How often would you say you make fried chicken, Alice—I mean, Margaret?

68 MARGARET: At least once a week—but I could increase it to twice a week, maybe three times, if you—

69 KINGSTON: How about macaroni and cheese?

70 MARGARET: (*brightening*) Certainly! And I also make excellent beef stew, glazed ham, burritos, vegetarian chili, lobster thermidor, banana fritters, mussels on the half shell, fish fingers—anything you want.

71 KINGSTON: (*holding his paws wide*) I was thinking of portion size. You know, somehow I feel better with a little extra meat on my bones.

72 MARGARET: Oh, I know what you mean. I never skimp on portion size. It's quantity *and* quality that counts.

73 KINGSTON: I have a feeling this might work out just fine.

74 MARGARET: Great! So how about it, sport? You want to come home with me? Right now? Tonight? I get off work at six. We'll go food shopping on the way home.

75 KINGSTON: (*sitting back and looking thoughtful*) I'll have to mull it over, consider my options, let you know—there are some other parties expressing interest—

76 MARGARET: Please, Kingston? We can have so much fun together—oh, please say yes!

✅ Comprehension Check

1. How are Margaret and Kingston similar and different?

   _____

   _____

   _____

2. Summarize the play *Animal Shelter*.

   _____

   _____

   _____

3. Read this line from the play.

   **MARGARET: . . . Actually, to be quite honest, I have no family . . .
   I live alone . . . It's a solitary life.**

   Write a sample dictionary entry for the word *solitary*. Include syllabication,
   part of speech, and a definition.

   _____

   _____

4. What point is Kingston getting at when he asks Margaret whether she
   rents or owns and what she prepares for dinner?

   _____

   _____

5. Read this line from the play.

> **KINGSTON: I've had kennel cough, ringworm, fleas . . . (*His voice trails off as he thinks of all the ailments he's had.*)**

The word *trails* has more than one meaning. Write the definition of the word *trails* as it is used in the play. Then write another meaning of the word *trails* and use it in a sentence.

_____

_____

_____

6. What do the stage directions reveal about each character? List two examples.

_____

_____

_____

7. How does Kingston help guide Margaret to change her attitude regarding him?

_____

_____

_____

8. Why is it important that the characters speak similar lines?

_____

_____

Poetry

Poetry is the oldest of all literary genres. Since the beginning of human language, poetry has expressed every possible emotion, from joy and love to sadness and grief. The poet Samuel Taylor Coleridge described poetry as "the best words in the best order." Poetry often rhymes and has a strong rhythm, or beat, so it is often set to music.

Each reader brings his or her own experiences to a poem and therefore responds differently to it. What thoughts and feelings might someone visiting this rocky coast want to express?

Skills Focus

The War God's Horse Song / The Tyger / Sea Fever

Visualize   **Word Choice and Tone**

Paul Revere's Ride / Remember

Paraphrase   **Poetic Structure: Narrative and Sonnet**

Practice the Skill

First Read **Visualize**

In a dark movie theater, an image of a tall sailing ship on a stormy, gray sea appears on the screen. The wind blows hard, filling the air with salty spray. Rolling waves tower over the ship. The camera closes in on an old sailor in a yellow raincoat, standing by the ship's railing. Suddenly a huge wave washes over the rail. The action continues in sharp, powerful detail. You can sit back while the movie does the visual work for you.

Seeing the visuals in a poem is quite different. You, the reader, must use the words of the poem to form a picture in your mind. You try to see, or **visualize**, the scene or action in the poem. Luckily, you have two essential tools to help you do this: your experience and the images that the poet creates through words.

Try It Read these opening lines from "The Eagle" by Alfred, Lord Tennyson.

> He clasps the crag[1] with crooked hands;
>
> Close to the sun in lonely lands,
>
> Ring'd with the azure[2] world, he stands.
>
> [1]**crag** edge of a cliff
> [2]**azure** clear blue

Discuss **Where is the eagle? Underline the words that tell you. What scene do you imagine as you read these lines?**

Try It Now read the rest of the poem.

> The wrinkled sea beneath him crawls;
>
> He watches from his mountain walls,
>
> And like a thunderbolt he falls.

Discuss **What does the word *wrinkled* help you visualize about the sea? What do the words *like a thunderbolt* help you visualize?**

As you read, complete the Visualization Chart on page 293.

Practice the Skill

Second Read **Word Choice and Tone**

Poets rely on **word choice**, or selecting exactly the right words, to convey their ideas. Meaning can change, depending on the words chosen. A person's lips described as "lovely rubies" are far different from those called "snarled roots." In choosing their words, poets consider every aspect of their poem, including its subject, structure, audience, and tone. The **tone** is the poet's attitude or feelings toward the subject. For example, the tone might be described as humorous, angry, bitter, sad, or joyful.

Word choice has an impact on tone through words' sounds, meanings, rhythms, and repetition. For example, a Halloween poem might have a spooky tone, and words like *somber*, *phantom*, or *creep* will help to convey that tone. To find the tone of a poem, ask yourself, "What feeling do these particular words convey?" and "What are the poet's feelings about the subject?"

Try It Read these lines from "The Raven" by Edgar Allan Poe.

> Once upon a midnight dreary, while I pondered, weak and weary,
>
> Over many a quaint and curious volume of forgotten lore[1]—
>
> While I nodded, nearly napping, suddenly there came a tapping,
>
> As of some one gently rapping, rapping at my chamber door.
>
> "'Tis some visitor," I muttered, "tapping at my chamber door—
>
> > Only this, and nothing more."
>
> [1]**lore** knowledge

> **Discuss** **What is the tone of this poem? What words convey that tone? Circle the words.**

> As you read, record your answers to questions about word choice and tone on the Close Reading Worksheet on page 294.

Purpose for Reading

Read along with your teacher. Each time, read for a different purpose.

First Read	Focus on using visualizing images from the poems.
Second Read	Focus on how word choice affects each poem's meaning and tone.
Third Read	Focus on evaluating the poems critically.

The War God's
Horse Song

a traditional Navajo poem

What image do you visualize in lines 7 and 8? Describe or draw your answer on the **Visualization Chart.**

Circle things to which the horse is compared. What tone do these things suggest?

I am the Turquoise Woman's son

On top of Belted Mountain beautiful horses
slim like a weasel

My horse has a hoof like striped agate[1]
5   His fetlock[2] is like fine eagle plume
His legs are like quick lightning

My horse's body is like an eagle-feathered arrow

My horse has a tail like a trailing black cloud

I put flexible goods on my horse's back

10   The Holy Wind blows through his mane
his mane is made of rainbows

My horse's ears are made of round corn

My horse's eyes are made of stars

My horse's head is made of mixed waters

15   (from the holy waters)
(he never knows thirst)

[1]**agate** a colored, striped stone
[2]**fetlock** tuft of hair on a horse's leg

My horse's teeth are made of white shell
The long rainbow is in his mouth for a bridle
 with it I guide him

20 When my horse neighs
different-colored horses follow

When my horse neighs
different-colored sheep follow

I am wealthy from my horse

25 Before me peaceful
Behind me peaceful
Under me peaceful
Over me peaceful
Around me peaceful
30 Peaceful voice when he neighs
I am **everlasting** and peaceful
I stand for my horse

What kind of horse do you visualize in this poem? <u>Underline</u> words throughout the poem that help you visualize. Describe or draw your answer on the **Visualization Chart**.

What does the poem suggest about traditional Navajo culture and values? Cite textual evidence to support your answer.

The Tyger

by William Blake

What do you visualize in the first three stanzas? Underline words that help you visualize. Draw or describe what you visualize in the **Visualization Chart.**

Tyger Tyger, burning bright
In the forests of the night;
What immortal hand or eye,
Could frame[1] thy fearful symmetry?

5   In what distant deeps or skies.
Burnt the fire of thine eyes?
On what wings dare he aspire?[2]
What the hand, dare seize the fire?

And what shoulder, & what art,
10   Could twist the sinews[3] of thy heart?
And when thy heart began to beat,
What **dread** hand? & what **dread** feet?

[1]**frame** make
[2]**aspire** aim for
[3]**sinews** cords connecting tissue

What the hammer? what the chain?
In what furnace was thy brain?
15   What the anvil? what dread grasp,
Dare its deadly terrors clasp!

When the stars threw down their spears
And water'd heaven with their tears:
Did he smile his work to see?
20   Did he who made the Lamb make thee?

Tyger Tyger burning bright
In the forests of the night:
What immortal hand or eye,
Dare frame thy fearful symmetry?

What is the tone of the poem? Circle specific words that affect the tone. In lines 1 and 21, what impact does the word *burning* have on the tone?

What does the poet mean when he asks the question in lines 23 and 24?

Sea Fever

by John Masefield

What is the poet describing in this poem? Underline the words that help you visualize the images. Draw or describe what you visualize in the **Visualization Chart**.

How do the descriptions of the sea, weather, and sea life support the title of the poem?

Judge

Which of the three poems do you think has the most powerful visual images? Cite textual evidence that supports your judgment.

I must go down to the seas again, to the lonely sea and the sky,
And all I ask is a tall ship and a star to steer her by;
And the wheel's kick and the wind's song and the white sail's shaking,
And a grey mist on the sea's face, and a grey dawn breaking,

5 I must go down to the seas again, for the call of the running tide
Is a wild call and a clear call that may not be denied;
And all I ask is a windy day with the white clouds flying,
And the flung spray and the blown spume,[1] and the sea-gulls crying.

I must go down to the seas again, to the vagrant[2] gypsy life,
10 To the gull's way and the whale's way where the wind's like a whetted[3]
    knife;

And all I ask is a merry yarn from a laughing fellow-rover,
And quiet sleep and a sweet dream when the long trick's over.

[1]**spume** foam
[2]**vagrant** wandering
[3]**whetted** sharpened

Vocabulary: Synonyms and Word Choice

The English language is rich in **synonyms**, or words that have similar meanings. If a poet wants to describe a *boring* day, the words *dreary*, *wasted*, *dull*, or *tiresome* are all available to choose from. The poet can choose the synonym for *boring* that best contributes to the poem's tone and rhythm.

Try It Read this opening line from a poem by William Wordsworth.

> My heart leaps up when I behold
>
> A rainbow in the sky

Suppose Wordsworth had chosen these words instead:

> My heart jumps up when I notice
>
> A rainbow in the sky

> **Discuss** **Does the meaning of the line change when synonyms are used for other words in the poem? In what way does the tone change?**

The phrases below appear in the poems you have just read. Think of a synonym for the underlined word in each phrase and replace the underlined word with your synonym. Discuss how the different words affect the tone of the poem.

1. **I am <u>everlasting</u> and peaceful,** p. 89 _____

_____

_____

2. **What <u>dread</u> hand? & what <u>dread</u> feet?** p. 90 _____

_____

_____

Practice the Skill

First Read **Paraphrase**

When you **paraphrase** a text, you restate what it is saying in your own words. Paraphrasing is a good way to check that you understand a text. When you paraphrase a poem, you use your own words to restate the poem in plain language. Often when you paraphrase poetry, your paraphrase will be longer than the actual lines of poetry. This is because poets can express big ideas in a few words.

To paraphrase a poem, first, give it a close reading. Look up any words you don't know in a dictionary, or try to figure out their meanings based on the words and phrases around them. Then, restate the poem's lines in your own words.

Try It Try paraphrasing these lines from a sonnet by William Wordsworth.

> The world is too much with us; late and soon,
>
> Getting and spending we lay waste our powers;—

Discuss Reread the lines, phrase by phrase. Restate each phrase in your own words. How could you restate the phrase "the world is too much with us"? How would you say in plain language, "We lay waste our powers"?

Try It Try paraphrasing the next two lines from the same poem.

> Little we see in Nature that is ours;
>
> We have given our hearts away, a sordid boon![1]
>
> [1]**sordid boon** distasteful benefit

Discuss What is the poet saying about our relationship with nature? Restate the first line in your own words. Then paraphrase the second line.

> As you read, record your answers to questions about paraphrasing on the Close Reading Worksheet on page 295.

Practice the Skill

Poetic Structure: Narrative and Sonnet

A **narrative poem** tells a story with a beginning, middle, and end and uses setting and characters. The lines don't have to rhyme, and the verses can be short or long.

In contrast, a **sonnet** has many rules about form. Sonnets are always fourteen lines long. They usually have two parts, an eight-line section and a six-line section. The first section describes a situation or problem, and the second section presents a new idea or solution to that problem. Sonnets usually have a strict rhythmic pattern of stressed and nonstressed syllables. Sonnets also have a **rhyme scheme**, the pattern of words that rhyme at the end of each line.

Try It Read "On the Grasshopper and the Cricket" by John Keats.

The poetry of earth is never dead:

    When all the birds are faint with the hot sun,

    And hide in cooling trees, a voice will run

From hedge to hedge about the new-mown mead;

That is the Grasshopper's—he takes the lead

    In summer luxury,—he has never done

    With his delights; for when tired out with fun

He rests at ease beneath some pleasant weed.

The poetry of earth is ceasing never:

    On a lone winter evening, when the frost

      Has wrought a silence, from the stove there shrills

The Cricket's song, in warmth increasing ever,

    And seems to one in drowsiness half lost,

      The Grasshopper's among some grassy hills.

Discuss **Put boxes around the two parts. What does each part describe?**

As you read, complete the Compare Poetic Structures Chart on page 296.

Paul Revere's Ride

by Henry Wadsworth Longfellow

On April 18, 1775, the American patriot Paul Revere rode to Lexington, Massachusetts, to warn Samuel Adams and John Hancock that the British army was coming to arrest them. Along the way, he gave warning of the troops' movements to townspeople and farmers.

Paraphrase lines 6–14, restating in your own words what Paul Revere says to his friend.

Who is the main character in this poem? What setting is described? Record your answers on the **Compare Poetic Structures Chart.**

How could you find out if the events in this poem are historically accurate?

Listen, my children, and you shall hear
Of the midnight ride of Paul Revere,
On the eighteenth of April, in Seventy-five;
Hardly a man is now alive
5   Who remembers that famous day and year.

He said to his friend, "If the British march
By land or sea from the town to-night,
Hang a lantern aloft in the belfry[1] arch
Of the North Church tower as a signal light,—
10   One, if by land, and two, if by sea;
And I on the opposite shore will be,
Ready to ride and spread the alarm
Through every Middlesex village and farm,
For the country folk to be up and to arm."
15   Then he said, "Good-night!" and with muffled oar
Silently rowed to the Charlestown shore,
Just as the moon rose over the bay,
Where swinging wide at her moorings lay
The Somerset, British man-of-war;

[1]**belfry** bell tower

20   A phantom ship, with each mast and spar
       Across the moon like a prison bar,
       And a huge black hulk, that was magnified
       By its own reflection in the tide.

       Meanwhile, his friend, through alley and street,
25   Wanders and watches with eager ears,
       Till in the silence around him he hears
       The muster[2] of men at the barrack door,
       The sound of arms, and the tramp of feet,
       And the measured tread of the grenadiers,[3]
30   Marching down to their boats on the shore.

       Then he climbed the tower of the Old North Church,
       By the wooden stairs, with stealthy tread,
       To the belfry-chamber overhead,
       And startled the pigeons from their perch
35   On the sombre[4] rafters, that round him made
       Masses and moving shapes of shade,—
       By the trembling ladder, steep and tall,
       To the highest window in the wall,
       Where he paused to listen and look down
40   A moment on the roofs of the town,
       And the moonlight flowing over all.

       Beneath, in the churchyard, lay the dead,
       In their night-encampment on the hill,
       Wrapped in silence so deep and still
45   That he could hear, like a sentinel's[5] tread,
       The watchful night-wind, as it went
       Creeping along from tent to tent,
       And seeming to whisper, "All is well!"

[2]**muster** gathering
[3]**grenadiers** foot soldiers
[4]**sombre** gloomy and dark
[5]**sentinel** watchman

What character does this part of the poem focus on? What actions does he take that move the plot along? Record your answers on the **Compare Poetic Structures Chart.**

Why would the poet describe the dead in the churchyard as being "in their night-encampment"?

Circle the important details that describe what Paul Revere is doing.

What plot development is described in lines 52–56? Record your answer on the **Compare Poetic Structures Chart.**

A moment only he feels the spell
50 Of the place and the hour, and the secret dread
Of the lonely belfry and the dead;
For suddenly all his thoughts are bent
On a shadowy something far away,
Where the river widens to meet the bay,—
55 A line of black that bends and floats
On the rising tide, like a bridge of boats.

Meanwhile, impatient to mount and ride,
Booted and spurred, with a heavy stride,
On the opposite shore walked Paul Revere.
60 Now he patted his horse's side,
Now gazed at the landscape far and near,
Then, impetuous, stamped the earth,
And turned and tightened his saddle girth;
But mostly he watched with eager search
65 The belfry-tower of the Old North Church,
As it rose above the graves on the hill,

Lonely and spectral and sombre and still.
And lo! as he looks, on the belfry's height
A glimmer, and then a gleam of light!
70 He springs to the saddle, the bridle he turns,
But lingers and gazes, till full on his sight
A second lamp in the belfry burns!

A hurry of hoofs in a village street,
A shape in the moonlight, a bulk in the dark,
75 And beneath, from the pebbles, in passing, a spark
Struck out by a steed that flies fearless and fleet;
That was all! And yet, through the gloom and the light,
The fate of a nation was riding that night;
And the spark struck out by that steed, in his flight,
80 Kindled the land into flame with its heat.
He has left the village and mounted the steep,
And beneath him, tranquil and broad and deep,
Is the Mystic,[6] meeting the ocean tides;
And under the alders[7] that skirt its edge,
85 Now soft on the sand, now loud on the ledge,
Is heard the tramp of his steed as he rides.

It was twelve by the village clock,
When he crossed the bridge into Medford town.
He heard the crowing of the cock,
90 And the barking of the farmer's dog,
And felt the damp of the river fog,
That rises after the sun goes down.

[6] **the Mystic** the Mystic River, which empties into Boston Harbor
[7] **alders** trees related to birches

Paraphrase lines 77–80.
What does this part
contribute to the poem as
a whole?

Underline the lines that
establish a new time and
place. Record these details
on the **Compare Poetic
Structures Chart.**

Write a paraphrase of
lines 107–110.

Underline phrases that
show a time change in
each stanza.

It was one by the village clock,
When he galloped into Lexington.
95 He saw the gilded weathercock
Swim in the moonlight as he passed,
And the meeting-house windows, blank and bare,
Gaze at him with a spectral glare,
As if they already stood aghast
100 At the bloody work they would look upon.

It was two by the village clock,
When be came to the bridge in Concord town.
He heard the bleating of the flock,
And the twitter of birds among the trees,
105 And felt the breath of the morning breeze
Blowing over the meadows brown.
And one was safe and asleep in his bed
Who at the bridge would be first to fall,
Who that day would be lying dead,
110 Pierced by a British musket-ball.

Statue of Paul Revere and Old North Church in Boston

You know the rest. In the books you have read,
How the British Regulars fired and fled,—
How the farmers gave them ball for ball,
From behind each fence and farm-yard wall,
115 Chasing the red-coats down the lane,
Then crossing the fields to emerge again
Under the trees at the turn of the road,
And only pausing to fire and load.

So through the night rode Paul Revere;
120 And so through the night went his cry of alarm
To every Middlesex village and farm,—
A cry of defiance and not of fear,
A voice in the darkness, a knock at the door
And a word that shall echo forevermore!
125 For, borne on the night-wind of the Past,
Through all our history, to the last,
In the hour of darkness and peril and need,
The people will waken and listen to hear
The hurrying hoof-beats of that steed,
130 And the midnight message of Paul Revere.

How many lines are in this poem? Do you see one stanza, or multiple stanzas? What is the rhyme scheme? Record your answers on the **Compare Poetic Structures Chart.**

Draw a box around the lines that show why Longfellow might have written about Paul Revere's ride.

Paraphrase the last two lines of the sonnet.

How many lines and stanzas are in this poem? Which lines rhyme? Draw boxes around the two main sections of the sonnet. Record your answers on the **Compare Poetic Structures Chart**.

Argue

Why is the sonnet a better poetic structure for the topic of "Remember" than the narrative poem?

Remember

by Christina Rossetti

Remember me when I am gone away,
　　Gone far away into the silent land;
　　When you can no more hold me by the hand,
Nor I half turn to go yet turning stay.
5　Remember me when no more day by day
　　You tell me of our future that you plann'd:
　　Only remember me; you understand
It will be late to counsel then or pray.
Yet if you should forget me for a while
10　And afterwards remember, do not grieve:
　　For if the darkness and corruption leave
　　A vestige[1] of the thoughts that once I had,
Better by far you should forget and smile
　　Than that you should remember and be sad.

[1]**vestige** a small trace of something

Vocabulary: Figurative Language

To help you visualize a subject or to show it in an unusual way, poets use **figurative language**, words or phrases that mean something other than their dictionary definitions. Similes, metaphors, and personification all add to a poem's tone and meaning. A **simile** compares two things using *like* or *as*: *My nose was as red as a rose.* A **metaphor**, however, directly compares two things without using *like* or *as*: *My love is a rose.* **Personification** gives human qualities to nonhuman things: *The wind danced through the fields.*

Try It Reread these lines from "Paul Revere's Ride."

> . . . He could hear, like a sentinel's tread,
>
> The watchful night-wind, as it went
>
> Creeping along from tent to tent,
>
> And seeming to whisper, "All is well!"

Discuss ▸ **Underline the simile. To what is the wind compared? Circle an example of personification. What human qualities does it attribute?**

Find the following lines in the poems, and identify whether the phrase is a simile, a metaphor, or personification. Then explain what it helps you visualize.

1. **A phantom ship, with each mast and spar / Across the moon, like a prison bar.**

   p. 97 _____

   _____

2. **Gone far away into the silent land;** p. 102

   _____

   _____

Respond to Text: Poetic Structure

Compare and contrast the poetic structure of "Paul Revere's Ride" and "Remember." Think about how the structure of a narrative poem is different from and similar to a sonnet. Consider how these differences affect what is being expressed in each poem.

Try It Think about how each poem's structure affects your understanding of its purpose, ideas, and tone.

> **Discuss** **What events and description did Longfellow relate to the reader? Why did he decide on a narrative structure for his poem? What topic did Christina Rossetti address in her poem? Why did she use the sonnet structure?**

On Your Own Write a paragraph in which you analyze the poetic structures used in the two poems, citing details to support your ideas. For example, in Longfellow's narrative, you might analyze how the verses organize the events of Paul Revere's ride. In Rossetti's "Remember," you could analyze how the sonnet form organizes the poet's thoughts. Use the next page to help you plan your response. Then write your paragraph on a separate piece of paper. When citing details, include the line number from the poem.

Checklist for a Good Response

A good paragraph

✔ states the subject of your analysis.

✔ explains the reasons why you think each poem's structure is appropriate for its purpose.

✔ includes details from each poem.

✔ shows your understanding of each poem.

✔ includes a topic sentence, supporting ideas, and a concluding statement.

How Poetic Structure Affects My Reading

1. **Topic Sentence** Include this information in your topic sentence:

    The _____ structure of "Paul Revere's Ride" organizes

    _____ , and the _____ structure of

    "Remember" organizes _____ .

2. **Detail Sentences** Explain how the structure of each poem affected your
    understanding and experience of the poem. Cite details that support your
    ideas. Use this chart to organize your ideas.

	"Paul Revere's Ride"	**"Remember"**
How did the structure and content of the poem work together?		
How did the poem's structure help me understand its tone and purpose?		
How did the poem's structure help me enjoy the poem?		

3. **Concluding Sentence** Your final sentence should restate in a fresh way
    how the poetic structure of each poem added to your understanding.

    _____

    _____

    _____

On a separate piece of paper, write your paragraph.

Read on Your Own

Read each poem independently three times, using the skills you have learned. Then answer the Comprehension Check questions.

First Read Practice the first-read skills you learned in this lesson.

Second Read Practice the second-read skills you learned in this lesson.

Third Read Think critically about the poems.

Sonnet 29
by William Shakespeare

Paraphrase Think about how you would restate the poet's feelings in the first eight lines.

Poetic Structure Consider the poetic structure of this poem. Draw a box around pairs of words that rhyme. Some rhyming words have been boxed for you.

When in disgrace with fortune and men's eyes,

I all alone beweep[1] my outcast state,

And trouble deaf heaven with my bootless[2] cries,

And look upon myself and curse my fate,

5　Wishing me like to one more rich in hope,

Featured like him, like him with friends possessed,

Desiring this man's art and that man's scope,

With what I most enjoy contented least;

Yet in these thoughts myself almost despising,

10　Haply, I think on thee, and then my state,

(Like to the lark at break of day arising

From **sullen**[3] earth) sings hymns at heaven's gate;

　　For thy sweet love remembered such wealth brings,

　　That then I scorn to change my state with kings.

[1]**beweep**　cry about
[2]**bootless**　useless
[3]**sullen**　dull, sad

The Listeners

by Walter de la Mare

"Is there anybody there?" said the Traveller,

    Knocking on the moonlit door;

And his horse in the silence champed the grasses

    Of the forest's ferny floor:

5 And a bird flew up out of the turret,

    Above the Traveller's head:

And he smote[1] upon the door again a second time;

    'Is there anybody there?' he said.

But no one descended to the Traveller;

10   No head from the leaf-fringed sill

Leaned over and looked into his grey eyes,

    Where he stood perplexed and still.

But only a host of phantom listeners

    That dwelt in the lone house then

15 Stood listening in the quiet of the moonlight

    To that voice from the world of men:

Stood thronging[2] the faint moonbeams on the dark stair,

    That goes down to the empty hall,

Hearkening[3] in an air stirred and shaken

20   By the lonely Traveller's call.

[1]**smote** hit or strike
[2]**thronging** crowding together in great numbers
[3]**hearkening** listening

Word Choice and Tone
Think about how the description of the house affects the tone of the poem. Circle adjectives that describe the house.

Poetic Structure Think about how you can tell that this is a narrative poem.

Visualize Think about what the house looks like. <u>Underline</u> words that suggest the appearance of the house.

And he felt in his heart their strangeness,

Their stillness answering his cry,

While his horse moved, cropping the dark turf,

'Neath the starred and leafy sky;

25   For he suddenly smote on the door, even

Louder, and lifted his head:—

Paraphrase Think about the phrase "the silence surged softly backward" in line 35. How would you restate the phrase in your own words?

'Tell them I came, and no one answered,

That I kept my word,' he said.

Never the least stir made the listeners,

30   Though every word he spake[4]

Fell echoing through the shadowiness of the still house

From the one man left awake:

Critical Thinking Think about who the listeners in this poem might be and why the poet doesn't say who they are.

Ay, they heard his foot upon the stirrup,

And the sound of iron on stone,

35   And how the silence surged softly backward,

When the plunging hoofs were gone.

[4]**spake** spoke

✓ Comprehension Check

1. In line 12 of "Sonnet 29," Shakespeare describes the earth as *sullen*. Think of some synonyms for the word *sullen*. Then use the word *sullen* in a sentence.

    _____

    _____

    _____

2. Write a paraphrase of the first eight lines of "Sonnet 29."

    _____

    _____

    _____

    _____

3. Read these lines from "Sonnet 29."

    Haply, I think on thee, and then my state,
    (Like to the lark at break of day arising
    from sullen earth) sings hymns at heaven's gate;

    Is this a simile, a metaphor, or personification? What is compared?

    _____

    _____

    _____

4. How does the poetic structure of "Sonnet 29" help you understand the ideas in the sonnet?

_____

_____

_____

5. Read this line from "The Listeners":

   'Neath the starred and leafy sky;

   Why is the sky described as *leafy*? What does this adjective add to the tone of the poem?

_____

_____

6. Why did the poet leave out important details in "The Listeners," such as why the Traveller is in the forest and who the listeners are?

_____

_____

_____

7. Did you find "Sonnet 29" or "The Listeners" easier to visualize? Why? What did you visualize?

_____

_____

_____

Lesson 5
Literary Nonfiction

Literary nonfiction

is often called creative nonfiction because it relates factual information in a literary style. Authors of literary nonfiction use storytelling techniques to lure readers into the text and make factual information read like fiction. Literary nonfiction includes biographies, autobiographies, memoirs, narratives, articles, and speeches. This photograph shows a sandstone rock formation called "The Waves," located in Arizona. What might someone write in a memoir about his or her experiences hiking through this area?

Skills Focus

Saving the Sun

Main Ideas and Details

Word Choice and Tone

An Extraordinary Imagination

Summarize   Author's Point of View

Practice the Skill

Every work of nonfiction has a main idea. The **main idea** is the most important concept the author wants to convey. You identify it by reading the selection and thinking about what it is mostly about. Sometimes, the main idea is stated directly in a topic sentence or even the selection title. Other times, you need to identify key details to figure out the main idea. The key details stated in each paragraph work to support the selection's main idea.

To distinguish between the key details and unimportant details, ask yourself, *Why did the author include this detail? Do I need it to help me understand the main idea of the whole selection?*

Try It Read the following paragraph.

> In the 1930s, a series of droughts devastated the Midwest, making conditions perfect for enormous storms that kicked up topsoil and blew clouds of dust for hundreds of miles. The dust storms raged over the flat prairies and plains, hitting southern Colorado, Kansas, Oklahoma, and the Texas Panhandle particularly hard. This area became known as the Dust Bowl.

Discuss **Underline the topic sentence that tells the main idea of the paragraph. Draw a circle around the supporting details.**

Try It Read the following paragraph.

> Living in the region known as the Dust Bowl was difficult. Because of the drought, people had very little water to grow crops. The air people breathed was full of dust, and there was no getting away from it. Many people left the area in search of better land.

Discuss **Underline the main idea of this paragraph. How does the main idea of this paragraph connect to the main idea of the first paragraph?**

As you read, record your answers to questions about main idea and details on the Close Reading Worksheet on page 297.

Practice the Skill

Second Read Word Choice and Tone

Authors of literary nonfiction use language carefully and selectively to convey tone and relay messages. **Tone** refers to the author's attitude toward the subject. The author can have a serious and formal tone, a hostile and dismissive tone, or a humorous and informal tone. The words the author uses help to convey that tone.

Beyond choosing their words precisely, authors can use figurative language, such as analogies, to convey tone. An **analogy** makes a comparison between two things that are similar in some ways but otherwise are not alike. An analogy helps readers think about the subject in a new way. These kinds of comparisons help the author explain concepts that are new to readers and may be difficult to understand.

Try It Read the following paragraph.

> The soldiers found themselves wandering through the forests of Vietnam, a place so lush and beautiful that it seemed like being on another planet. They felt displaced, far from home, and unprepared. They felt like there were surprises behind every tree, some of them frightening.

Discuss What comparisons does the author make? Draw a box around the analogy the author makes. Think about how the author's word choices help convey tone. Underline words or phrases that set the tone.

As you read, complete the Word Choice Chart on page 298.

Purpose for Reading

Read along with your teacher. Each time, read for a different purpose.

First Read	Focus on main ideas and details.
Second Read	Focus on word choice and tone.
Third Read	Focus on thinking critically about the selection.

Saving the Sun

The author states that ancient astronomers didn't understand what caused eclipses. What main idea does this detail support? Underline other details in paragraphs 1 and 2 that support the main idea.

What tone does the author convey in paragraph 1? Write the tone and the word choices that support the tone on the **Word Choice Chart**.

1   To people living in ancient times, eclipses of the sun and the moon were two of the most frightening events they would witness in their lifetimes. In a solar eclipse, the moon passes between Earth and the sun and either fully or partially blocks our view of the sun. It looks like the sun is disappearing. In a lunar eclipse, the moon passes through Earth's shadow and becomes partially or fully blocked from our view. The moon turns an eerie red color as a dark shadow crosses over it. A solar eclipse can be either partial or total, depending on where on Earth it is viewed from. A total solar eclipse is one in which the view of the sun is completely blocked by the moon. A partial solar eclipse is one in which the view of the sun is only partially blocked by the moon.

2   Ancient peoples did not understand what was happening in an eclipse. It was frightening to them to think the sun was disappearing. They feared that it might not come back. It was frightening to see the moon changing color. Ancient sky watchers told stories to explain what they saw in the heavens. They did not have the scientific background or tools to know that Earth revolves around the sun or that the moon orbits Earth. These **celestial** objects were important to the ancient sky

watchers. They believed that the moon ruled the night sky, and the sun ruled the day sky. The sun brought light and heat and ensured the survival of the world. People believed the sun and the moon maintained order in the heavens and were supposed to behave in an orderly fashion. When they turned red or disappeared, people were convinced something evil and chaotic was happening.

3   Myths ancient people created to explain eclipses typically told of a sky monster taking bites out of the sun or the moon, and in some cases, devouring them completely. The Chinese attributed eclipses to an enormous sky dragon that threatened the survival of the world by extinguishing light and heat. The Maya attributed eclipses to a giant serpent, a jaguar, or an army of ants. The Vikings attributed them to two wolves. No matter what beast threatened the order of the cosmos, however, ancient peoples recognized the importance of **averting** destruction. They beat drums and made noise to scare away the monster. They shot arrows at the beast that was threatening their existence.

4   In order to wage war against the sky dragon, the people needed advance notice so they could prepare. In China, the duty of eclipse prediction fell to the royal astronomers. These ancient "scientists" were high priests who were believed to have an understanding of the ways of the heavens. The emperor employed them to help him protect the world from destruction. The astronomers' job was to monitor the movements of the celestial bodies and predict when the sky monster would attack the sun and put the world at risk of eternal darkness.

5   The royal astronomers of ancient China were official timekeepers and used the sky as their calendar, announcing the first day of each month and tracking the passage of seasons. The people of China tied the constellations to earthly empires, and they viewed the sun as a symbol of the emperor himself. Because people believed that Earth and sky were very much linked, eclipses were believed to be supernatural signs that foretold the future of the emperor, the future of the empire he ruled, and the survival of the entire world.

What does the author mainly want readers to know about the royal astronomers? Underline the details.

What are the constellations and the sun compared to in paragraph 5? Circle the analogy. What does the author mean by this? Record your answer on the **Word Choice Chart**.

Why did eclipse monsters in ancient myths take so many different forms?

In a solar eclipse, the moon blocks our view of the sun, leaving only a ring of light around the moon visible.

What does the story of Hsi and Ho show about ancient Chinese astronomy?

How does the author's use of dates and sequence contribute to tone? What other words in paragraphs 7–9 contribute to tone? Write your answers on the **Word Choice Chart**.

Why did ancient people view meteors and comets in the same way they viewed eclipses?

6   The job of the royal astronomers was also to record and track the appearance of comets, meteors, and other astronomical events that threatened to disrupt the world order.

7   Ancient Chinese astronomers observed and recorded the supernova of 1054, and they considered it equally as threatening as an eclipse. A supernova is a star that explodes and can appear as bright as the moon for a short time. The Chinese, among other groups of people, recognized the supernova of 1054 as something beyond explanation. The Chinese referred to it as a guest star, and they viewed it as an intruder into an otherwise orderly universe.

8   Eclipses have been observed and recorded for thousands of years for exactly this reason—they seemed to be at odds with the natural rhythm of the cosmos. So, the royal astronomers attempted to track and predict them in order to prepare an attack. A legend from ancient China tells of an eclipse that occurred in 2100 BCE without warning, due to the **negligence** of two astronomers named Hsi and Ho. Hsi and Ho had been appointed by the emperor to watch the sky and inform him when the sky beast would make an appearance. The astronomers, however, failed to take their position seriously. As a result, they failed to predict a solar eclipse that was believed to threaten the empire. According to myth, the sun was devoured for a time before it emerged from the dragon's mouth and continued to light the world. Nevertheless, Hsi and Ho lost their lives for their blunder.

9   The significance of eclipses was an established part of the Chinese belief system. During an eclipse, the emperor would often perform rituals to rescue the sun or the moon, and he would eat only vegetarian food and remain outside the main palace. Often, he would take the blame for the chaos himself, or he would lay blame on his royal astronomers.

10   The connection that ancient astronomers believed existed between the celestial bodies and the earthly rulers made them excellent recorders of celestial phenomena. Consider the following, from an early Chinese text on astronomy.

> When a wise prince occupies the throne, the moon follows the right way. When the prince is not wise and the ministers exercise power, the moon loses its way. When the high officials let their interests prevail over public interest, the moon goes astray toward North or South. When the moon is rash, it is because the prince is slow in punishing; when the moon is slow, it is because the prince is rash in punishing.

Underline the details that support the idea that modern scientists think ancient Chinese astronomy is important.

11   Thus, in tracking the effects they believed the heavens had on their rulers, the ancient sky watchers made notations that can be used today to study some of the astronomical phenomena that occurred in early historic times. Ancient Chinese astronomical records serve an important function to modern scientists in their understanding of events such as eclipses.

What analogy does the author stress by including the excerpt from the ancient astronomy book? Write your answer on the **Word Choice Chart.**

12   The astronomers of those times were ambitious. Lacking the technology we have today, it is very hard to imagine how Chinese astronomers could even begin to understand what was going on. For example, whether observers on Earth see a partial or a total eclipse depends on their location. For any given location, the pattern of total solar eclipses is **erratic** rather than regular. This makes eclipse prediction difficult. However, ancient astronomers made the attempt nevertheless. Predicting a total solar eclipse requires a precise understanding of the moon's orbit and the ability to track it accurately—two things ancient Chinese astronomers utterly lacked. Yet however hopeless those astronomers' efforts may seem to us today, they were not in vain. During a partial eclipse, for example, the sky monster appeared to retreat before swallowing the sun completely. Therefore, the people—and the emperor—could believe that the astronomers' efforts had prevailed. Because partial eclipses are more frequent than total eclipses, the astronomers were able to maintain a decent track record.

Describe the overall tone of the selection created by the author's word choices. Write your answer on the **Word Choice Chart**.

Analyze

An oracle was originally a priestess of ancient Greece. People believed the gods spoke through her to answer their questions. The word has since come to mean someone giving wise or prophetic advice or opinions. Why did scientists and scholars use the term *oracle bones* to refer to the bones and shells described in paragraph 14?

13   Scientists have been able to trace the occurrences of eclipses far back in ancient history. Records show that Chinese astronomers had a good understanding of what caused eclipses by 20 BCE. The Chinese were among the first to recognize that eclipses occurred in regular patterns. By 8 BCE, they could predict them using a calendar they devised, and by 206 CE, they had learned to predict them by monitoring the motion of the moon.

14   Much of what we know today about astronomy in the ancient world has been reconstructed from records written by early Chinese astronomers. Sadly, though, most of these early records were burned upon the order of an emperor. Thankfully, the Chinese tracked eclipses long before the invention of paper. Much of the astronomy that exists from ancient China comes from inscriptions carved on what scholars call oracle bones. During the Shang Dynasty, from 1600 to 1050 BCE, people tracked and recorded the occurrence of eclipses on ox bones or tortoise shells. The bones were used for divination, or telling the future. Those oracle bones are the earliest record we have of eclipses.

15   The Chinese were astute astronomers, despite their attempts to wage war against sky dragons. They had calendars from as early as 1200 BCE. One was based on the moon and another was based on the movement of Jupiter. The calendar based on Jupiter is known as the Chinese calendar, and it is still popular in many places today. In Jupiter's twelve-year cycle, each year is associated with a different animal, depending on which part of the sky the planet passes through. They also have records of the sky dragon that showed up from time to time and took bites out of the sun or the moon.

Vocabulary: Context Clues

While reading, you can often figure out the meaning of an unfamiliar word by using context clues. **Context clues** are words near the unfamiliar word that give you clues to its meaning. When you have an idea of what the unfamiliar word might mean, check your definition in a dictionary.

Try It Read these sentences from the text.

These **celestial** objects were important to the ancient sky watchers. They believed that the moon ruled the night sky, and the sun ruled the day sky.

> Discuss **What words help you understand the meaning of** *celestial*? **Underline context clues that help you. Write a definition for** *celestial*. **Then check your definition in a dictionary.**

Read the sentences from the selection that contain the following words. Use context clues to help determine the meanings, and write a definition of each word. Use a dictionary if you need assistance.

1. **averting,** p. 115 _____

_____

_____

2. **negligence,** p. 116 _____

_____

_____

3. **erratic,** p. 117 _____

_____

_____

Practice the Skill

Summarize

A summary tells the main ideas and most important details of a text. A summary conveys the main ideas in a much shorter format than the selection. It includes all the major points but ignores the minor details. When you summarize, you tell about what the text is mostly about, who it is about, and the author's main points. Good summaries tell the main points and preserve the author's purpose and meaning.

Imagine you are telling a friend about a soccer tournament in which you just participated. You would tell your friend where it took place, which teams you played, who won the games and scored the goals, and the overall outcome of the tournament. You might even include details about the weather and other important events that occurred. You would leave out the minor details, such as that one player broke a shoelace during a game. Summarizing a selection is very much like telling a friend about an event that you participated in.

Try It Read the following paragraph.

A famous story explains how Benjamin Franklin learned to understand electricity by flying a kite in a thunderstorm and drawing lightning from a cloud. According to the story, Franklin and his son William attached a sharp metal wire to a kite and tied a silk ribbon to the kite string. Then they tied a metal key to the end of the ribbon. When lightning struck the wire, it traveled down the ribbon and caused the key to spark. Whether or not the story is true, it is used to explain how Franklin discovered that lightning was just a big electric spark.

Discuss Underline the main idea of the paragraph and the details that support it. Then summarize the paragraph by telling the main idea and most important details in your own words.

As you read, complete the Summary Chart on page 299.

Practice the Skill

The **author's point of view** is his or her opinion about a topic. An author's point of view can be influenced by his or her experiences, cultural background, age, or personal tastes. Whatever the author's point of view is, it will be supported by details. While reading, look for details that support and influence the author's opinion.

Your own point of view, or opinion, may differ from the author's. When you read, consider how the author's opinion is similar to your own or how it is different.

Try It Read the following paragraph.

> Francis Marion was a soldier who fought for the French against the British in the French and Indian War. He was known as the Swamp Fox because he learned the lay of the land from the American Indians, and he knew how to sneak through the forests and swamps and make surprise attacks. Fighting a war in the wilderness was a lot different from fighting a war on the battlefields, and Marion's unconventional tactics caught the British off guard. The Indians helped Marion and his French comrades protect their settlement in the Ohio River Valley. The French had established a fur trade and had become friendly trading partners with the Indians in that region.

> Discuss > **What is the author's point of view about Francis Marion? Double underline two or more details in the paragraph that show that the author considers Francis Marion to be clever. Do you agree that he was clever?**

As you read, record your answers to questions about the author's point of view on the Close Reading Worksheet on page 300.

An Extraordinary Imagination

What is the most important point in paragraph 1? Record this on the **Summary Chart**.

Double underline the details that show the author's opinion about Rowling.

Why does the author italicize the word *one* in paragraph 3?

1   What does it take to create a fantasy world—an entire imaginary group of people, an environment in which they live, and an entire system of knowledge and beliefs under which they operate? A woman named J. K. Rowling created such a world in her seven books about Harry Potter. She created the world in her imagination—and in doing so, she became one of the best-loved authors of her time.

2   Today, J. K. Rowling is wildly successful. Since her first novel, *Harry Potter and the Sorcerer's Stone*, was released in 1997, she has continued Harry's story in six more novels, which have sold millions of copies, been translated into multiple languages, and been published all over the world. The last book in her series sold 8.3 million copies in the first twenty-four hours of its going on sale, setting a record for U.S. book sales. Then there are the movies—Harry Potter's adventures on screen made J. K. Rowling's fantastical tale the highest-grossing movie series in history. Now, crowds of screaming fans line up for blocks to meet her and buy signed copies of her novels, and they send her wands and quills in the mail.

3   Before all that, though, there had to be an idea. Rowling never had trouble thinking of ideas to write about. She loved to write since childhood and wrote almost constantly through her teens and twenties. But thinking of that *one* idea—that *one* novel she was meant to write—for that she had to wait for a unique inspiration. So, for a long time, Rowling struggled to find the right story to tell.

4   Rowling explains now that she never imagined herself writing a fantasy novel. She had always loved to read, but she had never been a huge fan of fantasy novels in the past. In fact, she has been compared to J. R. R. Tolkien, the author of *The Lord of the Rings*, but she admits that she never finished reading his books. Rowling also admits that she never imagined herself writing for children or young adults, either. She certainly never imagined that she would become so successful. All she knew was that she wanted to write, and she felt that impulse ever since she was a child.

5   Once Harry introduced himself to Rowling's imagination, however, his stories came easily. His friends and acquaintances and their tales of adventure started popping into her head and wouldn't stop. And according to Rowling, Harry Potter *did* introduce himself. One day, without warning, he materialized before her eyes. When Harry appeared so suddenly, Rowling admits that she was dumbfounded and **exhilarated** by the vision, and she felt lightheaded. She was in England, traveling to London from Manchester on a train that had been delayed. Bored with waiting, she stared out the window and began to daydream. Then suddenly, as if by magic, Harry Potter appeared in her daydream.

6   Rowling could see the boy clearly, and to her surprise, she felt like she already knew who he was. He was a wizard, but for a long time he hadn't known he was a wizard. He had just discovered that fact recently, and he was on his way to wizard school. That day on the train, Rowling allowed her thoughts to carry her away to a different world. Slowly, over the next few hours, details of Harry's life and adventures at wizard school kept coming into view, and she longed to write them down to lock them into her memory. She had nothing to write with on the train, however, so she let her imagination take over, and she wrote the stories in her head.

Paragraphs 5 and 6 describe how Rowling came up with her ideas. Write the important details on the **Summary Chart**.

The author goes into great detail about how Rowling came up with her ideas. What does this say about the author's point of view?

Why do you think Rowling describes feeling lightheaded when she saw Harry for the first time? Circle textual evidence that supports your answer.

7   By the time she arrived in London, she had seen Hogwarts School of Witchcraft and Wizardry, the school for wizards that became the primary setting for many of the books. She raced home to write all about it and about the mysterious wizard-child who over the next years would prove to be Rowling's full-time companion.

8   For the next seven years, Rowling immersed herself in Harry's world. She knew that in order to make it real for her readers, she had to understand everything about it, down to the last detail. Before she sat down to write the first novel, she knew so much about Harry Potter that she had all seven novels outlined on paper. Rowling had been through some tough times before Harry Potter came into her life, and they continued until *Harry Potter and the Sorcerer's Stone* catapulted her to fame. While she was writing about Harry, she was a single mother struggling to support her baby daughter, Jessica. They were **destitute**. The lived on the dole, or state welfare. She received barely enough money to support herself and her child, let alone heat her apartment. So, oftentimes she walked to a nearby coffee shop where she would buy one cup of coffee and sip it all day while she sat and wrote her stories. Her baby slept safe and warm in her stroller while Rowling wrote for hours about Harry Potter and his adventures at Hogwarts.

9   The rags-to-riches story of the young mother who wrote *Harry Potter and the Sorcerer's Stone* in longhand[1] while she sipped coffee at a café has become legendary and, given the success of the novel, an inspiration for everyone who ever dreamed of writing a novel themselves. The story continues to tell us that Rowling lived in Edinburgh, Scotland, at the time; and, because she had no money for photocopying, she typed and retyped the book so she would have a second copy.

10   The most compelling characters in literature are often based on real people, for the experiences we have in our lives mold who we are, what we know, and what we are able to imagine. In a way, Rowling's characters were people she had known all her life. As a child, she lived next door to her friends Ian and Viki Potter, which was where she got Harry's last name. Rowling and the Potters played fantasy games back then, and Rowling organized games in which she wore wizard's robes and made magic potions. She had a vivid imagination, and there were a lot of stories racing around in her head. When she was six, she wrote a book about a rabbit that got the measles. She illustrated the book, too. She has a sister, Di, who is two years younger, and Rowling claims that she started telling stories to keep her sister entertained.

[1] **longhand** in cursive script, by hand with a pen or pencil; not typed

11   Rowling's girlhood school was nothing like Hogwarts, however, at least not on the surface. She went to St. Michael's Village School in Gloucestershire, England, a small school with strict teachers and nothing the least bit eccentric about it. However, the headmaster, an **elderly** gentleman named Albert Dunn, had a shocking resemblance to Albus Dumbledore, the headmaster at Hogwarts. Rowling herself was, she claims, somewhat like Harry's friend Hermione, the smart overachiever who befriends Harry by the end of the first book. Rowling wore thick glasses and spent a lot of time studying. Sean Harris, Rowling's close friend, was the model for Ron Weasley, the boy who immediately befriends Harry on their way to school. Her friend Sean had a bright turquoise car that Rowling loved, and in fact, the Harry Potter books would feature a flying turquoise car that was just like it—except for the fact that it could fly.

Underline the details that describe who Rowling's characters are based on.

What does the author say about how Rowling came up with her characters? Record your answers on the **Summary Chart.**

Fans at the premiere of the movie *Harry Potter and the Half-Blood Prince.*

What are the most important ideas the author wants readers to remember about J. K. Rowling's personal story? Write your answers on the **Summary Chart**.

How does the author feel about Rowling's books in the context of the classics mentioned in paragraph 13?

Analyze

What does the author imply about the genre of fantasy literature? Cite textual evidence that supports your ideas.

12   The editor who bought *Harry Potter and the Sorcerer's Stone* told Rowling that she had better keep her day job because she would never make money writing children's books. Anticipating that boys might choose not to read books written by a woman, he asked her to use initials instead of her first name. Rowling had no middle name, and so she borrowed the name Kathleen from her grandmother and became J. K. (Joanne Kathleen) Rowling, the author. The name bears a certain resemblance to J. R. R. Tolkien.

13   In the 1960s, people read Tolkien the way they read Rowling today. Tolkien created Middle Earth—and the host of characters that inhabited it and that drive the stories of *The Hobbit* and The Lord of the Rings trilogy. Other writers had created fantasy worlds before, such as Lewis Carroll, who created *Alice's Adventures in Wonderland*; and A. A. Milne, who created *Winnie the Pooh*. Like Tolkien before her, J. K. Rowling created a story so compelling that it defies classification of any sort. She created a tale so timeless that it defies the boundaries of the pure fantasy genre and it defies the classification as young adult literature—as evidenced in its inclusion on *The New York Times* Bestseller List. Rowling became one of the **wealthiest** women in the United Kingdom and one of the most successful authors of all time.

Vocabulary: Distinguish between Connotation and Denotation

Authors choose words based on the meanings they convey. The **denotation** of a word is the literal meaning—the dictionary definition of the word. The **connotation** of a word is the emotional meaning it carries. Words can have negative, positive, or neutral connotations. For example, *inexpensive* has a fairly neutral connotation. *Cheap* has a more negative connotation, and *thrifty* is positive. *House* has a neutral connotation, and *home* conjures feelings of being cozy and comfortable and safe, so it has a more positive connotation than *house*.

Try It Read these sentences from "An Extraordinary Imagination."

> While she was writing about Harry, she was a single mother struggling to support her baby daughter, Jessica. They were **destitute**. They lived on the dole, or state welfare.

Discuss How does a dictionary define the word *destitute*? What feeling or connotation does the word convey? What is another word you could use in place of *destitute* that has a different and less negative connotation?

Read the sentence in the selection that contains each word. Then look at the word in the middle column that has a similar denotation. Explain how the connotations of the two words differ in the last column. For example, does one word have a more positive connotation? Does one have a more neutral connotation? You may consult a dictionary.

Word from Text	Word with Same Denotation	Connotations
exhilarated, p. 123	excited	
elderly, p. 125	old	
wealthiest, p. 126	richest	

Respond to Text: Summarizing

The author of "An Extraordinary Imagination" includes important facts that explain J. K. Rowling's rise to fame along with details that make the story more interesting but are not essential. A good summary of the selection would include only the most important details.

Try It Read this summary of "Saving the Sun."

In ancient China, eclipses were feared as supernatural occurrences; intruders in the sky threatened the survival of the world. The people of ancient China attributed eclipses to a monster—a malicious dragon that invaded the sky and attempted to devour the sun or the moon. The fear of eclipses was an essential part of ancient Chinese beliefs. In order to reassure their subjects, emperors appointed royal astronomers to study the heavens and predict when dragons were coming to attack. This shows that celestial events were taken very seriously in ancient times and that events such as eclipses were considered bad omens. The people of ancient China believed that what happened in the sky reflected what happened on Earth, and an orderly sky meant stability in the empire.

Discuss Is this a good summary of the selection? What kinds of details did the author include? What types of facts from the story did the author omit? Which details might you have included in a summary?

On Your Own Write a summary of "An Extraordinary Imagination." Use the next page to help you plan your response. Then write your paragraph on a separate sheet of paper.

Checklist for a Good Response

A good summary

✔ provides a topic sentence that conveys the main idea.

✔ describes four key events that led to the publication of the Harry Potter books.

✔ omits unimportant details from the selection.

✔ provides a concluding statement.

My Summary

1. **Topic Sentence** Write a sentence that summarizes the main idea of the selection.

_____

_____

_____

2. **Detail Sentences** Complete the sequence chart to show the main events described in the selection.

1.	2.
3.	4.

3. **Concluding Sentence** Your concluding sentence should sum up and repeat the main idea of the selection in a fresh way.

_____

_____

_____

On a separate sheet of paper, write your paragraph.

Read on Your Own

Read the selection independently three times, using the skills you have learned. Then answer the Comprehension Check questions.

First Read   Practice the first-read skills you learned in this lesson.

Second Read   Practice the second-read skills you learned in this lesson.

Third Read   Think critically about the selection.

Keeping America Wild

Summarize / Main Ideas and Details
Circle the main idea of paragraphs 1–3. Underline the details that support the main idea. The first few supporting details have been underlined for you.

1   When Lynn Cuny was a child in the 1950s, her busy family home in San Antonio, Texas, housed not only her five siblings and her parents but also usually one injured wild animal or another. Their home was like an informal pet hospital. One day, Lynn's brother found a red-tailed hawk whose wing was badly injured. The animal was thin and close to death. Lynn's family carefully placed the hawk in an outdoor cage they kept in their backyard. The hawk was very scared and reluctant to be cared for. But the family gently set her wing with a makeshift cast and patiently fed her meat with a small pair of pliers.

Word Choice and Tone
Think about how the words *soothingly*, *strong bond*, and *unspoken understanding* in paragraph 2 contribute to the author's tone.

2   The bird began to recover, and surprisingly one morning she laid an egg. So Lynn's mother named her Lady Hawk. Each day, Lynn's mother would spend time outside talking soothingly to Lady Hawk. The two of them developed a strong bond and an unspoken understanding.

3   The family cared for Lady Hawk until her wing was healed and she was strong enough to live on her own. Then her brother drove out into the Texas Hill Country where he released Lady Hawk into the wild. Lynn remembers feeling elated knowing that Lady Hawk flew confidently back into the wild.

Critical Thinking Think about why the family decided to release Lady Hawk instead of keeping her as a pet.

4   The following autumn, the family returned to the Hill Country to spend time in the woods. A red-tailed hawk flew to a tree near Lynn's mother who called up to it, "Hello, Lady Hawk!" The bird dropped to a closer branch, and Lynn's mother and Lady Hawk admired one another. Then Lady Hawk flew gracefully away as if to demonstrate her strength and gratitude. This incident was formative for little Lynn because years later, she would grow up to be a wildlife rescuer and rehabilitator and a pioneer in finding and curing injured wild animals and then returning the animals to their natural environment.

Main Ideas and Details
Underline the details that describe what inspired Cuny to become a wildlife rescuer.

5   As a young adult, Cuny's desire to help animals led her to accept a job at the San Antonio Zoo. While working at the zoo, she had the revelation that she did not believe in keeping animals in confined spaces for human observation. She strongly objected to the practice of having wild animals permanently in captivity—unless, of course, they were unable to survive on their own.

Author's Point of View Read paragraph 6, and think about how the author feels about animals that are injured by humans. Double underline the words that show the author's point of view.

6   Cuny left the zoo and began rescuing wildlife that had been victimized in one way or another by human activities. She saved birds that had been hit by cars, raccoons that had been trapped in attics, and coyotes, skunks, and many other animals that had been injured or orphaned. She saw for herself that the lives of many wild animals were **jeopardized** due to encounters with humans. She also learned that many wild animals could be successfully returned to the wild.

Critical Thinking Many people consider zoos a valuable resource to introduce people to wild animals from all over the world. Think about the pros and cons of keeping animals in zoos.

7   Then in 1977, Cuny started a formal rescue group called Wildlife Rescue and Rehabilitation (WRR). Cuny operated WRR from her home in San Antonio. For a while she struggled to get her operation off the ground. She received some donations at first but not nearly enough to carry out the work she wanted to do. She took a job delivering newspapers in the early mornings in order to make money to care for injured and orphaned animals. She also printed business cards and gave them to police officers and firefighters, as well as to animal shelters, pest control companies, and tree trimmers who called Cuny when they came across animals in need of help. She covered every base she could think of. She was **persistent** in her devotion to her cause.

8   Then, slowly but surely, she received calls reporting animals in need of assistance. One by one, volunteers signed up to help. After a while, local newspapers began covering some of Cuny's success stories. Then she began to attract more volunteers and more donations.

9   Soon, her house and small yard were overrun by wild animals. She knew that she needed a bigger space where she could not only care for the wild animals that would be released back into the wild but also provide a sanctuary for animals who were too injured to survive in the wild.

Wildlife Rescue and Rehabilitation cares for many native and exotic birds.

Native birds, mammals, and reptiles are among the animals rescued at WRR.

10   In 1980, Cuny received a donation of ten thousand dollars for WRR. This allowed her to purchase four acres of land to build the sanctuary. Six years later, the land was threatened by floods. The story made national news. Viewers responded by sending more donations. Soon Cuny was able to move to a 21-acre facility in Boerne, Texas, not far from San Antonio. Then in 2004, she received a donation of one million dollars. That donation changed her life. WRR moved to a 187-acre site in Kendalia, Texas. A modern-day Noah's Ark, the sanctuary is now home to more than six hundred animals—from praying mantises to wolves and tigers, creatures that traditional rescue groups can't handle.

11   Some of the wild animals, like the praying mantises and wolves, come to WRR from the wild, where their interactions with humans have resulted in injuries. Other animals come from private homes, pet shops, or "roadside" zoos (small, privately run carnivals or zoos). These animals, like lions and tigers, are often indigenous to other countries. WRR takes in all these wild animals, from squirrels to apes—nearly five thousand animals each year!

12   Since those days in the 1970s in Cuny's backyard, WRR has grown to become a nationally renowned organization. WRR has seven thousand members nationwide, twenty-two paid staff workers, as many as eighteen interns and apprentices, and more than one hundred volunteers. WRR has been recognized as one of the best rehabilitation sanctuaries in the United States. It is one of only nine nationally accredited sanctuaries. In addition to rescuing animals each year, WRR has a 24-hour, 365-day-a-year hotline for any questions regarding wildlife emergencies. The organization also maintains a drop-off center in San Antonio. This makes it easy for people to rescue animals and surrender them to Cuny's care. The center admits close to eighty animals each day. The healthy ones are immediately relocated and released into the wild. The injured ones go to the sanctuary in Kendalia.

Main Ideas and Details
One main idea is that WRR does important work. Underline the details that support this idea.

Author's Point of View
Think about how the author feels about WRR. Double underline the words that show the author's point of view.

Summarize (Circle) two sentences that you would leave out of a summary of the selection.

Word Choice and Tone Think about why the author puts the word *pet* in quotation marks.

Critical Thinking Think about how Cuny's parents taught her to respect the freedom of wild animals.

13   Animal sanctuaries such as WRR have large enclosures for the animals, many of them designed like natural habitats. The caregivers respect the right of the animals to live as close as possible to the way they would live in the wild. They also respect the animals' rights to live with as little human involvement as possible. WRR is not open to the public. It does not use animals in its education programs. In fact, the organization does not encourage anyone who wants to know how to care for a wild "pet." Cuny feels strongly that a wild pet is like a fish out of water. She does not want to send the message to anyone that wild animals should be tamed.

14   However, Cuny and other wildlife rescuers do believe that the public should be educated about how they can be involved in the care of wild animals. Of course this does not involve personal care of animals, but rather protecting their environment and respecting the animals' need for wild spaces to live. To educate the public and advocate for wild animals, Cuny has written two collections of stories about the many animals that have come into her care over the years. In these books, Cuny explains how wild animals have touched her life. Not surprisingly, the story of Lady Hawk is the first one in Cuny's latest book. Cuny demonstrates that she first learned to love and respect wild animals as a child. Her parents taught her not only to care for the weak but also to respect the right of all creatures to be free.

✓ Comprehension Check

1. What does the author mainly want readers to know about wildlife rescue?

2. Pick two details from the text that you would not include in a summary, and explain why you would not include them.

3. Summarize the work of a wildlife rescue worker. Include details that describe what a worker does and why he or she does it.

4. How does the author feel about Lynn Cuny's organization?

5. Cuny feels that a wild pet is like a fish out of water. How does this choice of words and comparison contribute to her tone?

_____

_____

6. Why does the author choose to tell the story of Lady Hawk? What does it explain about Cuny?

_____

_____

7. Read these sentences from the selection. Underline the context clues that help you determine the meaning of *jeopardize*, and write its meaning.

   Cuny left the zoo and began rescuing wildlife that had been victimized in one way or another by human activities. . . . She saw for herself that the lives of many wild animals were jeopardized due to encounters with humans.

   Jeopardized means _____

   _____

8. Read this sentence from the selection.

   She [Cuny] was persistent in her devotion to her cause.

   How would it have changed the meaning of the sentence if the author had used the word *stubborn* instead of *persistent*? How are the connotations of these two words different?

   _____

   _____

Lesson 6
Historical Texts

Historical texts, nonfiction writing on historical subjects, depend to a large extent on the author's effective use of details and specific examples to communicate ideas. The author establishes credibility by using the right facts and details to create an effective narrative and make history come alive. Historical texts may be written by people who lived through a historic era or participated in a historic event. They can also be written by historians who study and research a past era before they write about it. What might a piece of historical nonfiction say about the people in this photo? What makes you think so?

Skills Focus

The Great Influenza Pandemic of 1918

Draw Inferences

Fact, Opinion, and Reasoned Judgment

Hairstory

Compare and Contrast   Text Structures

Practice the Skill

To **draw inferences** is to make an educated guess based on information from a text. When you draw an inference, you are reading between the lines, discovering ideas that are not stated directly. These ideas are often important when it comes to fully understanding what an author means.

Drawing inferences involves thinking about the author's purpose for writing and including particular details. When relevant, you can also use your own experience to help draw inferences from a text. Building inference skills involves understanding the facts and details of the text, thinking about why the author chose to include them, and looking for evidence in the text to support the inferences you make. The details you use to support the inferences you make must come from the text.

Try It Read the selection below.

There were great differences in the types of clothing worn by nobles and peasants in the Middle Ages. For the nobility, clothing was a sign of importance and power. They wore expensive outfits made of luxurious materials, such as silk and velvet. Peasants wore plain, inexpensive clothing to keep them warm and dry as they worked in the fields.

Fifteenth-century lawmakers made it a crime for commoners to dress like nobles and others who were considered above them. For example, apprentices in England who worked for expert craftspeople, called masters, could not dress like the masters. Townswomen in Florence, Italy, could not wear striped gowns or fabrics embroidered with gold and silver thread because they might be mistaken for noblewomen.

Discuss **What was a difference between the clothing of the nobility and the peasantry in medieval society? Double underline the lines that tell you. Why do you think laws had to be enacted to enforce this dress code?**

As you read, record your answers to questions about drawing inferences on the Close Reading Worksheet on page 301.

Practice the Skill

Facts are pieces of information that can be proved. **Opinions** are statements of belief or personal feeling. Only opinions that are supported by facts are valid opinions. Distinguishing facts from opinions requires evaluating the author's evidence. Watch out for clue words and phrases that signal opinions: *I believe*, *I think*, and *in my view*. Also be aware of over-the-top, or hyperbolic, expressions that can signal opinions, such as *She was the greatest actress of all time* or *Everyone agrees this is true*. After you've distinguished facts from opinions, check whether the author's reasoning is sound. A **reasoned judgment** is a conclusion based on facts and opinions and supported by evidence that is both relevant and sufficient.

When reading historical texts, ask yourself questions such as *Can this statement be proved? How can I check it? What do I already know about the topic that might help me decide whether this is a fact or an opinion? Do any of these statements simply tell what the author believes, as opposed to reasoned judgments based on good evidence?*

Try It Read the selection below. Pay attention to facts and opinions.

Numerous absolute monarchs in eighteenth-century Europe, including Frederick the Great of Prussia and Catherine the Great of Russia, championed the ideas of the Enlightenment. They corresponded closely with progressive philosophers such as Voltaire and Diderot. While they believed in the philosophy of improvement through empirical, or fact-based, knowledge, both of these leaders refused to give up complete rule, which to me demonstrates a contempt for individual rights. It is my opinion that history should judge these rulers harshly for their obvious hypocrisy.

Discuss **Look for evidence that supports the author's statements. Are these facts, opinions, or reasoned judgments? Underline facts, circle opinions, and box reasoned judgments.**

As you read, complete the Fact and Opinion Chart on page 302.

The Great Influenza Pandemic of 1918

Draw an inference about why the author begins this selection with a scenario for you to think about.

Look at paragraph 4. Choose one fact and one opinion, and write them on the **Fact and Opinion Chart.**

How would you go about determining whether the statements the author makes are facts or opinions?

1   *Imagine this: a mysterious, deadly plague has taken over your town. Most of the houses on your block are dark, and entire families have been wiped out. People on their way to work are dead before they get there. As the plague spreads, your city shuts down, and schools and businesses in your neighborhood close.*

2   *Imagine that the plague that has hit your town is also hitting most other towns in the world. Now imagine that it's all* true—*it happened about a hundred years ago, in 1918, in cities and towns just like yours.*

3   *The name of the plague? Influenza—also known as the flu.*

4   Influenza hit the world just as World War I was ending. This war was a terrible conflict that had begun in Europe in 1914, spreading from a small conflict between Austria-Hungary and Serbia and eventually involving the superpowers Germany, Russia, England, and France. The United States thankfully intervened in 1917, and the war ended in the fall of the following year. Unfortunately, the deaths did not stop with the coming of peace—in fact, influenza would make things much, much worse.

World War I and the Influenza Pandemic

5   The American military involvement in World War I and the influenza **pandemic** were closely intertwined. In the spring of 1918, at the height of the war, large numbers of soldiers fighting in trenches—long, deep ditches—in France became ill. This was the first wave of the pandemic. The soldiers complained of a sore throat, headaches, and a loss of appetite. Although the disease appeared to be highly infectious, recovery was rapid, and doctors gave it the name "three-day fever." Generalizations like these are the reason pandemics always become so deadly.

6   But the crowded conditions of trench warfare soon created an environment where the influenza virus could mutate into a lethal strain. At first, doctors were unable to identify the illness. Looking back, this seems impossible, considering how deadly it became. Eventually, however, they decided it was a new strain of influenza.

7   The pandemic started to spread. In one sector of the western front,[1] over seventy thousand American troops were hospitalized, and nearly one-third of these men died. By the end of the summer, the virus had reached the British and German armies, and in a matter of months, it killed hundreds of thousands of soldiers.

8   Unlike an epidemic that targets a smaller population, a pandemic is a disease that affects victims on a global scale. By early fall, the second wave of the influenza pandemic grew with a vengeance; the disease had spread from the military to the civilian population in Europe and then outward to Asia, Africa, and North and South America.

[1]**western front** a line of battlefields stretching from Belgium, through France, to Switzerland

What can you infer about the speed with which the lethal strain of the disease spread? Which details support this inference?

Underline one fact and circle one opinion from this section of text.

World War I soldiers fighting in a trench

The Pandemic Hits Home

Why was the disease so difficult to track? What details from the text support your inference?

9   Outbreaks of the flu occurred in nearly every inhabited part of the world, first in seaports, then spreading from city to city along the main transportation routes. In ancient times, new infectious diseases could spread only as fast and as far as people could walk, then as fast and as far as horses could gallop and ships could sail. With the development of global travel, such as cars and airplanes, more new diseases than ever before were potential pandemics. In just one more example of why modern transportation poses the deadliest threat to society, influenza was the principal infectious disease to be influenced by the growing global transport network in the twentieth century.

What is an example of a hyperbolic expression signaling an opinion in "The Pandemic Hits Home"? Write your evidence on the **Fact and Opinion Chart.**

10   Still, it took a while before the seriousness of the disease was recognized. Americans did not think influenza was a serious cause for concern. People were familiar with pandemics, so at first it wasn't cause for unusual alarm. By the time it had achieved the status of a pandemic, however, it was killing people faster than the countries could deal with it, and it traveled quickly from region to region.

Doctors and Nurses

What reasoned judgment does the author make in paragraph 11? <u>Underline</u> a fact that supports the judgment, and list the judgment on the **Fact and Opinion Chart.**

11   In 1918, the germ theory of disease was fairly advanced. The medical practitioners of the day had a pretty good idea that droplets from an infected person had a lot to do with the spread of respiratory illness. They also recognized that the virus could be spread through contact with contaminated surfaces, used handkerchiefs, water glasses, and so on. They did a good job of controlling as many of these factors as they could by educating the public with posted announcements (see Figure 1).

12   But despite an order from the Public Health Service mandating the reporting of influenza cases, few reports were received. Most states were unable to keep accurate records, and requests for information went unheeded. As a result, epidemiologists[2] were unable to thoroughly study the disease.

[2] **epidemiologists** doctors who deal with the incidence, distribution, and control of disease in a population

U.S. Army field hospital inside ruins of a church in France, 1918

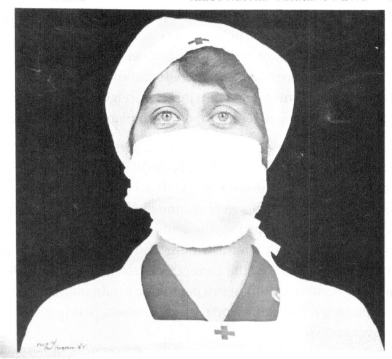

To Prevent
Influenza!

Do not take any person's breath.
Keep the mouth and teeth clean.
Avoid those that cough and sneeze.
Don't visit poorly ventilated places.
Keep warm, get fresh air and sun-shine.
Don't use common drinking cups, towels, etc.
Cover your mouth when you cough and sneeze.
Avoid Worry, Fear and Fatigue.
Stay at home if you have a cold.
Walk to your work or office.
In sick rooms wear a gauze mask like in illustration.

Figure 1

13   The seriousness of the situation was compounded by the fact that, because of the war, doctors and nurses were in short supply, so the beleaguered Public Health Service couldn't find enough medical professionals to work in hospitals and other medical facilities. Even when trained personnel were found, there was a good chance they'd get sick, too. Too frequently medical students would be enlisted instead of seasoned experts to staff the temporary hospitals that were set up in schools and community centers by local officials to address the shortage of hospital beds.

Prevention and Control

14   In many communities, **quarantines** were issued to prevent the spread of the pandemic. All public buildings were closed—even funeral parlors. Funerals were held outside to protect the mourners. Some policy makers demanded that people wear gauze masks in public and even passed laws requiring people to wear them. In some states, laws were passed that forbade spitting, which was thought to be a source of **contagion**. Enforcing these laws proved to be very difficult, as most people in times of great stress question authority.

> What does the author say about the public's cooperation with health officials? Is it a fact or an opinion? Cite the text evidence, and enter it into the correct column on the **Fact and Opinion Chart.**

> Why would states enact laws prohibiting spitting?

The End of the Pandemic

What can you infer about why the statistics regarding the numbers of people who died worldwide from the pandemic are so wildy different?

15   Two months after the pandemic struck, just as the war was winding down, the terrible second wave of influenza began to ebb. Slowly, people started to come out of their houses and celebrate the end of the war. Quarantines were lifted, and schools and shops reopened. Although the disease continued to be a threat throughout the spring of 1919, life was beginning to return to some semblance of normalcy.

16   By the time the pandemic had ended, in the summer of 1919, nearly 675,000 Americans were dead, and hundreds of thousands more were orphaned and widowed. No one can be sure how many died worldwide. Early estimates were around twenty million dead, but some say that number is far too low; these researchers posit thirty to fifty million dead, all told. By contrast, more than nine million soldiers died in World War I. No matter the correct estimate, this was still only a fraction of the number the influenza pandemic would ultimately kill worldwide, making it one of the worst, if not *the* worst, pandemics the world has ever known.

Argue

Given what people knew at the time, how could the spread of the disease have been slowed? Cite textual evidence to support your ideas.

17   After the war, however, many medical officers and military leaders would downplay the pandemic, which effectively erased this dramatic story from the American consciousness.

Bird's-eye view of returning World War I soldiers parading in Minneapolis

Vocabulary: Domain-Specific Vocabulary

It's important to know the meanings of words and phrases used in informational texts, including domain-specific words.

Domain-specific words include professional and technical terminology that are limited to use within a particular area. Typically, you don't come across these words in your everyday reading. However, they are essential to reading in different content areas. To determine the meaning of tough domain-specific words, try to use context clues, but sometimes you'll need to use a dictionary or glossary.

Try It Look at this chart that lists three professions and some domain-specific words relating to them.

Lawyer	Musician	Construction worker
arraign	acoustics	plumb
estate tax	treble clef	reciprocating saw

> **Discuss** **Talk about the words in the chart, and discuss how their meanings derive from a specific profession. Add one more word to the column for each profession.**

For each domain-specific word from the text, write its meaning, and underline the clues you used to figure it out. You may use a dictionary.

1. **pandemic,** p. 141 _____

_____

2. **quarantine,** p. 143 _____

_____

3. **contagion,** p. 143 _____

_____

Practice the Skill

Compare and Contrast

Compare and contrast means identifying how two or more things, ideas, people, or texts are alike and different. Understanding and expressing the relationship between things helps you understand both of them better. As you read, look for clue words and phrases that indicate a comparison or a contrast. Words such as *like*, *similar*, and *same* signal a comparison. Words such as *unlike*, *rather than*, *as opposed to*, and *but* signal a contrast.

To compare and contrast textual elements, ask yourself questions such as *How are these things alike? How are they different? What details in the text describe each of them? Are the details similar or different? Is there more than one way to compare or contrast these things?*

Try It Read the following sentences.

1. Various cancers are still classified as deadly, though many of them are not as untreatable as they once were.
2. Although they ran on their parties' usual platforms, one could argue that the three candidates had comparable agendas.
3. Sycamores shed their leaves in autumn, much as all deciduous trees do.
4. Teenagers frequently communicate by text message, while their parents prefer to speak to a live person.

Discuss **Underline what is compared or contrasted in each sentence. Double underline words that signal comparison or contrast. Talk about similarities and differences that the sentences express.**

As you read, complete the Compare and Contrast Chart on page 303.

Practice the Skill

Text structure refers to the way text is organized in a selection. In nonfiction, there are many ways to present information.

- **Chronology** tells a sequence of events in the order in which they occurred.

- **Comparison and contrast** tells the similarities and differences between ideas, events, and people. An **analogy** is an extended comparison in which one situation or idea is used to reveal information about a similar situation or idea.

- **Categorization** puts ideas, events, or people into separate categories to highlight their distinctions.

- **Cause and effect** tells the cause, or the reason for something happening, and the effects, or the results of the cause.

Being able to identify a text's structure is a key to understanding what the author is trying to say.

Try It Read the following selection.

> Scientist Cecily Veld likened the process of landing a rover on Mars to practicing an obstacle course in daylight, then running the course while blindfolded.
>
> "No matter how many times you've done it," she said, "when you don't have your own eyes on the experiment, everything changes. Even the smallest judgment error can lead to a major mistake. In the laboratory, when it's right in front of you, you know when to shift slightly. You know how to adjust to conditions as they arise. But with a camera and video lag and thousands of miles between the controls and the rover, it's like threading through barbed wire in the dark."

Discuss Talk about the effectiveness of this analogy. How does it help you understand the scientist's problem? To what other thing does she compare remotely maneuvering a Mars rover?

As you read, record your answers to questions about text structure on the Close Reading Worksheet on page 304.

HAIRSTORY

Explain how the author organizes the information in paragraph 2. Underline the clues that tell you.

Circle the words in paragraph 2 that give you an idea of the author's point of view. What might they suggest about the author's attitude toward hairstyle obsessions?

1   Student X is having a "bad hair day." That means he or she is experiencing a period in which the shafts of dead tissue that emerge from the follicles, or pits, below the surface of Student X's scalp don't flow in the right direction, have the desired texture, or are perhaps the wrong color or length. Why does Student X care about his or her hair? Whether we admit it or not, we think our hair says something about who we are and how stylish we think we are. People of all ages in our culture are expected to flaunt beautiful tresses. Has it always been this way?

2   Since the beginning of recorded history, men and women have yearned for perfect hair—perfect, that is, according to the notions of beauty of their time and place. Like Student X who is having the bad hair day, many otherwise intelligent people have gone to extravagant lengths to follow a trend. Like Student X, they wanted to look like the important and powerful people of their time—movie actors, pop stars, athletes, national heroes, or royalty—and sometimes suffered for it. It is easy to say these people—including Student X— were vain, but let's be fair: hair will always be associated with self-worth, and some people will pay too much money and undergo uncomfortable and sometimes even dangerous treatments to avoid bad hair days. The phrase "suffering for one's beauty" was at times particularly appropriate, and one can only shake one's head in amusement at what people throughout history have gone through to achieve good hair.

3   Let's take a quick tour of the "hairstory" of Western civilization, starting with the Middle Ages.

Medieval Europe

4   In fourteenth-century Europe, men's and women's hairstyles were an important indicator of their social status. Women of the nobility parted their long hair in the middle, pinned it up on the sides, and then covered it with a veil or linen cap. No doubt this practice kept their locks clean in an age without running water or shampoo. But fashion also dictated that the ladies have high foreheads. To achieve this effect, they plucked unwanted hair or rubbed it off with a rough stone. The noblewomen were also known to use a cream made of the chemical quicklime and water, which would burn off hair and irritate the skin. In addition, they plucked their eyebrows into thin lines and clipped their eyelashes short. The result was considered quite beautiful.

5   Men's hairstyles were also dictated by their positions in society. Men who served within the Roman Catholic Church wore a hairstyle called a tonsure. **Tonsure** referred to the act of clipping, or shaving, the crown of the head. This was part of the rite of inducting someone into the clergy. Tonsure was required for receiving clerical **orders**, such as deacon, priest, or bishop. According to **canon** law, all clerics were bound to wear the tonsure or else face certain penalties.

6   Laymen, or men not affiliated with the church, wore "bowl cuts." This hairstyle looks as if a bowl were placed on top of a person's head, and everything else cut off. Young laymen usually shaved, while older laymen sported beards that they parted into points and then waxed in place. Some got their beards wet and rolled them up, then let them dry overnight in bags called "beard bags." Even though this took time and effort, the shaping of beards was not nearly as dangerous as the women's use of chemicals.

What is a similarity and a difference between laymen of different ages? Record your ideas on the **Compare and Contrast Chart**.

How does the author organize the important points in "Medieval Europe"?

What determined how medieval men and women wore their hair? Circle the clues that tell you.

What is a major difference between how women styled their hair in the fifteenth and eighteenth centuries? Record your ideas on the **Compare and Contrast Chart.**

What were the effects of Francis I accidentally burning his hair? Underline the effects.

7   By the fifteenth century, women continued to desire high foreheads. Instead of plucking out the hair, however, they began to cover their hairlines with jeweled turbans. In addition, women became interested in changing their hair color. In order to achieve the blond hair of many northern Europeans, dark-haired women sat for hours in the sun in an attempt to bleach their hair. The women of Venice, Italy, took a somewhat outrageous step: they put blond highlights in their hair by pouring lion urine over it before sitting in the sun!

Sixteenth Century to Eighteenth Century

8   In the sixteenth century, royalty set fashion trends, some of which had negative health effects. Male aristocrats wore their hair long until Francis I of France accidentally burned off most of his with a torch. As a result, men began wearing their hair shortly trimmed. In England, noblewomen imitated the naturally red hair and pale complexion of Queen Elizabeth I by wearing orange wigs and thick coats of white face powder that contained ingredients later discovered to be toxic, including lead.

9   Powder continued to be an important cosmetic for men and women well into the eighteenth century in Europe and the American colonies. Stylish men wore white-powdered wigs with a braid at the back of the neck and a black bow. These wigs were practical because they allowed men to wear their own hair short so they did not suffer from lice. Women powdered their hair, which they also crimped and curled and adorned with wreaths or bows.

10   By the 1770s, however, wealthy French and English women's hairstyles became absurdly elaborate. For instance, it was popular to build coiffures[1] over and around horsehair pads or wire cages. Some coiffures extended three feet in the air, which could make them crushingly heavy and often resulted in headaches and neck injuries.

[1] **coiffures**   styles of arranging hair

Men and women of the early Victorian era wore their hair naturally and simply styled. The days of powdered wigs were long over.

Victorian Era to the 1920s

11   In the 1840s, women's hair was sleek and demure. It was oiled and smoothed down over the temples, with long sausage curls at the sides or a heavy knot of curls or plaits in the back. Men wore their own hair in a soft, floppy comb-over.

12   But during the "Roaring Twenties" (1920–1929), American society reacted against the late Victorian standards of beauty. Gone were the elaborately waved or curled hairstyles. In came the new, short "bobbed" hair that symbolized the growing freedom of women. Plus, for the first time, Hollywood was a factor. Women took their cues from the early film stars Louise Brooks, Josephine Baker, and Clara Bow, while men imitated the slicked-back style of Rudolph Valentino.

13   During this period, a series of contraptions became available that made the whole business of hair care more efficient. The portable hair dryer was the perfect solution for new bobbed styles, and the first handheld hair dryer was invented in 1920.

The 1930s and 1940s

14   In the 1930s and 1940s, women got serious about copying Hollywood stars. Rejecting the hard-edged styles of the 1920s, women favored the longer, softer hairstyles their idols were wearing: Dolores del Rio's curls; Bette Grable's topknot with ringlets. Men, however, preferred the short, flat-topped crew cuts worn by athletes. Many African American men wore the conk hairstyle, in which they chemically straightened their hair so they could style it in different ways.

Compare women's hair during the Victorian era and the Roaring Twenties. Include a similarity that shows their motivations. Record your ideas on the **Compare and Contrast Chart.**

What new invention made styling hair easier? How did this invention change how people styled their hair?

Why was Hollywood becoming a factor in the 1920s? How do you know?

Compare men's hair treatments to women's in the twentieth century. Record your ideas on the **Compare and Contrast Chart.**

How does the author feel about hairstyles and remedies? (Circle) words that show the author's feelings.

Assess

Assess the author's point of view and how it helps or weakens the argument. Cite textual evidence to support your ideas.

15   Women weren't the only ones to benefit from high-tech beauty tools. Around this time, a slew of bizarre contraptions were invented. Many of these treatments were for men who were losing their hair. An array of baldness-reversing devices flooded the market, all promising improved hair growth, but few delivered on those promises.

16   In 1923, some men treated their hair loss by using the Thermocap, a device developed by Merke Institute that delivered heat and blue light directly to the scalp, and thus supposedly encouraged dormant hair to grow. Another gadget stimulated the scalp by sending an arc of sparks from blown-glass attachments to the head. Ouch! Then in 1936, a company launched the Crosley Xervac, which was a suction machine whose purpose was to circulate the blood in the scalp, thus curing hair loss. These mechanisms were not comfortable, and they probably caused some men to yearn for the days of powdered wigs!

17   Do you still think a bad hair day is a terrible thing? It sometimes seems that our hair is more trouble than it is worth. So, the next time you look at your hair in the mirror, consider this: over the centuries, men and women have taken great pains (and experienced some great pain) in order to make their hair into something that it wasn't originally. They plucked, powdered, and piled it high, and they crimped, curled, and covered it—they even poisoned and shocked themselves—all in the pursuit of beauty. You really must admire their dedication.

Vocabulary: Consult Dictionaries and Glossaries to Determine Word Meaning

A **dictionary** lists words in alphabetical order. It provides information about words including their pronunciation, syllabication, part of speech, and meaning.

A **glossary** is a listing of the specialized, unusual, or domain-specific words in a text. The words are usually listed in alphabetical order in a special glossary section at the back of the text. Because glossaries are specific to one text, they tell you the word's meaning only as it pertains to that particular text's topic.

Try It Read this section from "Hairstory."

> **Tonsure** was required for receiving clerical **orders**, such as deacon, priest, or bishop. According to **canon** law, all clerics were bound to wear the tonsure or else face certain penalties.

Discuss **Suppose this selection appeared in a book about the history of fashion. The book contains a glossary that features the three boldface words in the paragraph.**

Write a glossary definition for each word from page 149 of the selection. Use context clues and a dictionary to help you.

1. **tonsure** _____

   _____

2. **orders** _____

   _____

3. **canon** _____

   _____

Respond to Text: Evaluate Evidence and Opinions

Authors of historical nonfiction should give a factual account of what they're writing about. As is often the case, though, authors may include their opinions or judgment about events, ideas, and people. It is important to evaluate what the author says and to figure out whether he or she is relating an opinion or a fact. This will help you understand which parts of the historical account actually happened and which parts are the author's own ideas about the account.

Try It "Hairstory" tells how hair has been perceived through history and how hairstyles have changed.

 Discuss **Evaluate this selection in terms of its facts and opinions. Do the opinions get in the way of the facts? Are the opinions well reasoned? Base your discussion on evidence from the text.**

On Your Own Write your own evaluation of the author's insertion of opinions throughout the text. How do the opinions factor in to the author's history of hairstyles? What effect does this have? Use the next page to help you plan your response. Then write your paragraph on a separate piece of paper.

Checklist for a Good Response

A good paragraph

✔ evaluates the text for evidence and opinions.

✔ explains the reasoning behind your answer.

✔ includes details from the text and other things you know.

✔ shows your understanding of the information.

✔ includes a topic sentence, supporting ideas, and a concluding statement.

My Evaluation of the Author's Evidence

1. **Topic Sentence** Include this information in your first sentence:

    The author of "Hairstory" uses both facts and opinions to tell the

    history of hair. The author's opinion of hairstyling and treatments is

    _____ .

2. **Explain Your Answer** The sentences of your paragraph should provide
    details that explain your answer. Use this chart to organize your ideas.

Hairstyles	Author's Opinion
Fourteenth-century women	
Fourteenth-century men	
Fifteenth-century women	
Eighteenth-century women	
Eighteenth-century men	
Twentieth-century women	
Twentieth-century men	

3. **Concluding Sentence** Your final sentence should restate your conclusions
    with a new twist.

    _____

    _____

On a separate piece of paper, write your paragraph.

Read on Your Own

Read the selection independently three times, using the skills you have learned. Then answer the Comprehension Check questions.

(First Read) Practice the first-read skills you learned in this lesson.

(Second Read) Practice the second-read skills you learned in this lesson.

(Third Read) Think critically about the selection.

Nuclear Disasters

Draw Inferences Think about why the governor evacuated children and pregnant women.

Text Structures How are the events that describe the disaster organized? Box words and phrases that tell you. The first answer has been boxed for you.

1   At 4:00 in the morning on March 28, 1979, several water-coolant pumps failed in the second reactor (TMI-2) at the Three Mile Island nuclear power plant near Harrisburg, Pennsylvania. This caused the reactor to overheat. The reactor shut itself down automatically eight seconds later. However, the temperature of the core—where the high-energy nuclear reaction occurs—continued to rise. This was because the valves controlling the emergency cooling water were stuck shut. The plant operators had misdiagnosed the problems of the stuck valve and made misguided decisions.

2   Sixteen hours later, the core was successfully flooded. Its temperature was brought under control. Years later, scientists confirmed that a partial nuclear meltdown had occurred. Half of the fuel rods in the core had melted, and part of the fuel had completely disintegrated. The danger of a meltdown is the potential release of radioactive materials into the air that can be deadly to people, plants, and animals.

3   So began the worst nuclear accident in U.S. history. During the tension-packed week that followed, confusing reports and contradictory information led to widespread panic.

4   On March 30—known as "Black Friday"—rumors began to circulate. It was believed that the incident had led to an uncontrolled release of radiation. Because the governor thought the situation was much more dire than it actually was, he ordered the evacuation of children and pregnant women living within five miles of the plant. More than 100,000 others voluntarily fled. Later, it would be learned that there had been a release, but that the release was planned. It had been done to ease the pressure within the system.

5   On April 2, five days after the meltdown, the crisis at Three Mile Island was officially declared over: TMI-2's **containment** had remained intact. This means that the safety barriers held strong. Only a tiny amount of radioactive material had been released. But the reactor itself was heavily contaminated. The TMI-2 reactor was eventually buried in concrete. TMI-1 was back in operation by 1986.

Impact of the Three Mile Island Disaster

6   The accident at Three Mile Island was blamed on a combination of things: equipment failure, human error, and bad luck. No immediate deaths or injuries occurred, either to plant workers or members of the community. However, the accident had a devastating impact. For one thing, it permanently changed the nuclear power industry in this country. The Nuclear Regulatory Commission has not reviewed an application to build a new nuclear power plant in the United States since the accident. For another thing, sweeping changes occurred in emergency response planning, operator training, radiation protection, and many other areas of nuclear power plant operations.

Health Effects of Three Mile Island

7   Some cancers are linked to increased radiation exposure. Therefore, it was imperative to gauge the effects of the Three Mile Island disaster on nearby residents. Several studies on health effects have determined the average radiation dose to individuals near Three Mile Island at the time of the meltdown was about one millirem. (A millirem is a small unit of radiation exposure.) Researchers found this was much less than the average annual dose for residents of the central Pennsylvania region in which Three Mile Island is located. Every person in the world experiences radiation from nature, outer space, and even elements in our bodies. Since then, there has been no real increase in cancer deaths among people living near the Three Mile Island plant. However, a study found a sharp increase in the deaths among infants, children, and the elderly in the region in the first two years after the accident. No explanation for the increase was given. However, the very young and very old are most susceptible to the effects of radiation. Some experts believe that the deaths are tied to the meltdown.

Text Structures
Think about how the subheadings help structure this selection and organize its information.

Critical Thinking
Think about the various negative and positive effects of the Three Mile Island disaster.

Aftermath

Compare and Contrast
How was the training of operators different after the accident? Underline a description of their training before the accident. Double underline a description of their training today.

Fact, Opinion, and Reasoned Judgment
Which sentence in *"The China Syndrome"* contains an opinion? Circle the sentence.

8   Social scientists also were interested in the accident at Three Mile Island. They studied it as an example of how groups of people act in stressful situations. They believed the incident at Three Mile Island would give them the opportunity to study the decision-making processes of people under stress. They found that there was a connection between the operators' unwise decisions and the stress they were under.

9   Because of their findings, the training of Three Mile Island operators has improved. Before the accident, operator training focused on figuring out the problem. After the accident, it focused on reacting to emergency situations. Part of the training involves checks to make sure that the core is getting enough coolant.

10   Cleanup of the reactor started in August 1979 and ended in December, 1993. From 1985 to 1990, almost one hundred tons of radioactive fuel were removed from the site. The cost of the cleanup was about $975 million.

The China Syndrome

11   The accident at the plant happened a few days after a movie called *The China Syndrome* appeared in theaters. In the movie, a reporter from a California TV station is doing a series of reports on nuclear energy. Suddenly, a meltdown almost happens at the plant from which she is reporting. She attempts to raise awareness of how unsafe the plant is. During one scene, a nuclear safety expert tells her that a meltdown could force an area "the size of Pennsylvania" to be evacuated. (Remember that Three Mile Island is located in Pennsylvania.) Far more bizarre, in both the movie and in real life, the plant operators were wrong about the amount of water in the core reactor.

The Chernobyl Nuclear Accident

12   The worst nuclear accident in history, however, was not at Three Mile Island. It occurred on April 26, 1986. It happened in Chernobyl, Ukraine, at the Chernobyl Nuclear Power Plant. At the time, Ukraine was part of the Soviet Union, a powerful country with which the United States was involved in the Cold War—a long period of rivalry and political tensions. At 1:21 a.m., the plant's fourth reactor released thirty to forty times the radiation released by the atomic bombs dropped on Nagasaki and Hiroshima during World War II combined.

13   An estimated four thousand people died, fifty of those being employees on duty during or just after the accident. A lethal dose of radiation is around 500,000 millirem over five hours. At Chernobyl, 20,000,000 millirem were released every *hour*. In some areas, unprotected workers got a deadly dose within minutes.

14   Although the exact causes of the explosion are not known, a possible scenario has been suggested. Researchers theorize that the plant's operators had been attempting to conduct an experiment with the emergency cooling system turned off. In the process, they made several fatal errors. Soviet officials claimed that if the technicians would have avoided at least one of those mistakes, the plant could have been saved. Instead, a deadly full-core meltdown occurred. It spread radiation so widely throughout Europe that it set off radiation sensors as far away as Sweden.

15   Although the exact causes of the explosion are not known, a possible scenario has been suggested. Ukraine continued using the unharmed reactors until the last one was finally closed down in 2000. As of December of that year, according to official post–Soviet era data, 350,400 people had been evacuated and resettled from the most severely affected areas. Because of the disaster and the fact that Soviet nuclear plants were known to operate with fewer safety measures than those built in the West, the world community began to question how safe the Soviet nuclear power industry was. The industry slowed down for a few years.

16   Health concerns still run high among the countries that were contaminated. Decontamination efforts are still under way. Scientists now believe that the radiation that covered Russia, Belarus, and Ukraine after the incident has greatly increased the risks of cancer in those areas.

Draw Inferences Think about an inference you would make about why people questioned the safety of the Soviet nuclear industry.

Text Structures Think about why this section on Chernobyl was included in the selection.

Lost city of Pripyat, Ukraine

Chernobyl and Three Mile Island

Compare and Contrast
Contrast the causes
of the accidents at
Three Mile Island and
Chernobyl. How were
they different?

Critical Thinking
Think about what facts
from this selection supply
reasons for people's
doubt regarding the
nuclear industry, and also
for others' faith in it.

17   Unlike Chernobyl, most nuclear reactors are encased in a steel or concrete dome. These are designed to prevent radioactive materials from escaping during an accident. The construction of the dome never took place at Chernobyl because of the cost of making it. If the dome had been in place, there would have been no damage to the inhabitants or the surrounding land. Because Chernobyl was all about human error, having a safety system that could not be turned off would have kept such a massive problem from happening.

18   In comparison, Three Mile Island was caused by a mechanical mistake, although the operators did have a role in the destruction of TMI-2. At Three Mile Island, the damage was at worst a partial meltdown, not a complete meltdown, as at Chernobyl. And although Three Mile Island was the worst commercial nuclear disaster in the United States, no one was harmed or killed as a result.

19   The safety of nuclear energy has been and will continue to be debated for many years. There are many people opposed to nuclear energy, though their claims seem quite exaggerated. Whether this opposition is justified or not, several nuclear accidents have occurred over the years that have caused terror among the citizens of the world.

20   Since the accidents at Three Mile Island and Chernobyl happened within a few years of each other, they were lumped together. However, the two incidents were very different. Still, most Americans' confidence in nuclear energy plummeted after Chernobyl's meltdown. They believed such a meltdown easily could happen within the United States. Others insist that a Chernobyl-style accident could never happen here because of the more stringent safety procedures followed by our nuclear industry.

✅ Comprehension Check

1. In "Nuclear Disasters," the author states that the Three Mile Island accident had a big impact on the nuclear power industry. How is the industry today different from the way it was before the accident?

2. "Nuclear Disasters" uses a combination of text structures. Give one example of how the author uses chronology and one example of how the author uses categorization.

3. What has been the overall impact of the two accidents on the nuclear industry in the United States and in the former Soviet Union?

4. The domain-specific word *containment* is used in paragraph 5. Use context clues to determine the definition. Write a dictionary entry for the word *containment* that includes the part of speech and a definition.

5. Why would it matter to people who were directly affected by the Three Mile Island meltdown that the radiation release had been purposefully planned?

6. Identify two sentences in the selection that suggest the author may be underplaying the potential dangers of nuclear power.

7. What inference can you make about the fact that the United States and Ukraine continued to use other reactors on the sites of the meltdowns?

Lesson 7
Scientific Texts

Scientific texts provide factual information about science-related topics. They can describe a natural event, such as the causes and effects of a hurricane, or explain a process, such as how a plant photosynthesizes. Scientific texts can appear in magazines, newspapers, books and textbooks, print or online encyclopedias, or on Web sites. Their goal is to educate and inform you about your world. What information might you want to learn about the kiwi, pictured here?

Skills Focus

The Great Pacific Garbage Patch

Summarize   Types of Evidence

Tracking Forest Fires

Paragraph Structure   Evaluate Evidence

Practice the Skill

First Read Summarize

When you **summarize** a selection, you take its big ideas and put them in your own words. To summarize a text, first, read the whole selection. Then, think about the main idea and locate the information that supports that idea. Decide which details best support the main idea. Once you have done that, restate what you've read in your own words. Because it restates only the main idea and important details, a summary will be much shorter than the original selection.

Your summary should be objective, meaning that it should not include your own opinions on the topic. For example, a summary of a scientific text about nuclear energy should not include whether you are for or against it. If the author has included his or her opinions and they are important to the main idea, you should include them in your summary.

Try It Read the paragraph below.

The kiwi, native to New Zealand, is one of the most unique birds known to us. It is flightless and has only tiny stumps where wings should be. These stumps are hidden under the strange, long, fine feathers that resemble fur or hair. Kiwis lay the largest eggs in relation to their body size of any bird species known. Unfortunately, most species of kiwi are highly endangered due to the destruction of their habitat.

Discuss Summarize the paragraph. Underline its main idea. Double underline two important supporting details.

As you read, record your answers to questions about summarizing on the Close Reading Worksheet on page 305.

Practice the Skill

Second Read Types of Evidence

Scientific texts are filled with information and **evidence** that support the main ideas presented. Some types of evidence are more reliable and valuable than others. As you read, consider the type of evidence being presented. Types of evidence can include the following:

- **Examples:** specific instances that illustrate a general idea

- **Research and survey results:** information gathered through scientific investigation

- **Statistics:** information in number form

- **Case studies:** long-term studies of a single person, thing, group, or event

- **Expert opinions:** judgments by someone who has researched the specific topic being discussed and is considered to be an authority on the subject

- **Anecdotes:** short, personal stories that illustrate an idea

- **Direct quotations:** the exact words someone has said, enclosed in quotation marks

Try It Read the paragraph below.

The platypus doesn't have teeth. Instead, it scoops up pebbles from the river bottom with its bill and uses them to "chew" its food. A platypus forages for food for up to twelve hours per day. Each dive to the river bottom can last twenty to forty seconds, and the animal then rests on the surface to chew for about ten seconds. In the course of an hour, a platypus can make up to seventy-five dives to look for food.

Discuss **Look at the types of evidence in the paragraph. Circle all the statistics. Is this type of evidence the best way to support the ideas presented? Why or why not?**

As you read, complete the Types of Evidence Chart on page 306.

Purpose for Reading

Read along with your teacher. Each time, read for a different purpose.

First Read Focus on summarizing the ideas.

Second Read Focus on identifying types of evidence.

Third Read Focus on thinking critically about the selection.

~~~ The Great Pacific ~~~
Garbage Patch

Summarize the description of a gyre.

What unusual thing did Captain Moore see? (Circle) **the direct quotation in the selection. Categorize and record your answer on the Types of Evidence Chart.**

Based on the text, in which hemisphere is the garbage patch located? How do you know?

1   In 1997, Captain Charles Moore made a huge discovery in the Pacific Ocean. He had been sailing in a race in Japan and decided to take a less-traveled route home to the United States. He sailed through an area called the North Pacific Gyre, which is between Japan and the U.S. mainland.

2   The National Oceanic and Atmospheric Administration (NOAA) defines a gyre as a "circular feature of ocean currents that spiral around a central point." In the Northern Hemisphere, gyres spiral clockwise, and in the Southern Hemisphere, they spiral counterclockwise. Gyres absorb everything that gets caught in their currents. They normally pick up things like driftwood and seaweed. But the North Pacific Gyre has picked up something else.

3   As Captain Moore sailed through the North Pacific Gyre, he observed something unusual. "Every time I came on deck to survey the horizon, I saw a soap bottle, bottle cap, or shard of plastic waste bobbing by. Here I was in the middle of the ocean, and there was nowhere I could go to avoid the plastic," he said.

4   Captain Moore had discovered the Great Pacific Garbage Patch.

5   The Great Pacific Garbage Patch is composed of two separate clockwise-rotating patches. One is the Eastern Pacific Garbage Patch, between Hawaii and California, and the other is the Western Pacific Garbage Patch, off the coast of Japan.

6   Measuring the Great Pacific Garbage Patch is difficult. It doesn't appear as a blanket of trash on the surface of the ocean—at least not everywhere. Satellite photos and surveys from planes do not reveal the true size of the garbage patch. Scientists instead have to use water samples taken from several depths. Some now **estimate** that the Great Pacific Garbage Patch is twice the size of Texas. In addition to spreading out across the ocean, the patch reaches hundreds of feet below the surface of the ocean, filling the pelagic zone[1] with trash.

7   It's not just any trash that ends up in the garbage patch. Most of it is plastic. Ten percent of the 260 million tons of plastic produced each year ends up in the oceans. Of that, 80 percent starts out on land, getting washed into streams and rivers and eventually out to sea. The other 20 percent of the trash is dumped from cruise ships, fishing vessels, and oil-drilling platforms, or is the result of natural disasters like the 2011 earthquake and tsunami in Japan.

8   Shipping containers that fall off the decks of cargo ships can be an "interesting" source of plastic debris. Some notable spills include 33,000 Nike® sneakers, 34,000 hockey gloves, and 29,000 rubber ducks. When these accidents are reported, oceanographers get to work. By tracking where spilled items, like rubber ducks, eventually wash ashore, these scientists have learned a great deal about ocean currents.

9   Scientists classify plastic as anything that contains artificial or human-made chemical compounds. Unlike paper or animal products, plastic is not biodegradable, meaning there is no natural process that breaks it down. Instead, it is photodegradable, which means it breaks into smaller and smaller pieces as a result of exposure to light, until the pieces eventually become microscopic in size.

[1]**pelagic zone** the part of the ocean not close to the bottom or the shore

Summarize what happens to plastic when it ends up in the oceans.

How much plastic produced each year ends up in the oceans? Circle the statistic that supports your answer. Categorize and record your answer on the **Types of Evidence Chart.**

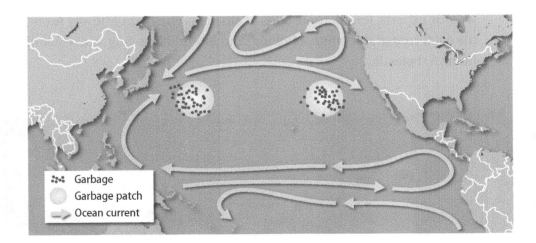

Garbage
Garbage patch
Ocean current

The North Pacific Gyre spins clockwise between Japan and the United States. Trash accumulates in the Western and Eastern Pacific Garbage Patches, known collectively as the Great Pacific Garbage Patch.

Underline the details that explain how albatross chicks die from plastic poisoning.

What animal population has been harmed by plastic pollution? Circle the sentence that contains the example. Categorize and record your answer on the **Types of Evidence Chart.**

What is one way the garbage patch will harm humans?

10   In some areas of the patch, there is so much plastic in the water that researchers say it looks like "plastic confetti." These tiny pieces of plastic are called microplastics or nurdles. Scientist who have **analyzed** nurdles from the Great Pacific Garbage Patch have found concentrations of PCB (polychlorinated biphenyls) that are 100,000 to 1,000,000 times that which occurs in plastic-free seawater.

11   Because of the water currents that form gyres, marine life collects in the centers, just as trash does. These areas of the ocean are teeming with life, from microscopic plankton to whales, and everything in between. Scientists have **evaluated** water samples from some areas of the garbage patch and found that there is more plastic in the water than plankton.

12   Estimates are that 1,000,000 seabirds and 100,000 seals, sea lions, whales, dolphins, and turtles die each year from ingesting trash. Nurdles look and move in the currents just like plankton and get eaten by marine life that eats plankton. The plastic can harm animals even when they don't eat it. Plastic bags and abandoned fishing nets can snare and injure sea turtles and other marine life.

13   Some populations of wildlife are declining dramatically because of plastic pollution. One example is the albatross that nest on Midway Atoll, an island that has been designated as a marine sanctuary. Midway Atoll is two thousand miles away from the nearest continent. However, it is in the path of the garbage patch, and ocean-borne refuse poses a major threat to its marine birds.

14   Albatross are huge seabirds that spot their prey from the air and swoop down to catch them. They then go back to their nests and regurgitate, or bring up, what they've eaten for their chicks. Unfortunately, from the air, floating bits of plastic look a lot like fish. The albatross eat the trash and take it back to their chicks. According to wildlife experts, tens of thousands of albatross chicks on Midway Atoll die each year of starvation, choking, and internal bleeding as a result of being fed plastic.

Albatross and chicks on Midway Atoll

15   In 2009, NOAA formed the Marine Debris Program to study the garbage patch, **calculate** its impact on marine life, and research methods of cleaning it. NOAA's goal is to combine rigorous scientific surveys with visual observation from volunteers at sea. They have gained the assistance of sailors participating in the Transpacific Yacht Race and the Pacific Cup to map the patch's location, photograph it, and collect water samples.

16   To measure the extent of pollution in the water, scientists drag a special "manta net" behind a boat. It measures the volume of water and collects tiny pieces of plastic in a fine mesh net. Once the researchers have their water samples, they analyze them to find the amounts of plastic toxins in them. They also examine any dead fish, birds, or other marine life for plastic toxicity.

17   Research, government, and environmental groups are studying different methods of cleaning up the plastic. In Hawaii, volunteers regularly sweep the beaches, picking up all the marine debris they can. The trash is then taken to a landfill and disposed of.

18   Hawaii has also launched a program that scoops abandoned fishing nets out of the ocean. The nets are taken to a special facility that incinerates them. The steam from incineration powers turbines that create energy. It's one excellent, but tiny, dent in a huge problem.

19   A possible cleanup solution is to drag nets behind ships and scoop up all of the trash. While this might work for any debris on or close to the surface, the plan has some serious drawbacks. First, the size of the area to be cleaned is so vast that it would take a fleet of ships working for years to cover it all. Then, there's the pollution that would be created by sending all of those ships to sea. Finally, what would happen to the trash after it is collected? There is no landfill big enough to handle that amount of garbage.

Summarize why scooping up the trash would not provide a solution to the problem.

What are scientists from the Marine Debris Program researching? Circle what they're studying and hoping to find.

Summarize ways to stop the garbage patch from getting bigger.

Complete the **Types of Evidence Chart** by filling in any boxes with additional evidence from the selection. If any types of evidence aren't used, write *none* in the box.

20   In addition to the size of the area to be cleaned and extra pollution caused by dragging nets through the ocean, there is the further damage such projects could cause the marine ecosystem. Because marine life tends to concentrate in the same areas as marine debris, dragging nets through the water would mean scooping up fish, seabirds, seaweed, and plankton from the ocean, along with the trash.

21   Most researchers agree that the best course of action is to monitor the Great Pacific Garbage Patch and stop it from growing any bigger. Captain Moore, one of the first to recognize the problem, has formed a research group that is doing just that. Scientists collect water samples and track the movement of the trash. Members of the group also provide education and outreach efforts aimed at spreading the word about the problem.

22   To stop the Great Pacific Garbage Patch from growing and to prevent any others from forming, there needs to be a worldwide effort to halt the flow of bottles, toothbrushes, shoes, bags, and all other forms of plastic into the oceans. Governments must encourage their countries to shift away from petroleum-based products—plastics—and toward ones made out of biodegradable materials.

23   You can help, too. Practice the "3Rs" whenever possible. Reduce, reuse, and recycle. It may not seem like a lot, but buying fewer plastic products is a good start. Use refillable water bottles instead of disposable ones. Remind your parents to use reusable bags at stores instead of single-use bags. And try getting into the habit of recycling what remaining plastic you must use. These actions can make a small difference in your own local impact. But that effort, if repeated by millions of people like you, will add up to a huge difference globally.

Connect

How can practicing the "3Rs" for plastic help your local environment? Cite textual evidence to support your ideas.

Vocabulary: Nuances in Academic Vocabulary

Have you ever noticed that certain words pop up over and over in different classes at school? Words like *analyze*, *explain*, and *evaluate* are **academic vocabulary**—words used in schools or texts to describe the thinking skills people use when they read about a subject. Because these words represent necessary skills that you will need to master and demonstrate throughout your school career, it's important that you understand the words and their nuances of meaning.

A **nuance** is a small but important shade of meaning in a word. To understand a word's nuance, ask yourself, *What does this word mean? How is it different from other words that are like it?*

Try It Read this sentence from "The Great Pacific Garbage Patch."

> Some now **estimate** that the Great Pacific Garbage Patch is twice the size of Texas.

> Discuss **What does *estimate* mean? What are other words similar to *estimate*? How is *estimate* different from these words?**

Find the following words in the selection. Read the sentence that contains each word. Write down a definition and at least one synonym—a word with a similar meaning. Explain how the vocabulary word differs from its synonym.

1. **analyzed,** p. 168 _____

_____

2. **evaluated,** p. 168 _____

_____

3. **calculate,** p. 169 _____

_____

Practice the Skill

Paragraph Structure

By paying attention to how a paragraph is organized, you can often get clues to its important ideas. In general, the first sentence of a paragraph contains its main idea in a **topic sentence**. It doesn't contain details, but instead introduces the overall idea of the paragraph. The sentences that follow the topic sentence contain specific details that support, or explain, the main idea. These sentences are called **supporting sentences**. In longer paragraphs, supporting sentences are sometimes followed by a **concluding sentence**, which restates the main idea of the paragraph.

Just as sentences in a paragraph support the paragraph's main idea, paragraphs in a longer text also work together to support the larger idea the text expresses. Authors might link their paragraphs by presenting a sequence of events or steps in a process, by comparing and contrasting important ideas, or by showing how causes create certain effects.

It is important to note that not every paragraph begins with a topic sentence. Sometimes the topic sentence comes at the end—the concluding sentence will be the topic sentence. And sometimes there is no topic sentence at all; you have to read the whole paragraph in order to determine its main idea.

Try It Read the paragraph below, and think about its structure.

Brown recluse spiders like to hide away from people and animals. They prefer small, dark places for their nests. Outdoors, their homes are under rocks and inside dead tree trunks. Inside houses, they will live anywhere dark and quiet. This can include storage boxes, corners of closets, and heating vents. Like their name implies, these spiders like to stay hidden from the world in these out-of-the-way places.

Discuss **What is the main idea of the paragraph? Underline the topic sentence. What details support the main idea? Double underline the supporting sentences. How do the supporting details develop the key idea in the paragraph?**

As you read, record your answers to questions about paragraph structure on the Close Reading Worksheet on page 307.

Practice the Skill

It's easy to think of science as a set of fixed, proven facts. Much of it is, but most of what scientists study is still unknown, and authors of scientific texts are presenting their theories and ideas about a topic. To support these theories, scientific texts are filled with **evidence**, such as statistics, expert opinions, and anecdotes. When you read these texts, you should **evaluate**, or decide, whether the evidence successfully supports the author's ideas. To evaluate evidence, ask yourself these three questions.

- Is it reliable? The evidence should come from a trustworthy source.

- Is it credible? The evidence should be believable.

- Is it sufficient? There should be enough evidence to support ideas.

Try It Read the paragraph below, and think about the types of evidence.

Last week's tornado destroyed four homes and one grocery store. Eyewitnesses to the twister said it touched down west of town and moved slowly to the southeast. One resident told reporters, "We saw it land back behind the mall. Then it spun its way down through our neighborhood. It jumped over the high school before hitting the grocery store." Meteorologists with the National Weather Service tracked the storm on radar and said that it travelled southeast at about ten miles an hour. Their data show the tornado was on the ground for five miles. Fortunately, no one was injured in the storm.

Discuss | Circle the evidence presented about the tornado. Is the evidence reliable, credible, and sufficient? Discuss why or why not.

As you read, complete the Evaluating Evidence Chart on page 308.

Purpose for Reading

Read along with your teacher. Each time, read for a different purpose.

First Read	Focus on paragraph structure.
Second Read	Focus on evaluating evidence.
Third Read	Focus on evaluating the selection critically.

Tracking Forest Fires

Underline the topic sentence of paragraph 3. How does the main idea of this paragraph develop the concept indicated by the title of the selection?

Circle the evidence that two different approaches are necessary. Is it reliable, credible, and sufficient? Write your answers on the **Evaluating Evidence Chart.**

1   Large and unpredictable fires impact human life on a global scale. Every year, fire destroys millions of hectares of vegetation throughout the world. When you consider that a single hectare equals about 2.5 acres of land, you can see that's a lot of destruction.

2   Annually in the United States alone, more than 100,000 forest fires burn at least five million acres. If they are not contained, these fires can destroy everything in their path, from large areas of national parkland right down to entire communities. A tragic number of people are killed by wildfires every year, so it's not surprising that research into fires— and forest fires in particular—has become a serious worldwide effort. This research falls into two basic categories, which line up with the two basic causes of wildfires: human beings and nature itself.

Two Approaches to Fire Research

3   Given the two basic categories of forest fires, it makes sense that the approach to fire research and fire management would be two-pronged. The first prong has been called the biophysical paradigm,[1] which focuses primarily on fires caused by nature, mostly those ignited by lightning. The second prong focuses on the eco-cultural paradigm, or the fires caused by human actions. Several scientific studies have shown this dual approach to be necessary because of large fires that show both natural and human causes.

4   The international scientific community shares a network of resources to research forest fires. However, before any work can be done, one question must be asked and answered, and **virtually** any fire researcher can answer this "burning" question in his or her sleep: What is fire?

[1]**paradigm** a typical example or pattern; a model

What Is Fire?

5   In western mythology and astrology, fire has long been associated with three other common aspects of the natural world. The ancients wrote about these four as a group, referring to them as the four elements—earth, water, air, and fire.

6   But science quickly **extinguishes** the idea that fire is anything like the other three. Earth, water, and air are matter. They are substances with an atomic structure, all composed of millions of atoms. Under the right conditions, matter can change form. Water, for instance, can become ice or steam.

7   Fire, however, is completely different. You can see it, you can smell it, and you can certainly feel its effects if you're not careful. But instead of being a material substance with a molecular makeup, fire is actually one stage in a chemical reaction. It is not matter, but rather *what happens* when matter changes its form.

Beginnings of a Blaze

8   It takes two substances to begin the chemical reaction that leads to fire: oxygen and fuel. Add heat to ignite the fuel, and you've got a fire. The graphic below shows how these components react to create fire.

> Look at the graphic. How can fallen power lines contribute to causing a fire?

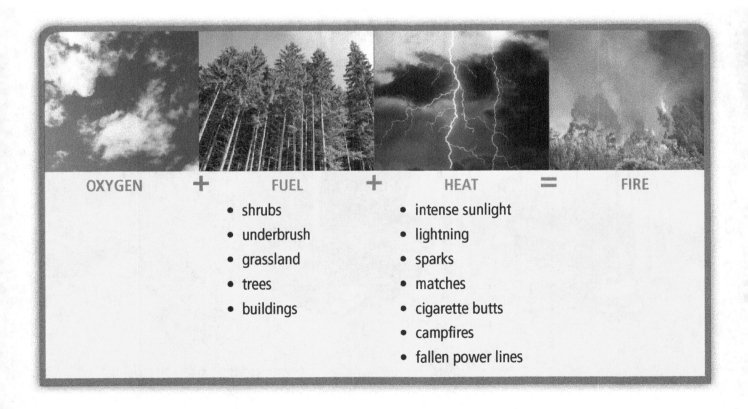

OXYGEN   **+**   FUEL   **+**   HEAT   **=**   FIRE

FUEL
- shrubs
- underbrush
- grassland
- trees
- buildings

HEAT
- intense sunlight
- lightning
- sparks
- matches
- cigarette butts
- campfires
- fallen power lines

The Human Factor

Circle evidence that humans cause nearly all wildland fires. Is it reliable, credible, and sufficient? Write your answers on the **Evaluating Evidence Chart**.

What are some examples of human carelessness that can cause wildland fires?

9   Fire researchers use the collective term "wildland fires" to refer to uncontrolled fires that occur in the countryside or in a wilderness area. Today, wildland fires are an ever-increasing threat to human life, livelihood, and property. Ironically, according to the United Nations Environment Programme (UNEP), human activities are responsible for about 90 percent of all fires around the world. People set off nearly all of the world's fires, which in turn have a direct effect on human life.

10   One research focus is on the impact of changing vegetation conditions, since vegetation is fuel. In many cases, people have altered the nature of the vegetation, and such changes often create greater potential for wildland fires. For example, reducing forests for farming and clear cut logging[2] can be disastrous. When thick forests are cut down, the canopy shade is destroyed. This causes the drying out of once-moist, lush woodlands. Along with these unnaturally dry conditions, human carelessness is always a risk. Forests left vulnerable like this are prone to massive, quick-spreading wildfires.

[2]**clear cut logging**   the practice of harvesting all trees in an area

Clear cut forest

El Niño and Climate Cycles

11   Other research is being done on the relationship between fire and climate change, including changing weather patterns. El Niño is one climate pattern that can have a destructive effect. Scientists at NASA have discovered that every three to seven years, the balance among global weather conditions becomes almost **catastrophically** disrupted by a phenomenon known as El Niño, Spanish for "the little boy."

12   During El Niño, which tends to occur in December and January, the delicate balance between ocean currents, atmospheric temperatures, wind, and other factors simply breaks down. When this happens, the trade winds—winds that circle the globe in a predictable pattern—become weak. This, in turn, disrupts the normal functioning of the oceans, which can result in violent storms, flooding, hurricanes, even droughts. And droughts cause forest fire conditions.

Explain how paragraph 12 is structured to explain the cause of forest fires.

Circle evidence that shows El Niño is responsible for forest fires. Is it reliable, credible, and sufficient? Write your answers on the **Evaluating Evidence Chart.**

Fighting Fire with Fire

Circle the evidence that explains why forest fires can be beneficial.

Why do you think the Forest Service originally put out every forest fire?

13   In the United States, the U.S. Forest Service is the primary force behind forest fire control. The agency monitors forest fires, coordinates firefighting efforts, works with local officials, and educates the public on fire **prevention**. The Forest Service maintains records on each forest fire that occurs in the United States each year, including where and when the fire took place, the number of acres burned, and the extent of property damage. After a fire has receded, the Forest Service sends people in to investigate the cause of the blaze.

14   When the Forest Service first began more than a hundred years ago, its policy was to put out every forest fire that burned. But doing so created even more fires, often much larger ones. This is because, in reality, forests benefit from fire in numerous ways, relying on regular blazes to stay healthy and to promote a **diverse** ecosystem.

15   On the positive side, forest fires burn out the underbrush and leaves that can choke seedlings. They can eliminate invasive species and insects that are harmful to the forest ecology. Forest fires take out dead trees, which creates room for new growth. They also destroy treetops, allowing sunlight to reach the forest floor.

16   Now with a good grasp of these facts, Forest Service officials set prescribed fires on purpose, and firefighters monitor them closely to ensure they don't get out of control. Such "controlled" fires are set only under very specific conditions, ideally on cool, humid days with no wind. The Forest Service allows these fires to burn themselves out, so in most cases, firefighters will only intervene to protect people and property.

All-Seeing Satellite Eyes

17   Tracking fires is a vital job. Knowing where a fire has broken out and where it might be heading can save lives and property as well as billions of dollars. In the twenty-first century, fire tracking has become a high-tech science, and at the modern-day heart of finding and following fires is satellite technology.

18   The Forest Service and firefighters alike could not do without NOAA. One of NOAA's stated missions is "To understand and predict changes in climate, weather, oceans, and coasts." It uses environmental satellite systems not only to forecast weather but also to look out for and report on forest fires.

19   Two NOAA satellite systems watch over the United States and the world. They are the Geostationary Operational Environmental Satellites (GOES) and the Polar Operational Environmental Satellites (POES).

20   GOES satellites capture photographic images every fifteen minutes, tracking serious weather threats and watching for anything that could escalate into real trouble. POES pick up environmental data of all kinds. While they are critical to climate research and weather forecasting, they can also predict where fires might easily break out, based on weather conditions.

21   Both POES and GOES work constantly to detect forest fires in progress. The satellites transmit images and data on the size, direction, and precise locations of these fires.

What is the main idea of the section "All-Seeing Satellite Eyes"? Underline the topic sentence. What details show that GOES and POES help track fires?

Circle evidence that fire tracking has become high tech. Is it reliable, credible, and sufficient? Write your answers on the **Evaluating Evidence Chart**.

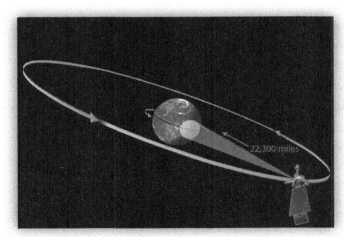

GOES maintain a constant orbit 22,300 miles above the equator.

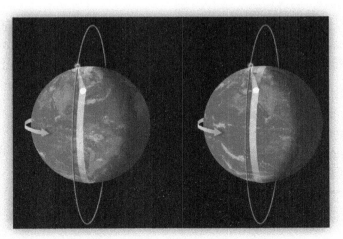

POES pass over both the North and South Poles about fourteen times a day while Earth rotates 500 miles below.

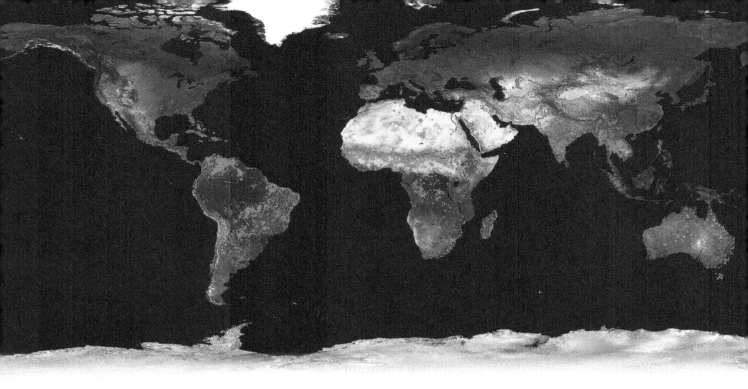

This global fire map shows worldwide fire activity occurring over a ten-day period.

Does the selection provide enough reliable, credible, and sufficient evidence to support the main points? Explain why or why not. Complete the **Evaluating Evidence Chart.**

Evaluate

Is it worth it to spend millions of dollars on high-tech equipment to track fires? Why or why not?

Where There's Smoke, There's Fire

22   Another aspect of NOAA's fire watching is its Hazard Mapping System (HMS). This system tracks the plumes of smoke that come from forest fires. HMS follows the smoke trails of every wildfire in North America. Meteorologists assess the movement of the smoke on computer screens. The smoke from a powerful blaze can travel thousands of miles from its source. It often travels into populated areas, destroying the air quality and, in some cases, endangering lives.

23   Armed with the up-to-the-minute and highly accurate data that NOAA provides, those battling fires on the ground have a tremendous advantage. Such an overview helps firefighters create a strategy to deal with out-of-control wildfires. By knowing in advance what is coming, people in general can be better prepared. Thanks to modern science working on all fronts to track and control wildfires, the threat the fires pose can often be greatly diminished.

Vocabulary: Using a Thesaurus

Good writers use a variety of words to describe events. Sometimes they run out of ways to describe a particular item or instance. In those cases, they can turn to a thesaurus to find synonyms, or similar words, for the word they want to replace. A **thesaurus** is an online tool or print book that provides lists of words that can be used in place of one another.

Try It Read the sentence below. Based on the context, brainstorm a definition for the word *catastrophically*. Then, look at the sample thesaurus entry for the word *catastrophic*.

Scientists at NASA have discovered that every three to seven years, the balance among global weather conditions becomes almost **catastrophically** disrupted by a phenomenon known as El Niño, Spanish for "the little boy."

catastrophic   calamitous, cataclysmic, disastrous, fatal, ruinous, tragic

> Discuss   **Which word(s) from the thesaurus entry might best fit in the sentence?**

Below are words from the selection you just read. For each word, consult a thesaurus and provide three words that mean the same thing.

1. **virtually,** p. 174 _____

2. **extinguishes,** p. 175 _____

3. **prevention,** p. 178 _____

4. **diverse,** p. 178 _____

Respond to Text: Evaluating Evidence

"Tracking Forest Fires" is a scientific text that provides factual information about forest fires. The article includes several kinds of evidence, including statistics, expert opinions, research, and case studies.

Try It Think about the types of evidence presented in "Tracking Forest Fires."

 Discuss **How did the author's use of evidence affect your understanding of the topic? Which pieces of evidence were most convincing? Could the article have been more effective if more or different types of evidence were used?**

On Your Own Write a paragraph in which you evaluate the types of evidence the author used to support the idea that scientists, researchers, and firefighters are doing a good job of fighting and tracking fires. Which types of evidence would have made the article easier to understand? Was the evidence used reliable enough? Was the evidence sufficient? Support your conclusions with details from the selection. Use the guide on the next page to help you write your response.

Checklist for a Good Response

A good paragraph

✔ summarizes the types of evidence offered.

✔ gives specific examples of effective evidence.

✔ explains which additional types of evidence could have been used.

✔ explains whether the evidence was reliable and sufficient.

✔ includes a clearly stated main idea, supporting details, and concluding sentence.

How Evidence Affected My Reading

1. **Topic Sentence** Include this information in the topic sentence:

   "Tracking Forest Fires" used these types of evidence to support its main ideas:

   1. _____   2. _____   3. _____

   This evidence (was / was not) effective.

2. **Detail Sentences** Tell what types of evidence were presented and how effective they were in supporting the author's ideas.

Type of Evidence	Is It Effective? Why or Why Not?

3. **Concluding Sentence** Your concluding sentence should restate how effective the use of evidence was in the article.

   _____

   _____

On a separate sheet of paper, write your paragraph.

Read on Your Own

Read the selection independently three times, using the skills you have learned. Then answer the Comprehension Check questions.

First Read · Practice the first-read skills you learned in this lesson.

Second Read · Practice the second-read skills you learned in this lesson.

Third Read · Think critically about the selection.

Toys in Space!

Summarize Double underline details that you would include in a summary of paragraph 4. One pair of details has been underlined for you.

Critical Thinking Think of reasons why it might be easier and less expensive to launch into near space.

1   For thirty years, NASA flew space shuttle missions. The shuttles carried astronauts into space to conduct experiments, repair telescopes, and build the International Space Station. The shuttle program ended in 2011. All of the shuttles have now been moved to their permanent homes at museums around the country.

2   However, the end of the shuttle program doesn't mean the end of space exploration or travel. American astronauts are still aboard the International Space Station. They get there and back by riding on the Russian Soyuz spacecraft. Private companies are now entering the space race. In 2012, an American company called SpaceX launched a supply ship that docked with the International Space Station.

3   But it doesn't take rocket scientists to launch things into space, or at least into near space.

4   Scientists define *near space* as the area between 60,000 and 328,000 feet above Earth. At these altitudes, the air pressure is so low that there is nearly a vacuum. Temperatures there drop to sixty degrees below zero or more. Because it is easier and less expensive than launching things into orbit, NASA sends equipment to near space to test its reliability in the cold and in the vacuum of space.

5   Weather balloons are large latex balloons measuring about five feet across or more when inflated. The balloons are thicker and more durable than the ones from party stores. Researchers launch weather balloons from more than eight hundred locations around the world each day to study weather conditions.

6   Scientists fill the balloons with helium, which weighs less than air. This causes the weather balloons to float up. As they rise, the air pressure outside the balloons drops compared to the pressure inside, allowing the balloons to expand. Depending on the size of the balloon and the amount of helium used, weather balloons can expand up to five times their original size. And, with enough helium, weather balloons can float to near space.

7   Scientists have identified separate layers of Earth's atmosphere by using special instruments suspended from the balloons. These instruments can **measure** the thermal characteristics, chemical composition, movement, and density of the air above us.

8   The troposphere is the layer closest to Earth. It extends four to six miles above the ground. The second layer is the stratosphere, and it extends from the edge of the troposphere to about thirty-one miles up. The next layer is the mesosphere, which extends up fifty-six miles, or 90,000 feet.

9   Weather balloons can soar to about 100,000 feet above Earth, into the mesosphere, before they burst. That's three times higher than passenger planes fly. At this altitude, the blackness of space and the curvature of Earth are visible. As the balloons rise, they expand to between twenty to twenty-five feet. Once the air pressure in the balloon gets too great, the balloon pops. The attached instruments fall back to Earth, slowed by small parachutes.

10   These days, high school students and ordinary moms and dads are launching all sorts of packages into near space using weather balloons. Notable things that have been launched include a toy train, a toy action figure, and an MIT[1] acceptance letter.

[1]**MIT** Massachusetts Institute of Technology, a university with a strong emphasis on scientific, engineering, and technological education and research

Types of Evidence
Circle the facts scientists know about Earth's atmosphere.

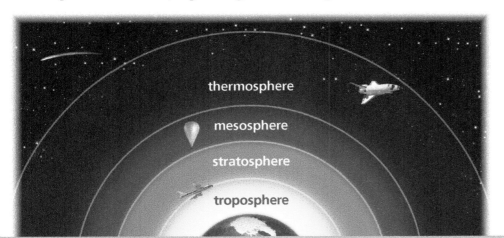

Layers of the atmosphere

thermosphere

mesosphere

stratosphere

troposphere

Paragraph Structure
Underline the topic sentence of paragraph 14. Double underline the supporting sentences. Think about how this paragraph contributes to the selection as a whole.

Critical Thinking
Think about why the FAA requires payloads to weigh less than four pounds.

11   Sending a package into space can be a weekend project for an amateur scientist. The most important piece of equipment is the weather balloon itself. They are available for purchase online and come in different shapes and sizes. The larger the balloon, the more helium it can hold. The more helium it can hold, the higher it can go. Adding a radar reflector helps make the balloon visible to aircraft.

12   Building a package to carry the payload, or cargo, is a crucial part of the plan. Federal Aviation Administration (FAA) requirements state that a weather balloon payload must weigh less than four pounds. The payload must also have a high degree of breakability. This is just in case it ends up in the path of a passing plane. A payload that breaks up will do less damage to the plane upon collision. In addition to being light, the package must be able to withstand extreme temperatures and the fall back to Earth.

13   Most people use lightweight Styrofoam drink coolers to carry their payloads. Many spray-paint them with neon colors for visibility and cut holes in the sides for cameras. People who want pictures of specific items in space build platforms on the outside of the coolers for the cargo and cameras.

14   Because near space is so cold, people who send up weather balloons often include chemical hand warmers intended for people's pockets. These small pouches generate enough heat to keep cameras and GPS equipment from freezing over. They stay warm for the entire trip to space and back.

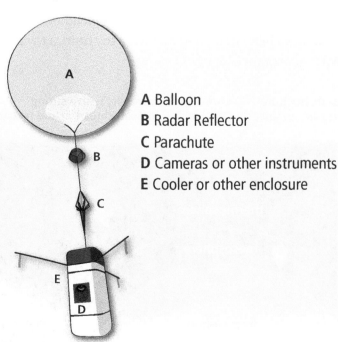

A Balloon
B Radar Reflector
C Parachute
D Cameras or other instruments
E Cooler or other enclosure

A man sends a weather ballooon into the air.

15   To help the payload fall back to Earth safely and to ensure no one gets hit by a plummeting cooler, the weather balloon package needs to include a small nylon parachute. These can be made at home or ordered online. The parachute is built to deploy after the weather balloon pops and the payload begins falling.

16   To record the trip, amateur scientists attach small cameras to the coolers. They use still cameras that snap pictures at regular intervals or video cameras with a two-hour recording time. The cameras can capture the balloons' ascent into space and descent to Earth. People who have launched things like toy trains have set the cameras so that they get pictures of their favorite item against the curve of Earth.

17   In order to retrieve their equipment, people who launch weather balloon packages include some sort of GPS-enabled device to help them track down the payloads on the ground. A cell phone with GPS is the best option. Special programs allow an amateur scientist to track the GPS signal as the balloon ascends for as long as it remains in range of cell phone signals. When the package falls back to Earth, the cell phone towers will pick up the signal again and **transmit** the package's final location. Mapping programs will allow the person to determine the package's general location based on the GPS readings.

Summarize
Think about how you would summarize the processes involved in sending objects into near space.

Critical Thinking Think about why a person might temporarily lose track of a balloon during its trip.

18   Travelling to near space takes longer than the trip back. The trip up takes about an hour. The return trip is much faster, only about twenty minutes. Balloons often drift dozens of miles during the ascent. In addition to tracking payloads with GPS, balloon owners can plot likely landing places online. Web sites exist that factor in wind speed and direction and weather conditions in order to predict likely landing spots.

19   When launching a balloon, it is important to think about landing sites. It is crucial not to launch a balloon from a location where winds can blow it into an airport or city. It's best to launch from a site where the balloon will land in an empty field.

20   Two Canadian teenagers almost learned this lesson the hard way. When they plotted the likely landing spot for their package, they discovered that the balloon would drift across the border with the United States. Not wanting to start an international incident, the boys had to map alternate launch sites until they found one that would allow their package to fall back to Earth in Canada.

21   Launching weather balloons has become so popular that there are now clubs of amateurs who work together to send up payloads. The clubs also provide how-to information and tutorials for people who want to launch their own weather balloons.

22   Looking for a good science fair project? Want to take a one-of-a-kind picture of your favorite action figure or stuffed animal? Consider launching your own package into space.

✔ Comprehension Check

1. How is paragraph 17 structured to explain methods for tracking a weather balloon?

   _____

   _____

   _____

2. Which detail about weather balloons could be left out of a summary of paragraph 6?

   _____ They are made of latex.

   _____ They measure about five feet across.

   _____ They are thicker and more durable than party balloons.

   _____ They are launched daily from more than eight hundred locations.

3. Give an example of a type of direct quotation or statistic that could be added to the selection to strengthen its support.

   Direct quotation: _____

   Statistic: _____

4. Summarize the information about payloads in paragraph 12.

   _____

   _____

   _____

5. Evaluate the evidence about why it's important to know where a payload is going to land. Explain your answers.

reliable: _____

_____

credible: _____

_____

sufficient: _____

_____

6. Why would someone send an MIT acceptance letter into near space?

_____

_____

_____

7. The word *transmit* is used in paragraph 17. List two synonyms that would be found in a thesaurus and could be substituted in the paragraph.

_____

8. Read this sentence from the selection.

   These instruments can measure the thermal characteristics, chemical composition, movement, and density of the air above us.

   Write a definition and a synonym for the word *measure*. Explain how the vocabulary word differs from its synonym.

_____

_____

Technical Texts

Technical texts explain how things work or how to do things. When you read the instructions that tell you how to play your new video game, you are reading a technical text. The purpose of technical texts is to provide information in a straightforward way. Technical texts do not contain opinions or first-person narrative. Numbers or bullets are usually used to show the steps in the process. Directions, explanations, help manuals, recipes, and schedules are all types of technical texts. What kind of technical text might this woman be using? What information would be in that text?

Skills Focus

Canned Heat: How to Build a Solar Heater

| Sequence | Author's Purpose |

Driving Greener

| Ask and Answer Questions |

| Graphics and Visuals |

Practice the Skill

Sequence is the order in which things happen. Sequence can be a very important part of a technical text. Imagine that you are using instructions to put together your new bike. Just think what would happen if you followed the steps out of order! You probably wouldn't be very happy with the end result.

It's often easy to understand the sequence in a technical text because the steps are numbered or placed in a bulleted list. Even if they're not, words like *first*, *next*, *then*, *last*, and *finally* can help you figure out the sequence of events.

Try It Read the following technical text that explains how to install new software programs.

Installation Instructions

- Insert the flash drive containing the program download into the USB port.

- Double-click the file to extract it. (The file name extension **.exe** indicates that it is a self-extracting compressed file.)

- Double-click **setup.exe** to start installation. The process can take several minutes to several hours.

- When prompted, type your registration number and password. (You can find it on the sticker on the back of the packaging.)

- The program will then launch. Check to make sure it is working correctly.

Discuss **What tells you the sequence of these instructions? Circle the design element that indicates the sequence. Then underline the step that tells you how long the process might take.**

As you read, complete the Sequence Chart on page 309.

Practice the Skill

Second Read Author's Purpose

All authors have a purpose, or a reason, for writing. Authors of technical texts inform the reader about a specific topic or subject. Their purpose is to explain complicated concepts and vocabulary in language that all readers can understand. To best achieve their purpose, they have to use straightforward language in clearly organized ways.

Try It Read the following paragraph.

> If you like to dance but you don't want to pay a lot of money for dance classes, you should try the Dance-O-Matic 2000. It's so easy to use! Thousands of people have gone from stumbling over their own feet to looking like professional dancers in a matter of hours. You only need a television and a Zcube gaming system, and you'll be ready to glide across the dance floor!

Discuss **Does the author do a good job of informing the reader about how to use the Dance-O-Matic 2000? Why or why not?**

Read on and compare this paragraph to the previous one.

> The Dance-O-Matic 2000 can be installed in fifteen minutes. First, remove the pad from the box and unroll it so it is flat on the floor in front of your television. Then, place the motion-detection sensor on top of your television. Next, place the Dance-O-Matic 2000 CD into the Zcube gaming system. Follow the directions that pop up on your television screen that explain how to synchronize the mat and the sensor. Finally, click the symbol to choose the dance you want to learn first.

Discuss **Which author does a better job of informing the reader? Why do you think so? Draw a box around the paragraph that you think is more informative.**

As you read, record your answers to questions about the author's purpose on the Close Reading Worksheet on page 310.

Purpose for Reading

Read along with your teacher. Each time, read for a different purpose.

First Read   Focus on sequence.

Second Read   Focus on the author's purpose.

Third Read   Focus on thinking critically about the selection.

CANNED HEAT:
How to Build a Solar Heater

Circle the sentence that indicates what the directions in this technical text tell you to make.

What does the author imply about drawing energy from the sun?

Are you worried about an impending energy crisis? Our world's supply of traditional energy resources, such as coal and oil, grows smaller every year. Soon, we'll need to rely on new forms of energy. Would you like to reduce your use of traditional resources? It's a far simpler task than you may think—for instance, solar heaters use energy from the sun to heat your home. To build your own solar heater for a small space with just a few inexpensive materials and a big pile of recycled aluminum cans, just follow the directions below.

Supplies

- An adult to supervise and help
- Safety goggles
- A large sheet of glass (about 4' x 8')
- A tape measure
- Pencil and paper
- A hand saw
- Three 2" x 6" boards (8' in length)
- Nails and a hammer
- Heat-treated particleboard
- One tube of adhesive caulk
- Rubber window molding
- Reflective roof insulation (same size as glass)
- Aluminum cans (about 200)
- Drill with ¾" drill bit
- One can of black BBQ paint
- Two small solar fans
- Dryer vent piping
- Small thermometer (optional)
- Duct tape (optional)

Instructions

Caution: Remember to ask an adult for assistance when using the saw and drill, and always wear safety goggles when using any tools.

1. Draw a plan for your solar panel based on the size of the glass you have found. The box will be the same width and length as the glass, and the cans will be stacked in columns inside the box. Once you've drawn the plan, you can use the **dimensions** of the box to figure out how many cans you'll need. Leave a few inches of space between the top and bottom of the can columns and the top and bottom of the box to allow air to flow through the cans.

2. Use the hand saw to cut the 2" x 6" boards according to the exact dimensions on your plan.

3. Nail the 2" x 6" boards together to make a frame. Then nail the particleboard to the back of the frame to make the box. Glue a strip of molding to the inside of your box on each of the long sides to keep the glass from touching the cans.

4. Seal the seams of the interior of the box using the **adhesive** caulk. Then use caulk to glue reflective insulation to the interior back of the box, leaving 12" of space at the top and bottom. Finally, seal the exterior seams of the box using the caulk.

> What is the first step you need to take to build this solar heater? Record your answer on the **Sequence Chart**.

> How do the illustrations add to the text?

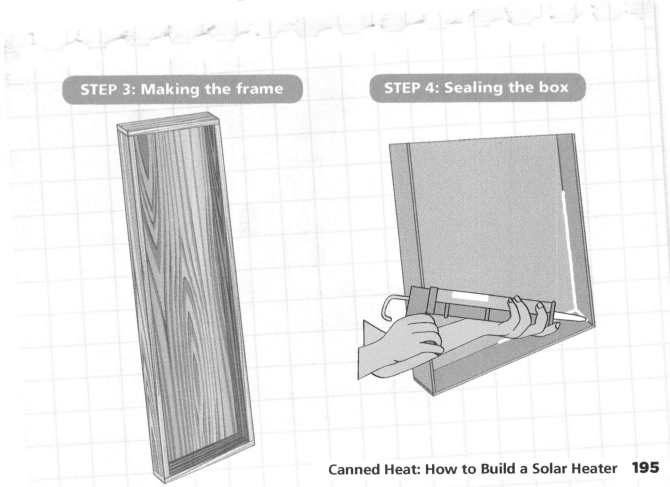

STEP 3: Making the frame

STEP 4: Sealing the box

Summarize step 5. Record your summary on the **Sequence Chart**.

5. Rinse all of the aluminum cans clean and remove their pop tops. Drill a hole in the bottom of each can, except for the cans that will be making up the bottom row of the box. Drill holes in the sides of the cans that will be placed in the bottom row.

6. Place a ring of adhesive caulk along the top and bottom of each can, then stack the cans into columns that match the size of your plans. Let the caulk dry.

7. Paint each column of cans with black BBQ paint, which can withstand high temperatures, and leave them to dry.

8. While the paint is drying, cut two 2" x 6" boards that fit across the width of the box, a few inches down from the top (header) and a few inches up from the bottom (footer). Use your plans to determine the measurements of a series of holes in these boards into which you will pop the top and bottom of each can column after the paint has dried. Drill these holes.

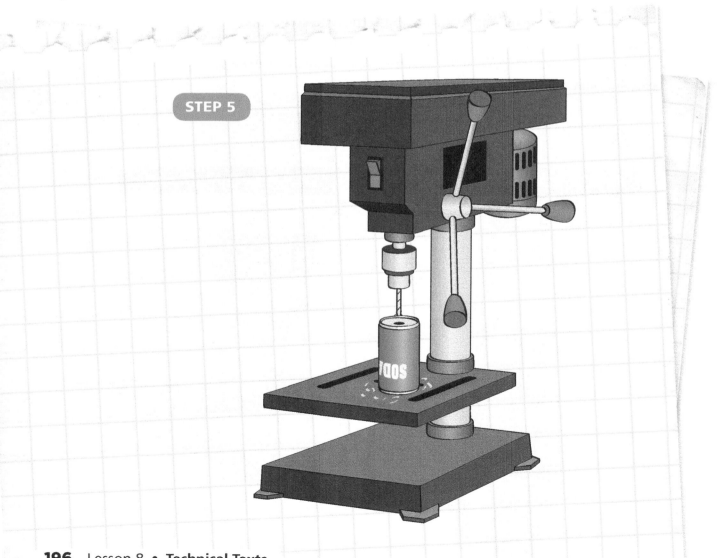

STEP 5

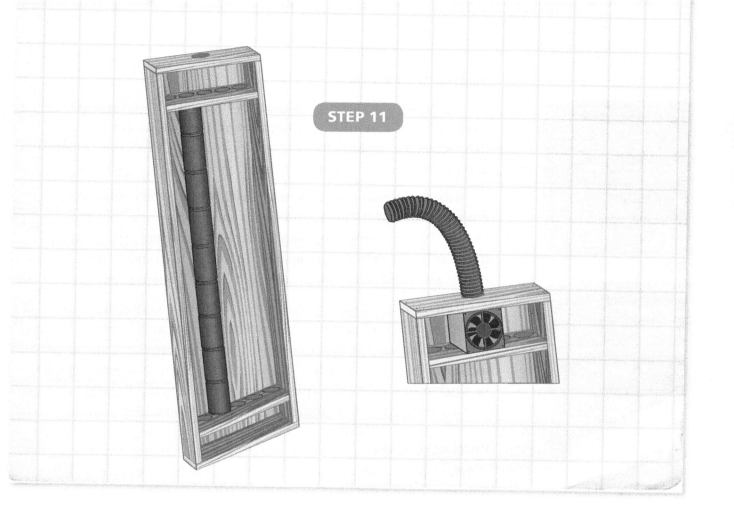

STEP 11

9. Put reflective insulation into the footer and header spaces of the box. **Install** small solar fans into the header and footer sections as well. Set the fan in the footer so that it will pull in cool air from the outside room, and set the fan in the header so that it will push out hot air into the room.

What do you do after you place the can columns into the box? Record your answer on the **Sequence Chart.**

10. Drill a hole in the back wall of the box in the header and footer sections, through both the particleboard and the reflective insulation. The hole should be the same diameter as the dryer vent piping you are using. Place a piece of piping into each hole.

11. Place the header, footer, and can columns into the box. If you like, you can place a small thermometer, such as an aquarium thermometer, onto the side of the glass that will be inside the box.

Circle the optional steps the author lists. What is the author's purpose for doing this?

12. Secure the glass to the front of the box using caulking if you want a permanent seal or using duct tape if you want to be able to remove the glass. Once the seal is tight and secure and the glass is flush to the box frame, your solar heater is complete!

13. Let the solar panel rest flat until the caulking has dried, then take it outside and place it in a sunny spot.

Why does the seal between the glass and the box frame need to be tight?

What should you do if you see that the temperature difference inside and outside the box is not significant? <u>Underline</u> the sentence that tells you.

The writer divided "Canned Heat" into three parts. Describe the information given in each part.

Evaluate

Why is it worth the time and effort to make a solar heater? Cite textual evidence that supports your evaluation.

Testing Your Panel

If you put a thermometer inside of your solar heater, it will tell you whether the air inside is getting hot. You can use an outdoor thermometer to make comparisons between the outdoor temperature and the temperature inside the box.

If the temperature is not warmer inside the box than outside the box when the sun is shining and the air temperatures are cool, the heater might be **malfunctioning**. It may be that the hot air is escaping from the box in a place you can't see. To fix this, use caulk to reseal all of the seams and places where air might escape from the box.

If the air is warming up inside the box but not entering the room, place your hand at the end of the dryer vent piping at the top and feel to see if air is being pushed through it. (You'll want to check this when the sun is shining.) If you don't feel a strong air current, something may be blocking the air inside of the pipe, or the fan may not be working. You'll need to check both things and fix them if something is wrong.

Putting It to Use

Once you've determined that your solar heater is working, it's time to put it to good use. Remember that the solar panel needs to be located outside in a sunny spot, but close to a window or other entry into the room. You can connect longer lengths of dryer vent piping to the heater and run them through a window. You will need to use insulation to seal the spaces in the window around the dryer vent piping.

The best thing about building your own solar heater is that, if you're happy with the way it works, you can keep building more!

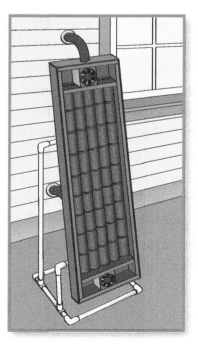

A completed solar heater

Vocabulary: Domain-Specific Vocabulary

Domain-specific vocabulary refers to words that have a special meaning in a particular kind of work, activity, or field of study. For instance, if you were talking to a friend about camping, you might say, "It is important to get enough kindling to start your campfire." The word *kindling* is a domain-specific word used to refer to small pieces of wood used in building a fire. When reading, look for context clues that help you understand the meaning of domain-specific words.

Try It Read this sentence from the text.

> If the temperature is not warmer inside the box than outside the box when the sun is shining and the air temperatures are cool, the heater might be **malfunctioning**.

Discuss **What does *malfunctioning* mean? What other words could the writer have used? Why might *malfunctioning* be the best choice?**

Read the sentences from the text that contain the following words. Complete the chart by writing a definition for each word and using the word in a sentence. Look for context clues that might help you understand what each word means.

Word	Definition	My Sentence
dimensions, p. 195		
adhesive, p. 195		
install, p. 197		

Practice the Skill

Good readers ask questions before, during, and after they read, and they read closely to find answers to them. There are the different types of questions you should ask as you read technical texts.

- **Literal questions** ask about the main details. *What ingredients do I need to make brownies?*

- **Interpretive questions** ask about the details that the author doesn't explicitly state. These questions require you to connect details. *Why does a hamster need a cage with a top?*

- **Evaluative questions** ask judgment questions about a text. *Does the author do a good job of explaining the steps? Is this step essential or optional?*

As you read, ask yourself questions about things you want to know or parts of the text that seem confusing. Then look closely at the text to determine whether the answers can be found there.

Try It Read the following selection.

> The first thing your pet hamster needs is a place to live. You can keep your hamster in a wire cage or an aquarium with a mesh top. Hamsters love crawling, climbing, and running, so make sure to include things that help your hamster exercise. Fancy cages with tubes and tunnels are great, but you can make your own with clear PVC pipe and fittings. Put bedding such as hay or shredded paper on the bottom of the cage or tank. Add a place where your hamster can hide and sleep, such as a small box with an entrance hole or a small flowerpot.

Discuss What is the purpose of the information in this paragraph? Underline the sentence that tells you.

As you read, record your answers to questions on the Close Reading Worksheet on page 311.

Practice the Skill

Second Read **Graphics and Visuals**

Technical texts often contain graphics and other visuals that give you information about the content in a form other than words. **Diagrams** show technical information, such as the names and locations of specific parts, how to complete a specific step in a process, and how parts might work together. Charts, graphs, and time lines display number data in easier-to-understand formats. As you read, it's important to take the time to look at and "read" the graphic elements on the page. Read the title and labels of the graphic, and then connect the information to the text to see how they work together.

Try It The diagram below shows the parts of a hot-air balloon.

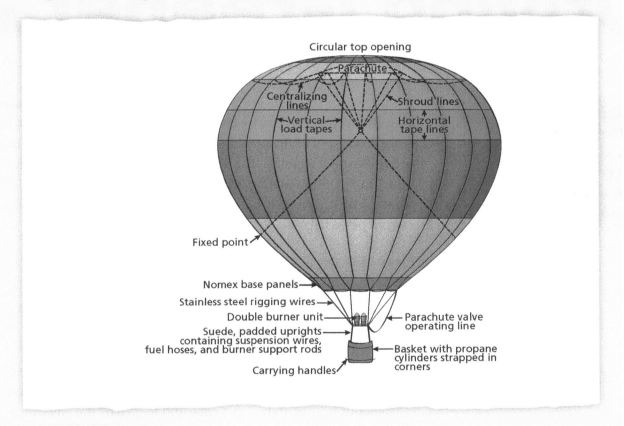

Circular top opening
Parachute
Centralizing lines
Shroud lines
Vertical load tapes
Horizontal tape lines
Fixed point
Nomex base panels
Stainless steel rigging wires
Double burner unit
Parachute valve operating line
Suede, padded uprights containing suspension wires, fuel hoses, and burner support rods
Basket with propane cylinders strapped in corners
Carrying handles

Discuss **What can you learn from the diagram? Circle what you think is important, and tell what you might be able to learn from it that you couldn't learn from text.**

As you read, complete the Graphic Information Organizer on page 312.

Purpose for Reading
Read along with your teacher. Each time, read for a different purpose.

First Read	Focus on asking and answering questions.
Second Read	Focus on graphics and visuals.
Third Read	Focus on thinking critically about the selection.

Driving Greener

Literal Question: What is a fossil fuel, and in what ways is it bad? Underline at least three sentences that helped you answer the question.

1   It is one of the basic laws of physics. Energy—the ability to do work or bring about change—can be changed from one form to another, but it cannot be created or destroyed. We change energy to different forms every day. We do it when we eat a bowl of cereal before going out for a morning run, or when we plug a light into an outlet and use electricity to turn it on, or when we fill our cars with gasoline and then drive them to get from place to place.

Different Forms of Energy

2   Some energy, like light from the sun (solar power), heat from deep inside Earth (geothermal energy), or power from the wind, is renewable. We don't have to worry that it will run out, and we can harness it at any time. Most of the energy that we use, however, is nonrenewable. In the United States, more than three quarters of the energy we use comes from fossil fuels.[1] We use fuels like gas, oil, and coal to heat our homes, to fuel our cars, and to give us the electricity we need to turn on our televisions and computers. This energy poses problems for a society. Since fossil fuels take millions of years to form, they are nonrenewable, and we know that one day they will run out. There are more immediate problems, too: burning fossil fuels for energy can cause hazardous air pollution, and many scientists believe it is leading to global climate change.

[1]fossil fuels natural substances found deep underground that are the remains of ancient plants and animals; over time, heat and pressure turned the ancient remains into fuels that store energy

A Hybrid Solution

3   There are more than 200 million cars registered to owners in the United States. The average American uses more than five hundred gallons of gasoline every year. Combined, we use billions of barrels of oil—which is used to make gasoline—a year, consuming an incredible amount of Earth's natural resources. Scientists, car companies, and the government have been working together to find alternative ways to power the cars we use. One of the alternatives is known as the hybrid.

4   Hybrid-electric vehicles (HEVs) are combinations of gas- and electric-powered cars. They have both a gasoline engine and an electric motor. The engine and the motor are each used to power the car in different ways.

Gas Engines vs. Electric Engines

5   Every gas-powered car has a fuel tank. It supplies gasoline to the engine, which turns a transmission. A **transmission** is the system of speed-changing gears and the shaft that takes the engine's power and uses it to turn the wheels. Every electric car has a set of batteries. Electricity from the batteries powers the electric motor, which turns the transmission, which turns the wheels. Electricity can be generated using renewable energy sources.

6   Since an electric car produces almost no pollution and doesn't use gas, why do we even need a hybrid? The problem is distance—an electric car can only go between fifty to one hundred miles between charges, whereas gas-powered cars can go a few hundred miles between refuelings. Moreover, since electric cars are not as common, there are fewer charge stations than gas stations.

Interpretive Question: What would happen if you needed to make a two-hundred-mile drive in an electric car? Why is an electric car not a good solution?

In what ways are hybrid-electric cars better than gas- or electric-powered cars?

Electric car at a charging station

Literal Question: Which part of the diagram shows how you refuel or recharge these types of cars? Circle the labels in the diagram that tell you.

What information does each diagram show? What information do you learn in each diagram that you don't learn from the text? Record your responses in the **Graphic Information Organizer**.

Take a Peek Inside

7   The following diagrams show a comparison of a gas car and an electric car. Notice how both types of car rely on a single power source to run the transmission.

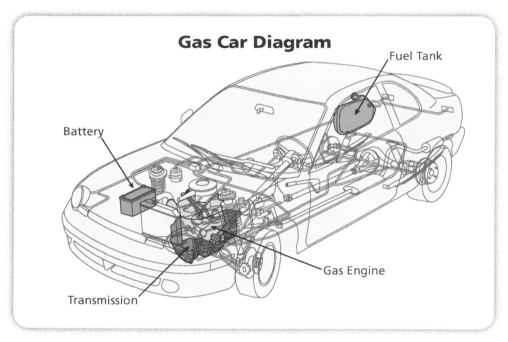

Gas cars rely on a large gas engine, lots of fuel, and a tiny battery to run.

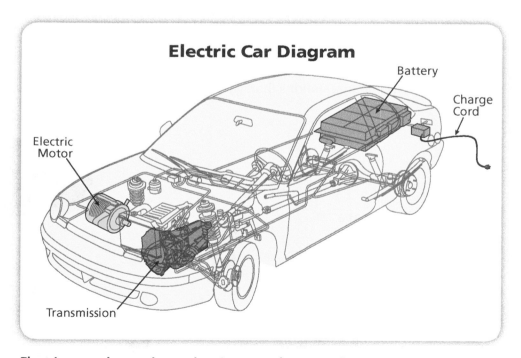

Electric cars rely on a large electric motor, frequent charges, and a big battery to run.

The Hybrid Difference

8   Hybrids have a gasoline engine and a fuel tank, but the engine is smaller on a hybrid than it is on a gasoline-powered car. Hybrids also have an electric motor and batteries, just like an electric car. They have a transmission, like the gasoline-powered and electric car both do. The ways the power sources are combined depends on the design of the hybrid.

Series Hybrids

9   A **series hybrid** is the simplest form of hybrid engine. It is designed so the gas engine turns a generator that charges the car's batteries or provides power to the electric motor. Only the electric motor is connected to the transmission in a series hybrid.

How does this diagram help you understand how the power sources in a series hybrid car are organized? Record your answer in the **Graphic Information Organizer**.

Why exactly would a series hybrid be useful for city buses?

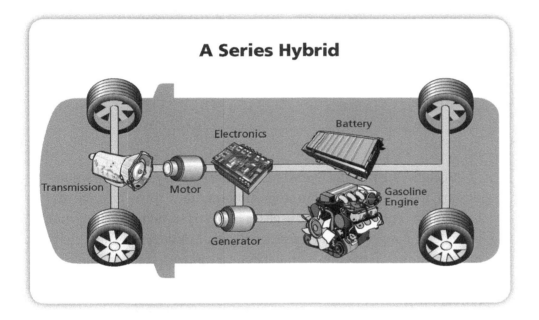

A Series Hybrid

Transmission · Motor · Electronics · Battery · Generator · Gasoline Engine

10   One of the biggest wastes of gasoline is in stop-and-go driving, such as in a city with many traffic lights. Electric motors do not waste as much gasoline because they utilize the electric motor in traffic. The advantage of a series hybrid is that because everything runs through the electric motor, it is much more efficient than other cars. The gas engine is smaller in this type of car, however, so it is less powerful on the open highway. These are both reasons why series hybrids are being considered for city buses and work vehicles.

How does this diagram show how a parallel hybrid car is different from a series hybrid car? Record your answer in the **Graphic Information Organizer**.

Parallel Hybrids

11   A **parallel hybrid** is designed so both the gas engine and the electric motor connect to the transmission. Each can be used to provide the power needed to turn the wheels.

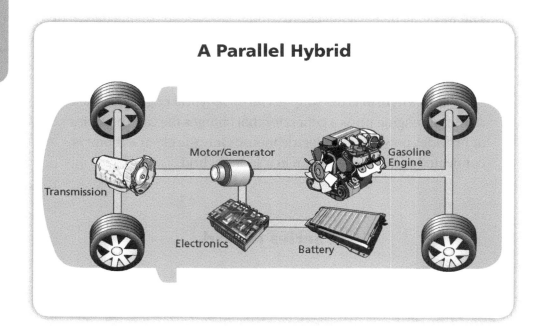

12   Because the parallel hybrid relies more on the gas engine while driving, it is more wasteful in stop-and-go traffic. However, once the car is up to cruising speeds, the gas is both consumed efficiently and provides more power than a series hybrid's. Moreover, because they depend more on gasoline, parallel hybrids utilize a smaller battery, which makes them significantly cheaper to purchase. Batteries are expensive!

The Efficiency of Hybrid Cars

13   The engine of a hybrid can be much smaller than the engine in a gas-powered car. This makes the car more efficient. A smaller engine weighs less, and therefore uses less power to move the automobile.

14   Other factors make the hybrid more efficient than the gasoline-powered car as well. Every time a driver slows or stops the car by stepping on the brakes, energy is lost in the form of heat. In a hybrid, the electric motor works together with the brakes to stop the car. Then the hybrid captures some of the energy and stores it in the battery for later use.

15   At other times, hybrids can turn off the gasoline engine completely when it isn't being used, such as when the car is going down a hill or is stopped at a light. Many hybrid designers also incorporate features such as special tires, aerodynamic[2] design, and lightweight materials to increase the car's efficiency.

Evaluative Question: Why would someone choose to buy a hybrid car over a gasoline-powered car? Box two sentences that show different reasons for buying a hybrid.

Why do hybrid car designers include other features that increase the car's efficiency?

Price and Pollution

16   Hybrid cars are more efficient than gasoline-powered cars, but they can cost thousands more. Still, if you consider the environmental costs, a hybrid may be well worth the price.

17   When gas is burned to power a car, waste materials are emitted from the tailpipe. They include carbon dioxide (CO_2), a form of pollution that some scientists believe has been contributing to global warming. The more gas a car uses, the more CO_2 it sends into the atmosphere, so because hybrids use much less gas, they produce less air pollution.

18   Gasoline is also relatively expensive, and prices have risen dramatically in the past few years. Owners of hybrids may pay more up front, but they can save money long-term because they'll use less gas.

[2]**aerodynamic** having a shape that reduces the drag from air moving past

A futuristic car design,
Concept Car 1

The Future of Cars

Interpretive Question:
What do most ideas for
the future of cars have in
common?

19   HEVs are a relatively recent car development, designed to increase fuel efficiency and reduce the amount of pollution emitted by cars. While they are becoming more popular, the number of hybrids on the road still doesn't come close to the number of gasoline-powered cars. With government incentives and rising gas prices, those numbers may change. One gas company predicts that by 2040, hybrids will make up half of all new cars being produced. Or maybe a new car design will replace the hybrids.

20   Car companies are constantly looking for ways to make better, more efficient cars. European automakers are researching car parts that can store energy in panels. The panels could reduce the car's weight *and* capture energy when the car brakes or when it's plugged into an electric outlet. A Japanese carmaker is looking at similar panels that store energy, but the company is researching panels that could capture solar energy.

Defend

Hybrid cars still use
gasoline. Explain why
hybrid cars are better
alternatives to gas-powered
cars than electric cars
are. Cite textual evidence
to support your ideas.

21   Other ideas for car design include cars that are fueled by pure hydrogen fuel cells,[3] like the type that powered the electric equipment on the space shuttle. Some car designers dream of a car that is powered by water. They believe there is a way to convert the hydrogen and oxygen in water into electricity the same way a fuel cell does. Others wonder if we can use products from plants and other biomaterials, such as ethanol or even coffee grounds, to fuel cars.

22   In the future, you may fill up your car's tank at the kitchen sink. You may even buy a car that drives itself!

[3]**fuel cell** a device that converts chemical energy (such as from hydrogen) to electricity

Vocabulary: Technical Vocabulary

Technical vocabulary consists of words or phrases that you need to know to in order to understand a specific concept. Technical vocabulary relates to language that is used in a technical field, such as engineering. If you work with computers to develop Web sites, for instance, you need to know technical vocabulary such as *absolute link*, *JAVA*, and *analytics*. Very often these words will only have a clear meaning when used in the context of a certain field, so use context clues or a dictionary to be sure you understand them.

Try It The following technical words are found in the text. Read the sentence that contains each word. Look for context clues from the text that help you understand what each word means. Then write a definition of each word.

Word	Definition
transmission, p. 203	
series hybrid, p. 205	
parallel hybrid, p. 206	

Discuss **Do any of these words have uses outside of car mechanics? If so, how are they used?**

Think about a profession that you find interesting. What technical vocabulary words might be important for you to know? List the words below.

Respond to Text: Evaluate the Advantages of Different Media

Different types of media can be useful in explaining technical concepts. Many types of media are readily available to choose from. Video, images, audio presentations, interactive exhibits, and text can work separately or together to provide an explanation, describe a procedure, or demonstrate an experiment.

Try It Think about the two articles you just read, "Canned Heat: How to Build a Solar Heater" and "Driving Greener." The author of each article explains how to build something or how something works. Is a technical text the best way to communicate that information? What other forms of media could you use to teach someone how to build a solar heater or explain how a hybrid car works?

 Discuss **Imagine that you have to explain how to build a solar panel or how a hybrid car works. What media format would be best to use? What graphic information might be useful to explain the concepts?**

On Your Own Choose one of the articles you read in this lesson. Think about how the author conveyed the information to the reader. Then consider how you could use other forms of graphic media, such as video or a Web site, to present it. Write a paragraph in which you evaluate how using different media would be more or less effective to deliver the information. Use the guide on the following page to plan your response. Then write your paragraph on a separate sheet of paper.

Checklist for a Good Response

A good paragraph

✔ explains how the technical text delivers the information.

✔ lists the positives and negatives of each media format.

✔ explains which format would be the best for the content.

✔ includes a topic sentence, supporting details, and a concluding sentence.

My Evaluation of Media

1. **Topic Sentence** Include this information in your topic sentence:

   In "_____," the author uses _____ to teach readers

   _____ .

2. **Detail Sentences** List the positive and negative aspects of using different media formats. Use this chart to organize your ideas.

Media	Positive	Negative
Technical Text (Print)		
Video		
Web site		

3. **Concluding Sentence** Your concluding sentence should state your evaluation about which media format would be best to use.

   _____

   _____

   _____

On a separate sheet of paper, write your paragraph.

Read on Your Own

Read the selection independently three times, using the skills you have learned. Then answer the Comprehension Check questions.

First Read Practice the first-read skills you learned in this lesson.

Second Read Practice the second-read skills you learned in this lesson.

Third Read Think critically about the selection.

Death-Defying Dive

Ask and Answer Questions In what two ways did Baumgartner plan a safe jump? Underline the answers. The first answer has already been underlined for you.

1   One Sunday morning in October 2012, people all over the world watched as a man attempted to make history. Felix Baumgartner, an Australian daredevil, jumped from a capsule nearly 24 miles above Earth's surface. His mission: to free-fall faster than the speed of sound, about 760 miles per hour.

2   People watched as a helium balloon carried Baumgartner's capsule 128,000 feet above Roswell, New Mexico. Some worried that he would be seriously injured or that his body might break apart. They were wrong. Baumgartner had technology and science on his side.

Planning the Jump

Author's Purpose Why do you think the author wrote this technical text? Circle a sentence that informs the reader.

3   In the past, a daredevil who was planning a stunt could make calculations and draw diagrams on paper, build models to test the feasibility of the stunt, and do a few test jumps. Today, computers are used to run simulations that take many details into account. The simulations can tell not only the best ways to be successful, but also how to be safe, too. Mathematical formulas can predict the effect of the physical forces on the body of a diver like Baumgartner.

4   Baumgartner's leap was planned to be record-setting in two ways: it would be the world's highest skydive, and Baumgartner would be the first person to free-fall at supersonic[1] speeds. Baumgartner worked with a team of three hundred people that included engineers, scientists, and doctors. They hoped that Baumgartner's success would show how humans can survive extremely high altitude escapes. High-altitude pilots could use that information if they had a problem during a mission.

[1]**supersonic** faster than the speed of sound

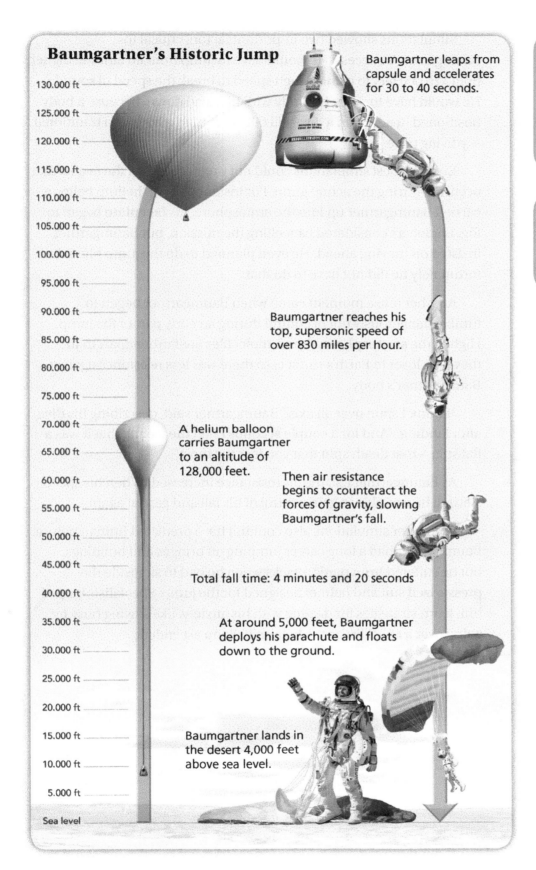

Baumgartner's Historic Jump

Baumgartner leaps from capsule and accelerates for 30 to 40 seconds.

130.000 ft
125.000 ft
120.000 ft
115.000 ft
110.000 ft
105.000 ft
100.000 ft
95.000 ft
90.000 ft

Baumgartner reaches his top, supersonic speed of over 830 miles per hour.

85.000 ft
80.000 ft
75.000 ft
70.000 ft
65.000 ft

A helium balloon carries Baumgartner to an altitude of 128,000 feet.

60.000 ft

Then air resistance begins to counteract the forces of gravity, slowing Baumgartner's fall.

55.000 ft
50.000 ft
45.000 ft

Total fall time: 4 minutes and 20 seconds

40.000 ft
35.000 ft

At around 5,000 feet, Baumgartner deploys his parachute and floats down to the ground.

30.000 ft
25.000 ft
20.000 ft
15.000 ft

Baumgartner lands in the desert 4,000 feet above sea level.

10.000 ft
5.000 ft

Sea level

Sequence What did Baumgartner do after accelerating for thirty to forty seconds? Draw a box around the label that tells you.

Graphic Information Think about what you can learn by reading the labels on the diagram.

Ask and Answer Questions How did Felix Baumgartner deal with the anxiety he felt? Underline the answer.

Critical Thinking Why is learning about the scientific principles involved in skydiving an advantage for someone like Baumgartner?

5   Simulations showed two important factors critical to Baumgartner's success. He would have to jump from an altitude higher than 120,000 feet to gain enough speed to break the speed of sound. He would have to angle his body with his head down, because a body positioned headfirst in a dive will fall faster than a body in a traditional skydiving pose.

6   Even the best simulations could not predict some of the events that occurred during the actual jump. For instance, as the helium balloon carried Baumgartner up into the atmosphere, his **faceplate** began to fog. Engineers considered cancelling the mission, but Baumgartner insisted on moving ahead. He even planned to do the jump blind, but fortunately he did not have to do that.

7   Another tense moment came when Baumgartner began to tumble dangerously out of control during an early part of the jump. High in the **stratosphere**, the air molecules are farther apart than they are closer to Earth's surface, so there was less resistance against Baumgartner's body.

8   "I think I spun over all axis," Baumgartner said, describing his dive after landing. "And for a couple seconds I had the feeling that it was a flat spin—that death spin that you fear the most."

9   As Baumgartner fell, the air resistance increased. When his speed slowed, he was able to gain control of his fall and get flat again.

10   Computer simulations also couldn't have predicted human nature. Baumgartner had a long career jumping off bridges and buildings, but he suffered from panic attacks when he had to sit inside the pressurized suit and helmet designed for the jump. Specialists helped him learn strategies for dealing with his anxiety, like staying busy by going over a checklist as the helium balloon ascended.

What Is Terminal Velocity?

11   Terminal velocity is the maximum speed reached by a falling object. Two opposing forces work against each other during a fall. Gravity is the force that pulls the object to the ground. Resistance, also called "drag force," pushes the object upward as it collides with the air molecules.

Graphic Information Think about how the information in the graphic helps you understand the text.

12   Faster-moving objects experience greater air resistance. At terminal velocity, the two forces balance each other. The object's fall no longer accelerates. When all other forces are constant, the speed of the object's fall stays the same once it reaches terminal velocity. The forces during Felix Baumgartner's fall, however, were not constant. Air molecules high up in the atmosphere are more spread out than those at lower altitudes, so the air resistance increased the farther Baumgartner fell. That's why he went so fast and spun out of control in the thin air at the top of the jump and was able to regain control later as he slowed.

Critical Thinking Think about how Baumgartner's fall would have been different if air resistance were constant from higher to lower altitudes.

13   In those conditions, the terminal velocity decreases and the object—in this case, Baumgartner—continues to slow gradually. At that point, Baumgartner's fall turned into a typical skydive.

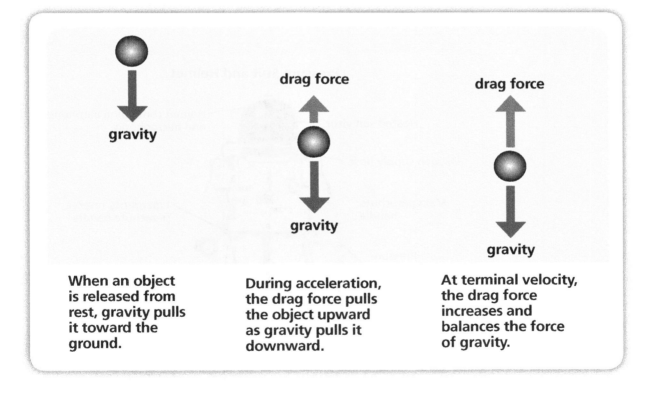

When an object is released from rest, gravity pulls it toward the ground.

During acceleration, the drag force pulls the object upward as gravity pulls it downward.

At terminal velocity, the drag force increases and balances the force of gravity.

Ask and Answer Questions Without the special suit, what would have happened to Baumgartner? Underline the details that tell you.

Graphic Information Draw a box around the part of the suit that would help Baumgartner if his parachute handle were broken.

14   Scientists also weren't able to predict what would happen to the human body when it broke the sound barrier. They knew that aircraft produce a sonic boom[2] when they break the sound barrier. They didn't know what effect this would have on Baumgartner, though. As Baumgartner collided with the gasses of the atmosphere, he was enveloped by a sonic boom. He also had to withstand a huge amount of heat produced by the fall. However, his suit protected him in both cases.

15   The suit that was designed for Baumgartner perfectly protected him from these effects. Its four layers protected him from shock waves. The suit's outer layer was insulating and fire retardant, ensuring that Baumgartner wouldn't go up in flames during his free fall. He didn't, and Baumgartner landed on his feet without any injuries at all.

16   Even though it caused Baumgartner great anxiety to be cooped up in the pressurized suit, he wouldn't have been able to survive, or to break records, without it!

[2]**sonic boom** a loud explosive noise caused by the shock wave from something airborne traveling faster than the speed of sound

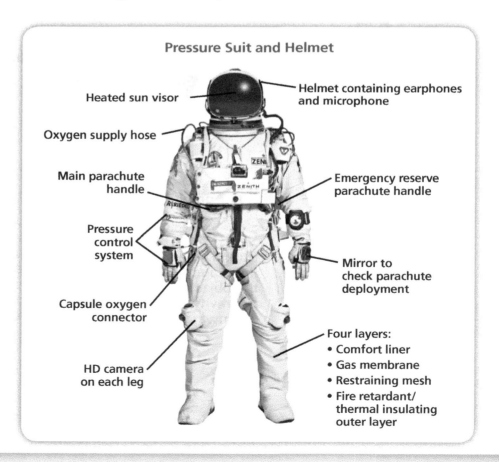

Pressure Suit and Helmet

Heated sun visor

Oxygen supply hose

Main parachute handle

Pressure control system

Capsule oxygen connector

HD camera on each leg

Helmet containing earphones and microphone

Emergency reserve parachute handle

Mirror to check parachute deployment

Four layers:
• Comfort liner
• Gas membrane
• Restraining mesh
• Fire retardant/ thermal insulating outer layer

✓ Comprehension Check

1. What is the sequence of events that led to Felix Baumgartner's record-setting skydive?

2. What is the author's specific purpose for writing this article? How do you know?

3. Name two events that the simulations failed to predict.

4. How did technology help Baumgartner succeed in completing his free fall?

5. What knowledge did Baumgartner learn that could be used for other purposes?

_____

_____

_____

6. Read this sentence from the selection.

> **High in the stratosphere, the air molecules are farther apart than they are closer to Earth's surface . . .**

What does the word *stratosphere* mean?

_____

_____

7. Read this sentence from the selection and look at the Pressure Suit and Helmet diagram.

> **As the helium balloon carried Baumgartner up into the atmosphere, his faceplate began to fog.**

Write a definition of *faceplate* using details from the sentence and the diagram.

_____

_____

8. Why did the author include the section about terminal velocity? How do you know?

_____

_____

_____

Persuasive Nonfiction

Persuasive nonfiction

seeks to convince the reader of a particular point of view. Usually a persuasive text is out to prove one particular point, trying to make the case so strongly that no reader can resist the author's argument. One way to make a persuasive text truly powerful is to use strong and well-researched facts. Another is to use powerful language that moves a reader emotionally. This photo shows a playground that has been uncared for. What might you say to your town officials to persuade them to either rebuild the playground or develop the land for something else?

Skills Focus

Newspapers vs. the Internet

Make Predictions   **Evaluate Author's Argument**

Fighting for Keiko / Freedom Isn't Free

Identify Author's Purpose   **Argument and Counterargument**

Practice the Skill

First Read Make Predictions

When you **make predictions** about a persuasive argument, you consider what's been stated so far and make a forecast about what will be said next. You might consider the opening argument and predict the reasons the author might give to support it. You might also predict whether the author will address the other side of the issue—the counterarguments that an opponent might make against the author's point of view.

Try It Read the following persuasive text. After you read the first paragraph, predict what the author might argue.

Shooting for the Moon

When John F. Kennedy announced in May of 1961 that this nation would put a man on the moon by the end of the decade, he was certainly going all out. And as crazy as it may have sounded at the time, we know now that it was not. Nor have the decades since that time dimmed the power of that momentous achievement.

Now the heavenly body in question is not Earth's moon but Mars. In a straight cost-benefit analysis, one could argue that we can't afford to send rovers to examine alien soil on Mars for signs of life. And yet, when we look back at what NASA's achievements did for science and industry in the previous century and for this nation's global reputation, we can conclude that these forays into space are worth every penny.

Discuss What prediction did you make? Underline parts of the text that support your prediction.

As you read, record your answers to questions about making predictions on the Close Reading Worksheet on page 313.

Practice the Skill

The ability to evaluate an author's argument is vital for determining whether you should be persuaded by a speech or written text. First, you need to identify the claim the author makes—what he or she is arguing or what he or she wants you to believe. Then, you need to identify the evidence the author uses to support the claim.

Evaluating an argument well means weighing the author's reasons and evidence. Make sure that the author's evidence is credible, or believable. Evidence should also be relevant to the topic and sufficient to persuade you. You also have to look for the author's bias. **Bias** is the attitudes or beliefs that influence a person's argument despite contrary facts or evidence. Authors use two types of appeals to try to persuade you.

- **Emotional appeals** may sweep you off your feet emotionally; they use strong language that makes you angry or excited.
- **Appeals to reason** are logical arguments based on facts, evidence, and expert testimony.

Try It Read the following paragraphs.

It's absolutely crazy that more people don't spend more time on bikes than they do in cars. Half the trips we take are short distances that would take minutes on a bike, saving buckets of gas a day and improving our health and well-being.

In cities like Amsterdam, everyone rides everywhere. Snarled traffic? Not a problem. You just pedal right past and arrive at your destination in a great mood, heart beating hard, hair a bit tousled. You're ready to tackle anything.

The advantages don't stop at health or saving fossil fuels, either. It stands to reason that maintaining a car—if you must—costs less if you use it less. Right? And, obviously, the less often you have to fork over four dollars for a gallon of gas, the happier your wallet will be. So don't just sit there. Saddle up and ride!

Discuss **Draw a box around the sentence that states the author's main argument. Circle the evidence that supports the author's claim.**

As you read, complete the Argument Evaluation Chart on page 314.

Newspapers vs. the Internet

by Harry Cardigan, Editor in Chief of the *Smithville Daily News*

Based on the title and the opening quotation, what can you predict the author will argue?

What is the author's argument? Circle an appeal to reason the author uses to support his argument. Write your answers on the **Argument Evaluation Chart.**

What information about the author should you bear in mind as you read? Why might the author be biased?

1   In 1787 Thomas Jefferson said, "Were it left to me to decide whether we should have a government without newspapers, or newspapers without a government, I should not hesitate a moment to prefer the latter." His reasoning implies that citizens who know what's going on in the world around them can pretty much govern themselves. The key, however, is in the quality of the news—is it accurate? Is it being gathered by professionals who know their jobs, people who can tell truth from fiction? Increasingly, the idea of what news even is has come under fire.

2   The newspaper is starting to appear as useless and outdated as the horse and buggy. Today more people get their news online than they do from newspapers, and they're happy with it—their mobile devices allow them constant contact with events as they happen. It seems that people are even reading more news than Jefferson ever thought possible. All in all, it appears to be a win-win scenario for the people and for democracy, if not for the *Smithville Daily News*.

3   But is online news really better? The question must be asked: What is news? It's the events of the day, it's opinion, it's politics, it's about where to eat and what to see at the movies and other subjects too numerous to mention.

4   The first thing a reader should ask about the news, whether from paper or a screen, is how true is it. No one cares about facts in an interview with a celebrity—it's written for pure entertainment, likewise with movie reviews and social commentary. But for issues that really matter, whether it's whom to vote for or what new medicine has proven effective for a disease, facts must be true and supported with evidence.

5   From the earliest days of our country, the power of the press and its right to tell things as they are has been a hot issue. This was part of Jefferson's deep concern for a free press because he knew that what people believed influenced behavior then as it does now, and an electorate moved by facts rather than by gossip tends to make better decisions. Jefferson correctly noticed that the quality of the information the people receive truly becomes the quality of their government—a democracy, in other words, runs on news.

6   But does the physical format news takes really matter?

7   Of course it doesn't—the heart of a newspaper is journalism: getting the facts and getting them straight. Get enough facts straight enough for long enough, and your journal becomes an organ of public discourse, a source for others—the foundation of a thousand other articles.

Based on the information in paragraph 4, what can you predict about how the author will compare journalists who write for the Internet to those who write for newspapers?

What appeal to emotion—expressed as bias—does the author make in paragraph 4? Underline it and write your answers on the **Argument Evaluation Chart**.

Having now compared how journalistic mistakes of fact are handled in a print newspaper and on the Internet, what do you predict the author will say about which source is probably more reliable and true? Why?

What arguments does the author make against newspapers in paragraph 8? Write your answer on the **Argument Evaluation Chart**.

8   *The New York Times* proudly describes itself as a paper featuring "all the news that's fit to print." While there are plenty of papers that seem to print "any news that fits," America is still rich in high-quality newspapers. Still, not all newspapers or journalists get it right. Reporters often take shortcuts in the interest of a more dramatic story—and a possible Pulitzer Prize.[1] But when a journalist at a newspaper fails to do thorough research, plagiarizes another reporter's work, or fails to get reliable and credible sources, there are consequences. If the infraction is serious enough, the journalist is fired, often becoming a public laughingstock, his or her career in tatters. The media universe uses the occasion for a "much needed" public dialogue about journalistic standards. Retractions are published, apologies are made, and the paper reaffirms its higher ideals—until the next time.

9   This is not so with the Internet—it can't be. When a story "goes viral," it reaches every corner of cyberspace—it's read by everyone because the story can be e-mailed, shared on social networks, and posted on endless Web sites and blogs. If at some later point the story is proved wrong, that correction will almost certainly not go viral—retractions almost never do, nor will the original online source be criticized for all to see, like a newspaper, which must keep its reputation bright because it lives in the public eye.

[1]**Pulitzer Prize** an annual award given to writers for outstanding achievement in literary or journalistic work established by the will of Joseph Pulitzer

10   Online journalism has two major defects. On the one hand, because an online article gets to the reader much quicker than a newspaper article, those online articles are often hastily written; facts go unchecked, and mistakes are made. On the other hand, the suspicion on the part of readers that such news is not, in fact, really news at all but some sort of "truthiness," as the comedian Stephen Colbert would say, becomes commonplace. A discerning reader sees that online journalism is faulty. When statements are presented with the look and feel of fact but have no reliable source to back them up, the very idea of news is undercut. The reader's trust is diminished.

What appeal to reason does the author introduce to suggest that newspapers are better? Write your answer on the **Argument Evaluation Chart.**

11   Internet advocates will always point to the advantage print newspapers can't utilize—the link. With a link, a reader can travel at the speed of light to all the sources cited by the journalist, which often turn out to be—you guessed it!—newspapers. The ability to deliver high-quality, fact-checked news rests almost exclusively with sources that employ whole staffs of professional reporters, editors, and fact-checkers. In other words, newspapers. It's the staffed, professional newsroom that makes those online articles possible.

What values does the author hold in the highest esteem? How do you know?

12   Without the existence of newspapers and the trust they manufacture, no one would take an online journal seriously.

13   In case this seems too strong to say, ask yourself, *What equivalent of a full newspaper exists on the Internet?* There are various news-magazine–style forums that derive all their journalistic heft from citations. Their credibility depends on links to truly professional outfits that can back up their "breaking stories." Isn't it admirable that these so-called online journalists get credit for essentially stealing the work of their print counterparts?

Assess whether the author's argument is valid and reasonable based on the appeals and reasoning he gives. Write your answer on the **Argument Evaluation Chart.**

Analyze

Having read the argument, do you think the author's role as a newspaper editor may have influenced his point of view on this topic? Why or why not?

14   The chief reason such independent online newspapers don't exist is the very economic doomsday that threatens the print industry. Cutting staff to save money means fewer reporters to chase stories and less depth in the stories that are chased.

15   The threat is not just to newspapers but to the very concept of news itself. As with any professional service, you get what you pay for. When an online news site gains its authority (or reliability) from a link to a newspaper, the news it offers is no better than that source. Online news sites exist currently as collectors of news that slice and dice but do not generally investigate and report.

16   Without a concentrated source of fact-checked, professionally edited news—the newspaper—Internet news will be as meager as an unlinked article. The core will fall out of the media itself. If our news cannot be trusted, and journalists cannot investigate deeply and publicly and be held accountable, Thomas Jefferson's faith in the power of news to preserve the republic will be empty. Indeed, without the journalistic values only newspapers uphold, that republic might well vanish from Earth.

Vocabulary: Verbal Irony and Puns

To make their arguments more persuasive, authors sometimes use language for humor and persuasive effect. **Verbal irony** is a technique in which what is said contrasts with the literal or usual meaning. For example, someone might say on a gloomy, miserable day, "What wonderful weather we're having!"

Puns are verbal jokes that depend on a word or phrase with more than one meaning. For example, a runner might joke, "I used to have a fear of hurdles, but I *got over it*!" The phrase *got over it* has two meanings: the runner *got over* the hurdle, and the runner *got over* his fear of running over hurdles.

Try It Read this sentence from "Newspapers vs. the Internet."

> *The New York Times* proudly describes itself as a paper featuring "all the news that's fit to print."

> Discuss **The newspaper's motto is a pun. Which word has a double meaning? How is each meaning used in the motto?**

Read the following examples of verbal irony from the selection. Explain the meaning of each and the effect it has on the selection.

1. **Retractions are published, apologies are made, and the paper reaffirms its higher ideals—until the next time.** p. 224

_____

_____

2. **Isn't it admirable that these so-called online journalists get credit for essentially stealing the work of their print counterparts?** p. 225

_____

_____

Practice the Skill

Whatever you read, behind it lies the **author's purpose**. Every author has a reason for writing: to entertain, to inform, to explain, or to persuade.

In a persuasive text, the author is trying to convince the reader to do something or to believe something. Often, the author's purpose is clearly stated at the beginning of a text, so his or her purpose is clear to the reader. Other times, you need to infer the author's purpose from the facts, explanations, and words the author uses to persuade you.

To identify the author's purpose in a persuasive text, ask yourself, *What is the author trying to make me think and why?* The answers to this question will either be stated clearly or inferred from the details the author gives to support the purpose.

Try It Read the following persuasive essay.

> ### Vampires in Your Walls
>
> Every electric socket in your house is a vampire. It's a vampire waiting to suck the energy—and the money—right out of you. This has to stop.
>
> Once upon a time, electricity was so cheap that we barely noticed the meter running. These days, we know the importance of conserving resources. The second you plug in your TV or toaster oven, the power suck begins. You may believe that when you turn it off, it's off—but this isn't so. There's a power draw to keep it in "ready" mode.
>
> So what's the answer? Well, it's simpler than you might imagine: unplug, unplug, unplug. Obviously you won't do this every day for items you use constantly, but if you leave the house for a week, the difference will be noticeable. Not just on your bill, but when millions of other Americans join you, it will show in our shining energy future.

Discuss What is the author's purpose? Underline a sentence that tells what the author is trying to persuade you to do. Are you convinced? Think about how you could follow the advice given in this essay.

As you read, record your answers to questions about the author's purpose on the Close Reading Worksheet on page 315. ✏️➡️

Practice the Skill

Argument is a form of nonfiction writing in which an author seeks to change your mind or influence your opinion. The most persuasive arguments use reasons supported by logic, facts, and passionate appeals to convince you. Of course, some arguments are not balanced—they only fire up emotions. Poor arguments may use false logic or phony facts to convince you to believe a claim that isn't supported by evidence.

A good persuasive writer must address **counterarguments**. This means that the author will acknowledge and speak against, or refute, the arguments of the opposing side in order to show you that she has considered all sides of the issue. The author should provide facts and details that help explain why the counterargument is not valid.

When you read a persuasive text, you must compare the author's argument to any counterarguments. This will help you to understand the entire issue. Then you can weigh the facts and opinions and make an informed decision to agree or disagree with the author.

Try It Read the following paragraph that the author of "Vampires in Your Walls" added to the essay.

> Some people will make the argument that the little bit of energy that an individual device draws can't make much of a difference. But studies that show the energy wasted just to run the "on" light and clock on a coffeemaker indicate that that argument doesn't hold water.

Discuss Circle the sentence that indicates the counterargument. How does this paragraph help support the author's argument overall?

As you read, complete the Argument Chart on page 316.

Fighting for Keiko

by Dawn Corbett

What does the first sentence tell you about why the author is writing this piece?

What argument does the author make in paragraph 1? Enter it into the **Argument Chart**.

Circle the counterargument the author addresses. How does the author refute this counterargument? Enter this information into the **Argument Chart**.

1   The twenty-five-year odyssey of Keiko the orca is a tale of cold indifference, greed, and, finally, unexpected triumph. Our rescue of this one whale is the rescue of everything that makes us human.

2   Born in the wild near Iceland around 1977, the whale we came to know through his work in the Hollywood movie *Free Willy* (1993) was captured at age two. Dubbed Keiko, he became the main draw at a series of aquariums in Mexico and Canada. It was cruel to capture a two-year-old mammal and imprison him in a tank, cut off from his natural world of sounds and sea life. For a creature that depends on sonar, a pool is like a sensory deprivation tank.

3   And yet this act was just the beginning of Keiko's mistreatment. In 1992, production began on *Free Willy* at Reino Aventura in Mexico City, where Keiko was then on exhibit. The film centers on a whale's rescue from an evil marine park owner. After the film came out, *Life* magazine published a dramatic article on the inhumane conditions at Reino Aventura, and the public outcry began: Free Keiko.

4   Whales are large mammals, and they require special conditions to thrive. Right from the beginning it was clear that if Keiko were to be rescued, the effort required—and the cost—would be huge.

5   Some will say the rescue of an individual whale is not worth the price tag. But the money didn't come from public funds. The cost of Keiko's rescue was paid by private donors and environmental advocacy groups like Earth Island Institute. Further, the effort involved shows an increase in awareness of the plight of our fellow species on this planet.

6   It must be made crystal clear—the work and cost of saving this one whale represent not just an act of kindness but also the payment of a historic debt owed to sea mammals everywhere. In rescuing Keiko, everyone involved realized how closely related we humans are to other species on this planet. People are moved to action not by abstract concepts but by living examples, by the acts of individuals on behalf of other individuals.

Underline the sentence in paragraph 6 that seems to clarify the author's purpose even further.

7   To the many people involved in his very real—as opposed to Hollywood—rescue, Keiko was an individual, living and breathing and thinking. And in 1994, that individual was very near death. To pull him back from the brink, the Free Willy/Keiko Foundation was founded, partly with $4 million donated by Warner Bros. The Reino Aventura marine park donated Keiko, and in 1996 the United Parcel Service provided a C-130 Hercules aircraft—one of a few planes large enough to handle the truly Herculean task of carrying a 7,720-pound whale to his new home.

Circle the counterargument the author addresses about Keiko's appearance in movies. How does the author refute this counterargument? Enter this information into the **Argument Chart.**

8   Starved and ill, Keiko was placed in a specially built pool at the Oregon Coast Aquarium in Newport, Oregon. The pool was built with $7.3 million raised by a partnership between Keiko's foundation, private donors, and the Humane Society of the United States. Under the direct care of the Ocean Ventures Society run by Jean-Michel Cousteau, Keiko soon gained 1,800 pounds.

9   Afterward, Keiko appeared in two more *Free Willy* films and at least one documentary. One might ask why Keiko was allowed to return to the screen at all—is this not more exploitation? And yet it was these sequels that kept up the pressure to return him to the wild. Ironically, without this further exposure, Keiko's remarkable journey might never have happened.

Keiko lived in captivity for many years before he was finally freed.

How does including the detail about Keiko's elaborate home in Iceland further the author's purpose?

Why was it important for Keiko to learn to hunt for his own food?

10   In preparation for his return to the open ocean, Keiko was retrained to feed on live fish. By 1998, he was getting more than half his calories from large steelhead salmon he hunted and ate in his tank. He continued to gain weight, and a medical board determined that he was ready to return to life in the wild.

11   After much consideration, the south coast of Iceland was chosen for Keiko's final training before reintroduction to the wild. Klettsvik Bay in Iceland was chosen for both its sheltered location and its closeness to where it was believed Keiko had originally lived. The bay was also narrow enough to allow a net to be placed across its mouth.

12   Of course by 1998, when the transfer was made, Keiko was considerably larger, which made things more difficult. This time an even bigger plane—a C-17 Globemaster—had to be used to transport the 6-ton mammal, at a cost to the foundation of around $300,000.

13   The first task was to build the largest whale pen ever constructed. Called the Bay Pen, this new 250-by-100-foot enclosure within the bay would house Keiko until he was ready to explore the larger bay. In preparation for that eventuality, a 925-foot net was constructed across the bay's open end. The net was so strong and well crafted, it survived 130-mile-per-hour winds without tearing.

Keiko arrives back in Iceland in 1998.

14   Keiko was first released into the bay in March of 2000. A sonar device was attached to the whale to allow his handlers to follow his movements, but he was allowed to feed freely, practicing his skills of hunting and feeding in the wild.

15   In 2002, the final and in many ways most dramatic phase of Keiko's lifelong odyssey began when he was released from Klettsvik Bay. The whale spent more and more time with fellow orcas, finally starting out on what would prove to be a 1,000-mile journey across the North Atlantic to the Faroe Islands and then up the coast of Norway.

16   Keiko was soon sighted, and it was determined that after sixty days in the wild, he was feeding himself without human assistance. It appeared that Keiko's return to the wild had been accomplished. It is only due to his natural curiosity about humans that we know how the story ends.

17   Fascinated by a local fishing boat, Keiko followed the vessel into a Norwegian fjord that quickly became a tourist destination. A year later, after careful monitoring by the foundation and the Humane Society of the United States, it was determined that the whale was suffering from a lung infection. Soon afterward, Keiko beached himself and died.

18   The lesson from this story could not be more obvious. This one whale, for all his star status, was simply a representative of all whales and indeed all sea creatures the world over. Personalizing this message—making it widely and wildly popular news—was the work of many people and was done at great cost. The real question we have to ask is not whether the job was worth it or whether the whale was worth it. The question to ask is, what are we worth as a species?

19   It would be difficult to dispute that Keiko the orca made it through years of cruelty and exploitation to finally benefit from the efforts of better examples of humankind. Those people never let him down, and in the process, they reminded all of us of our connection to all living things, a true measure of our humanity. It is a lesson without price.

What does paragraph 19 show you about the author's deepest concerns?

How does the author's answer to the question she asks in paragraph 18 help her argument? Enter this information into the **Argument Chart**.

Freedom Isn't Free

by Ned Gillespie

In paragraphs 1–4, what does the author reveal about his purpose? How do you know?

What does the author bring up and imply in the first sentence of the selection? How does he refute it? Enter both into the **Argument Chart**.

1   To object to the rescue of a beloved Hollywood whale would not seem to be a great idea. You just shouldn't do it. Better to become the evil marine park manager in the *Free Willy* movies. Better to climb into a tank with the whale itself—but no, we're told that whales will not attack people, that in fact, they are almost human, representatives of all that is good and wholesome, and that they would never eat a baby seal. Except they would—seals are definitely on the menu for orcas.

2   The problem with the rescue of Keiko, the real-life whale behind the three *Free Willy* movies (*Free Willy, Free Willy 2: The Adventure Home,* and *Free Willy 3: The Rescue*) is not that the rescue was the wrong thing to do; the problem is that there is far worse exploitation and crime on our planet, and humanitarian causes suffer for funds every day because they lack one key ingredient—they don't have a Keiko.

3   Keiko was captured in 1979 and went on to become the number-one attraction in marine park aquariums from Canada to Mexico until, in 1992, he became the star of a movie about a whale rescue. From that moment on, Keiko's smiling face was his own best friend; each movie and documentary brought him closer to his destiny: an expensive return to the wild—to a world he had, by that point, probably completely forgotten.

4   Actually, we do know that Keiko had in fact forgotten how to live in the wild because he had to be retrained in how to catch and consume living fish. Adding up all the costs, you have to wonder whether it was worth it. He was shipped by UPS to his new home in Newport, Oregon, a trip that required a C-130 transport plane and cost hundreds of thousands of dollars. Across the country, people starve and suffer every day in silence, and yet this massive sea mammal can charter a plane and be transported to an expensive new home, no expense spared, not once but twice.

5   In Oregon, Keiko successfully began recovering his health, literally putting on more than a ton of weight, going from just under 8,000 pounds in 1994 to nearly 12,000 pounds in 1998. Then he was transported in 1998 on an even larger plane. His new home in Iceland was a huge pen inside a natural bay, designed at enormous effort and expense by a firm in Washington State, and was the largest such enclosure ever built. One end of this bay was also sealed by a net almost 1,000 feet long that was specially built for the purpose—it was strong enough to resist 130-mile-an-hour winds.

6   All this for the comfort and security of one individual—a whale. In the olden days, there were people who got treated similarly. They were known as kings.

7   And yes, we love our kings and queens. The whole world loves royalty, and we make arguments every day for their continued existence. Who can resist the pageantry of a royal wedding? And, not to be harsh, who can resist the glory of a breaching whale?

Underline the phrases in paragraphs 4–6 that use humor to make a point. How does this reveal more about the author's purpose?

In paragraphs 6 and 7, why does the author compare Keiko to a king?

The enclosure built for Keiko inside the bay in Iceland was 250 feet long, 100 feet wide, and 24 feet deep.

What counterargument does the author make about the exploitation of sea mammals? What is his answer to it? Enter this information in the **Argument Chart**.

8   The intent here is not to rain on anyone's parade. The effort to rescue Keiko and return him to the wild was no doubt well intentioned, and no taxpayer money was involved.

9   The real issue is whether such a rescue accomplishes what it intends to. There is a tendency in society to address evils in flashy and public ways, and Keiko's rescue is a perfect example. Exploitation of sea mammals occurs; the public grows increasingly aware of the exploitation; the public, private individuals, or organizations like the Humane Society of the United States step in to right the wrong; and the battle ensues.

10   The story runs its course, huge amounts of money are pledged and spent, and the whale is saved—but for how long? By 2003, within months of his release into the wild, Keiko was dead.

11   Is it possible that Keiko's twenty-five-year-long journey was not a rescue at all? Might it be more realistic to say that this whale was simply being kept alive, and that once the paid human handlers were out of the picture, the great beast simply succumbed to the inevitable?

12   It may be obvious, but it must be said: freedom isn't free—it never is. We pay for our freedoms with blood and money. In this case, society used its collective will and energy to pick up the tab for Keiko's long journey back to the wild, and in doing so, enacted a pageant that allowed society to pat itself on the back and assuage some of the guilt people feel over the exploitation of sea mammals. Then it was back to business as usual—the exploitation of humans.

Evaluate

Which essay does a better job of persuading you? Cite textual evidence to support your evaluation.

Vocabulary: Allusions and Analogies

Allusions are references to commonly known characters or situations—often myths or figures from literature or popular culture. If you say, "My father's boss is the Mr. Burns of his company," many people will recognize the allusion to the vile nuclear power plant owner in the television show *The Simpsons*. **Analogies** are a type of figurative language in which one kind of event or situation is used to explain another, as in "Her attention comes and goes like the tide; half the time it's there, half the time it isn't."

Try It Read this sentence from "Fighting for Keiko."

> . . . In 1996 the United Parcel Service provided a C-130 Hercules aircraft—one of a few planes large enough to handle the truly Herculean task of carrying a 7,720-pound whale to his new home.

In Greek mythology, Hercules was the son of Zeus, the king of the gods, and was known for his strength and his mighty deeds.

Discuss **What connection can you make between this information about Hercules and the way his name is used in the selection?**

Read the following sentences that contain an allusion or an analogy. Based on the information given, explain each allusion or analogy.

1. An odyssey refers to the long and difficult journey, filled with many adventures, twists, and turns, in Homer's epic *The Odyssey*. **The twenty-five-year odyssey of Keiko the orca is a tale of cold indifference, greed, and, finally, unexpected triumph. Allusion,** p. 230

2. **For a creature that depends on sonar, a pool is like a sensory deprivation tank. Analogy,** p. 230

Respond to Text: Comparing Points of View

"Fighting for Keiko" and "Freedom Isn't Free" present two different views on the same topic. The opposing points of view of these authors provide the material for a lively debate and allow for a more interesting view into the issues at stake when it comes to rescuing large mammals—or not.

Try It After reading both selections, with which author did you agree more?

 Discuss ▶ **Why did you agree with one author over the other? Was the evidence more convincing in one selection? Did you like one author's attitude better than that of the other?**

On Your Own Write a paragraph that compares the arguments expressed in "Fighting for Keiko" and "Freedom Isn't Free." What sorts of facts do both selections cite? How do the styles of their arguments differ? How are they the same? Do you find one argument to be more persuasive than the other? Use the guide on the following page to plan your response. Then write your response on a separate sheet of paper.

Checklist for a Good Response

A good paragraph

✔ clearly states the nature of the arguments being described.

✔ explains how they are alike and different.

✔ includes an opinion about which argument is most effective and why.

✔ shows your understanding of the topic.

✔ includes a topic sentence, supporting ideas, and a concluding statement.

My Comparison of the Points of View

1. **Topic Sentence** Include this information in the first sentence of your paragraph:

   While both "Fighting for Keiko" and "Freedom Isn't Free" address Keiko

   the orca's rescue, _____

   _____ .

2. **Sentences** The sentences of your paragraph should provide details that support your comparisons. Use this chart to organize your ideas.

Compare and Contrast the Arguments	
Facts Cited by Both Selections	
Paraphrase of Argument in "Fighting for Keiko"	
Paraphrase of Argument in "Freedom Isn't Free"	

3. **Concluding Sentence** Your final sentence should clearly state and sum up why you preferred one argument to the other.

   _____

   _____

On a separate sheet of paper, write your paragraph.

Read on Your Own

Read the selection independently three times, using the skills you have learned. Then answer the Comprehension Check questions.

First Read — Practice the first-read skills you learned in this lesson.

Second Read — Practice the second-read skills you learned in this lesson.

Third Read — Think critically about the selection.

Trolleys vs. Big Oil

by Marlene Frazier

Identify Author's Purpose Underline the phrases that give you a clue to the author's purpose. Some details have been underlined for you.

Evaluate Author's Argument Think about what kind of appeal the author is making so far—logical or emotional?

Critical Thinking Think about how a phrase like "darker stories in American energy history" appeals to your emotions.

1   One of the darker stories in American energy history began in the 1920s. The main means of urban mass transit was the electric trolley. A group of oil and tire companies worked together to systematically replace the trolleys with buses. There is no question which system was more efficient. Electric trolleys moved more people faster at far less cost. They used less energy. They also caused less wear and tear on the roads. Of more importance to the health of the planet, the trolleys also used far fewer natural resources, including fossil fuels.[1]

2   It's not too late to return to this sane mode of transport. At some point, after a major oil shortage, this could become a necessity. If the change were made before we were in an acute oil shortage, we could make the change calmly rather than in desperation. To understand just how superior electric transport can be to our current modes of transport, it helps to take a look back.

3   The modern electric streetcar developed by the President's Conference Committee (PCC) in 1930 could start and stop faster than most cars. The trolley used six dollars' worth of electricity per hour, as opposed to thirty-two dollars' worth of heavily polluting diesel fuel used by a city bus. The PCC trolley carried twice as many passengers as a bus. These cars were built so sturdily that many are still in use today. But these streetcars came too late to save electric transit.

[1] **fossil fuels** natural substances, found deep underground, that are the remains of ancient plants and animals; over time, heat and pressure turned the ancient remains into fuels that store energy

4   By the 1950s, General Motors, Standard Oil, and Firestone Tires had bought up most of the trolley companies under the umbrella company National City Lines (NCL). They then replaced trolley lines with bus service. Now, more than a half century later, the effects of this shift are clear. America is more polluted and dependent on foreign nations for its primary energy source—oil—than it ever needed to be.

5   To understand just how unnecessary—and unwanted—the changes brought about by the automobile, oil, and rubber companies were, you have to look back in time. Early on, many cities made the choice for rail-based public transportation. New York City kicked things off in 1832 with horse-drawn cars that traveled over iron rails laid out along city streets. The rails reduced friction, allowing these nineteenth-century centaurs to pull heavier loads while offering passengers a smoother ride.

6   Naturally, horse cars were not pollution free. The streets of nineteenth-century cities became a sort of stable, always in some state of disarray. And the carts were slow. However, they transported people from their places of work to train stations and ferries. The carts were reliable, and they also provided shelter from the weather.

Make Predictions
Make a prediction about the sort of solution the author will propose to the problems outlined in the argument so far.

Electric trolleys became so popular with the public that the industry experienced exponential growth almost overnight.

Make Predictions What do you predict these companies will do to undermine the use of streetcars?

Evaluate Author's Argument What fact-based appeal does the author make in paragraphs 8–11? (Circle) the argument.

7   Like a nervous cat, though, innovation is jumpy, always moving. Along with the Civil War, the 1860s brought the cable car. Cable cars were propelled by a moving cable running through a slot beneath the street. The car engaged with the cable to get momentum, easing off—braking—when it needed to stop or slow down. But this wasn't ideal. While it did use the innovation of rails very well, the fact that the cable and therefore the cars moved at a constant speed made the cars dangerous to operate around turns. The cars themselves were also costly to run and maintain.

8   In 1888, Richmond, Virginia, became the first U.S. city to electrify its cable cars. The new streetcars, as they were called, used the power from electric generators. The cars moved silently and powerfully at greater rates of speed than ever before. The use of electric streetcars quickly spread across the country. Coney Island, Brooklyn, had the first system in New York in 1890. The electric streetcars were known as trolleys for the way the early versions got their electricity through overhead "trawlers." By the 1920s, trolleys were everywhere. They connected suburbs to downtowns. They brought new businesses and new customers to the areas they served.

9   Most trolley companies were privately owned, and yet they were subject to city-imposed maximum fares. They charged only a nickel in New York, even during a time of inflation. When a company repaired its trolley lines, it often wound up needing to repair side streets as well. Trolleys also had to compete with automobile traffic for the limited street space.

10   Nevertheless, the electric streetcar became the dominant mode of transport in American cities. In the 1930s, PCC was formed to address the problems of streetcars. Sadly, just as the PCC developed plans to perfect the modern streetcar, the oil, auto, and rubber companies began their scheme to end this mode of transport.

11   The NCL took control of and dismantled the electric streetcar systems in eight American cities. They began replacing the streetcars with buses.

12   The expansion of buses over streetcars progressed rapidly. Many cities embraced free-roaming buses. Buses, admittedly, did have some advantages. They needed no rails to get around, so they could go more places and take people closer to where they lived and worked. They also allowed the streets to become smoother, with the removal of the rails. But bus travel could be bumpy and uncomfortable. So, just as oil, auto, and rubber executives were hoping, people turned to individual transport—cars—in numbers greater than ever before.

13   All this took place despite the massive popularity of the electric streetcar lines. People had adapted well to the convenience and ease of streetcar travel. They enjoyed cleaner air and took it for granted. Now, that clean air is only a faint memory. Once the smooth, cheap, and clean option of electric travel was no longer a possibility, the public's clear preference was for individual automobiles.

14   This wasn't true in all American cities. Boston, Cleveland, Philadelphia, and New Orleans, along with a few others, still maintain their streetcars. And in 1989, when an earthquake shut down the Nimitz Expressway, the city of San Francisco instituted a new light rail project using restored PCC cars. That innovation has boosted ridership by 300 percent. This has been a tremendous boon for local shops and restaurants along these routes and for the city's tourist industry in general.

Counterargument Think about how the author acknowledges the benefits of bus transportation.

Argument Circle the dramatic, number-based fact the author gives in paragraph 14.

Critical Thinking Which advantage of electric streetcar travel would be most important to you? Why?

Some cities maintained their streetcar lines and still use them today.

Make Predictions What do you predict will be the role of electric streetcars in the cities of the future?

Critical Thinking Think about whether it would be fair to make oil, auto, and rubber companies help pay for the reintroduction of streetcars in cities.

15   Portland, Oregon, also adopted streetcars into its transportation mix. It has a line running through the heart of the city, including the recently developed Pearl District. Quiet, efficient, street-level transportation service is ideal for an urban area redesigned around the idea of pedestrian traffic and restaurants and shops to which you can walk. Since 1997, Portland investors have poured more than $3.5 billion into the area adjoining its new streetcar line. This investment has helped the Pearl District become a major destination for residents and visitors alike.

16   Light rail—automated electric railcars—remains the gold standard for urban mass transit. It is by far the most efficient system and has much lower operating costs than buses. Light rail systems built the old-fashioned way can cost one-hundredth of what subways or elevated trains cost to build. Operating at street level, they're also easier for passengers to board and use.

17   If this story tells us anything, it is that when it comes to our transportation habits, nothing is permanent. When the cost of oil reaches astronomical heights or when oil runs out, the cities that are ahead of the curve on adopting electric mass transit will be the first to profit by reaching into the past to solve the problems of tomorrow.

✔ Comprehension Check

1. What is the author's main argument? Explain why the argument is effective or not effective.

   _____

   _____

   _____

2. Read this sentence from the selection.

   The rails reduced friction, allowing these nineteenth-century centaurs to pull heavier loads while offering passengers a smoother ride.

   Here the author makes an allusion to a centaur—a strong mythical creature with the legs of a horse and the upper body of a human. Circle words in the sentence that give you context clues to the meaning of the allusion. What does the author convey with this allusion?

   _____

   _____

   _____

3. Identify a counterargument the author addresses. Evaluate whether the author does an effective job of refuting the counterargument.

   _____

   _____

   _____

4. What can you tell about the author's purpose from the last sentence of the selection?

_____

_____

_____

5. Solar power is believed to be a cleaner form of energy than coal power. Given the author's point of view about electric streetcars, what can you predict she would argue about coal power versus solar power? Why?

_____

_____

_____

6. Read the last sentence of the selection below.

> **When the cost of oil reaches astronomical heights or when oil runs out, the cities that are ahead of the curve on adopting electric mass transit will be the first to profit by reaching into the past to solve the problems of tomorrow.**

What irony is expressed about time?

_____

_____

_____

Primary and Secondary Sources

Primary sources tell about events through someone's direct experience. A letter written by a soldier who fought in World War II is a primary source.

Secondary sources use information gleaned from primary sources to describe an event and have a much broader view of the subject.

Think about a possible primary source and a secondary source to describe the event taking place in this photo. How would the two sources be similar and different? What is one thing that each could describe that the other could not?

Skills Focus

Mars Attacks

Main Idea and Details   Primary Sources

Panic on the Airwaves

Draw Inferences   Secondary Sources

Practice the Skill

First Read Main Idea and Details

The **main idea** is what a selection or paragraph is all about—the overall concept or thought it expresses. Sometimes the main idea is stated directly in the text, but when it is not, you have to figure it out based on information in the selection. To identify a selection's main idea, look for the one idea that all the important details in the selection point to.

Try It Read the following excerpt from a speech by Susan B. Anthony.

> The only question left to be settled now is: Are women persons? And I hardly believe any of our opponents will have the hardihood to say they are not. Being persons, then, women are citizens; and no state has a right to make any law, or to enforce any old law, that shall abridge their privileges or immunities.

Discuss **What is the main idea of this speech? Underline any phrases or sentences that help you understand the main idea.**

Now look for the main idea of this paragraph from a nonfiction magazine article.

> On November 18, Susan B. Anthony was arrested and fined $100 for casting an illegal ballot in the 1872 presidential election. One week earlier, Anthony and three other women had entered a barbershop in Rochester, New York, where voter registration was being held. Anthony read the Fourteenth Amendment to the U.S. Constitution aloud and pointed out that it did not contain any language that restricted the privilege of voting to men. She demanded her constitutional right to vote. After an initial refusal, the electoral registrars allowed Anthony and the other women to register. Four days later, Anthony cast her ballot in the election.

Discuss **What is the main idea of this paragraph? Underline phrases or sentences that help identify it.**

As you read, complete the Main Idea Chart on page 317.

Practice the Skill

Second Read Primary Sources

When you are researching a topic or an event, you have to act like a detective. You need to look at **primary sources**—such as letters, diaries, speeches, photos, and such family documents as birth, marriage, and death certificates—for a firsthand account of what happened at a particular time and place. Any document that was created at the time of the event can be a primary source if it helps answer your questions. Primary sources provide information and reveal things that only firsthand witnesses could have seen or felt.

To evaluate a primary source, first start with the basic questions: *Who? What? When? Where? Why?* You need to understand how and why a source was created, the forces that shaped it, and its limitations. What questions can this source help you answer? What questions can it not help you answer? Is this account biased?

Try It Read the following excerpt from a diary entry written by a grandmother in 1906. As you read, consider its value as a primary source.

> I had been setting the table for supper when a neighbor came running with the news that a tremendous earthquake had devastated the city of San Francisco, California. Though I was safe here in Missouri, my neighbor kindly remembered that my son and grandson were on their way to San Francisco. I could do nothing but wait for news. It was five nerve-wracking days before a telegram arrived on April 23 telling of their safety. It was the happiest day of my life.

Discuss What questions does this primary source help you answer? How might this be a valuable source for a report on the San Francisco earthquake or life in America in the early twentieth century?

As you read, record your answers to questions about primary sources on the Close Reading Worksheet on page 318.

Purpose for Reading
Read along with your teacher. Each time, read for a different purpose.

First Read Focus on the main idea and the details that support it.

Second Read Focus on aspects of the primary source account.

Third Read Focus on thinking critically about the selection.

Mars Attacks

How do you know the documents are primary sources?

On October 30, 1938, many people who turned on their radios were surprised to hear an urgent and official-sounding news report about an alien invasion from Mars. Spaceships were reportedly landing around New York and New Jersey. Some people panicked and ran into the streets. Others called the police. Some hid in their basements. However, those who understood they were listening to a dramatization of H. G. Wells's science fiction story *The War of the Worlds* enjoyed the show. The broadcast, which was directed by Orson Welles, was the subject of controversy in the weeks after it aired. Thousands of people wrote to the Federal Communications Commission (FCC), a government agency in charge of regulating radio content.

The first letter is from the city manager of Trenton, New Jersey. It describes the panic and fear in that city during the broadcast. The second letter is from a satisfied listener in South Dakota.

CITY OF TRENTON
NEW JERSEY

PAUL MORTON
CITY MANAGER
M.AM.SOC.C.E.

RAYMOND F. RICHTER
EXECUTIVE SECRETARY
AND
PERSONNEL OFFICER

October 31, 1938

WAR OF THE WORLDS

Federal Communications Commission

Washington, D.C.

        COMPLAINT — WABC BROADCAST

Gentlemen:

    To avoid a recurrence of a very grave
and serious situation that developed in this
community last night due to the public's
misinterpretation of the broadcast through
WABC at about 8:15, dramatizing H. G. Wells'
"War of the Worlds", which completely
crippled communication facilities of our
Police Department for about three hours,
I am requesting that you immediately make an
investigation and do everything possible to
prevent a recurrence.

What is the main idea of the first paragraph of the letter? Underline the phrases or sentences that help you identify the main idea. Record the main idea on the **Main Idea Chart**.

What is the writer's purpose for writing the letter? Use details from the letter to support your answer.

How did the author of the letter feel? Use details from the letter to support your answer.

The situation was so acute that two thousand phone calls were received in about two hours, all communications lines were paralyzed and **voided** normal municipal functions. If we had had a large fire at this time it could have easily caused a more serious situation. Tremendous excitement existed among certain areas of this community and we were receiving constantly long distance phone calls from many states making inquiries of relatives and families thought to have been killed by the catastrophe that was included in the play.

I can conceive of no reason why the name of Trenton and vicinity should have been used on this broadcast. The State Police were equally handicapped and it is indescribable the seriousness of this situation.

Your prompt attention will be appreciated.

Very truly yours,

PAUL MORTON
CITY MANAGER

PM/mlw

FILED IN
1938

Circle details that support the idea that the letter writer thinks the broadcast was a serious situation.

What questions does this primary source help you answer?

Aberdeen, S. Dak.
November 1, 1938

Federal Communications Commission
Washington, D. C.

44-3 WAR OF THE WORDS

Gentlemen:

I have read considerable [reports] concerning the program of Orson Welles presented over the Columbia Broadcasting System Sunday evening. I suppose that by this time you have received many letters from numerous cranks and crackpots who quickly became jitterbugs during the program. I was one of the thousands who heard this program and did <u>not</u> jump out of the window, did <u>not</u> attempt suicide, did <u>not</u> break my arm while beating a hasty retreat from my apartment, did <u>not</u> anticipate a horrible death, did <u>not</u> hear the Martians "rapping on my chamber door," did <u>not</u> see the monsters landing in war-like **regalia** in the park across the street, but sat serenely entertained to no end by the fine portrayal of a fine play.

What is the main idea of the second letter? Underline phrases or sentences that help you identify it. Record the main idea on the **Main Idea Chart.**

How are the main ideas of the two letters similar or different? Explain your answer at the bottom of your **Main Idea Chart.**

What questions does this primary source answer?

What is the second letter writer's attitude toward those who thought the alien invasion was real? How do you know?

What does the second letter writer want the FCC to do? <u>Underline</u> the sentence or sentences that tell you.

The "Mercury Theatre" has been one of the radio highlights of the week for me this fall. The program Sunday, I felt, was one of their better programs.

Should your commission contemplate serious measures toward the Columbia Broadcasting System my suggestion would be that the "Mercury Theatre" be directed to re-broadcast this program and the reaction of all the listening audience be **solicited**.

It is in the interest of a continuation of the fine things in radio today, I am,

Very respectfully yours,

J. V. Yauke

FILED IN
DEC 15 1938
D. M. & F. SEC.

P.S.- I am in the State Administration office of the South Dakota State Employment Service and every member of staff who heard the program **subscribes** to what I have had to say.

Argue

Which letter writer makes the better argument? If you were the director of the FCC, which suggestion would you take?

Vocabulary: Consult Dictionaries

Old primary source documents often contain outdated or unusual vocabulary words that may no longer be commonly used or that have come to be used differently now. This is especially true of primary sources that are generated by people in such professions as law, government, science, law enforcement, or the military. If you come across a word you don't know, check a dictionary.

Try It Read the following sentence from the second letter in "Mars Attacks."

> I suppose that by this time you have received many letters from numerous cranks and crackpots who quickly became **jitterbugs** during the program.

The word *jitterbugs* is not used much anymore. Can you use the context to guess its meaning? If not, a dictionary will help. Here's one entry.

> **jit•ter•bug** ('jit-ər-bəg) *noun.* **1:** a fast dance popular in the 1940s; **2:** (obsolete) a nervous person

Discuss **Which meaning of *jitterbug* is intended in the letter?**

Read the sentence in the selection in which each word below appears. Check a dictionary for the word's meaning if necessary, and then write the definition on the lines.

1. **voided,** p. 252 _____

2. **regalia,** p. 253 _____

3. **solicited,** p. 254 _____

4. **subscribes,** p. 254 _____

Practice the Skill

When you **draw inferences**, you make educated guesses based on information in the text. You draw inferences about things in real life all the time. Let's say you observe your dad cooking soup on the stove. You come back to the kitchen a few minutes later, and the stove is turned off. Would you touch the burner? No, because you put together what you observed (your dad cooking) with what you know (the metal of the burner stays hot after the burner is turned off) to draw an inference that the burner is probably still hot.

As you read, you should draw inferences. Think about the details the author shares with you, and combine them with your own knowledge to figure out what the author means but has not stated directly.

Try It Read this excerpt from a magazine article written during the Civil War.

> General Thompson is a strict leader. He enforces the regulations requiring tidiness in and about the camps, and in the persons of the soldiers. Shoes must be polished until soldiers can see their own reflections in them. Bedrolls and knapsacks must be packed correctly and neatly. Missing uniform buttons are not tolerated. The general inspects his troops carefully each day for flaws in their appearance.
>
> The soldiers receive special privileges if they meet and maintain General Thompson's standards of tidiness. Unlike the soldiers under General Marshall's command, they are allowed second helpings at mealtimes and may have one evening off per month.

 **Discuss** What inferences can you make about the soldiers under General Thompson's command? Underline details that help you draw your inference.

As you read, record your answers to questions about drawing inferences on the Close Reading Worksheet on page 319.

Practice the Skill

Second Read | **Secondary Sources**

Secondary sources are valuable research resources. They include magazine, encyclopedia, and Web articles, documentary films, and books written by experts, such as historians and journalists. Secondary sources are written after an event has occurred. The authors did not witness the event, but instead gathered information from primary sources to create a comprehensive picture. Authors of secondary sources have access to information that witnesses to the event could never know. Because secondary source writers have access to so much information and data, they often quote from primary sources and then organize and display information graphically by using charts, graphs, or time lines.

Just as with a primary source, you should ask questions that help you evaluate a secondary source. *Why was it written? Does the author have an expert background in the subject area? What primary sources has the author used? Are those sources valid and appropriate?*

Try It Read this excerpt from a biography about General Thompson.

> General Tyler J. Thompson commanded the Union army division that marched from Wisconsin to Mississippi. His troops were filled with young farm boys who had little experience in battle; however, they were highly regarded on the battlefield.
>
> General Thompson grew up in Corinth, New York, and graduated from West Point at the top of his class. He was known for his attention to detail. Every bullet in every gun was accounted for, and no soldier marched out of step. By the end of the war, Thompson's men grew resentful of his fastidiousness and attempted to stage a mutiny.

Discuss Compare the information in the biography above to the magazine article on the previous page. What information did the author of the biography have that the magazine writer could not have known? Draw a box around it. What does this information add to your knowledge of General Thompson?

As you read, complete the Sources Chart on page 320.

Purpose for Reading
Read along with your teacher. Each time, read for a different purpose.

First Read   Focus on drawing inferences.

Second Read   Focus on secondary sources.

Third Read   Focus on thinking critically about the selection.

Panic on the Airwaves!

Based on what you have read so far about Orson Welles, how would you describe him? Underline textual evidence that supports your inference.

Is this text a primary or secondary source? What information does the author have that people in 1938 could not have had? Record your answers in the appropriate column of the **Sources Chart.**

In 1938, many Americans were worried about World War II. How might that have affected people's reaction to Welles's broadcast?

1   Someone asks you, "Did you know the word *gullible* is not in the dictionary?" "Really?" you might respond before realizing you'd been tricked by one of the oldest jokes around. Of course, *gullible* is in the dictionary. Falling for a goofy joke is one thing, but imagine if you checked the TV, Internet, or radio—sources you trust—for news and saw a serious-looking report that Martians were invading the United States. Would you get scared, call the police, or run outside to see for yourself? That's what thousands of people did one evening in 1938. That's when a radio broadcast of the science fiction novel *The War of the Worlds* was aired. The program sounded so real that many people who tuned in late believed the world—which was already on the verge of World War II—really was under attack, and they panicked.

2   The broadcast took place between 8:15 and 9:30 p.m. on October 30, the night before Halloween. But Orson Welles, a young actor, writer, and director, had set the production in motion earlier. Welles had wanted to lure listeners away from a rival radio show. The popular *Chase and Sanborn Hour* was a musical program that aired on another station at the same time as Welles's show, *Mercury Theatre on the Air*. His plan was to update H. G. Wells's classic novel *The War of the Worlds* in a way that would **transfix** his listeners. As luck would have it, he succeeded only too well.

On the Air

3   Instead of presenting the show in typical dramatic fashion, Welles had the writer Howard Koch revise the story in an **inventive** way. The story of the Martian invasion would be presented as a series of important news reports. The audience would hear the regular musical programming suddenly interrupted by a news flash, something that often happened. They would hear announcers, news reporters, and scientists supposedly reporting about an actual Martian invasion. In fact, the speakers and musicians would all be in the studio following a script as directed by Welles.

4   According to *The New York Times*, Welles claimed that he had almost cancelled the show because he thought "perhaps people might be bored or annoyed at hearing a tale so improbable." Yet, the show went on as planned. It began with this introduction: "The Columbia Broadcasting System and its affiliated stations present Orson Welles and the *Mercury Theatre on the Air* in *The War of the Worlds* by H. G. Wells." Anyone who heard the announcement understood the fictional nature of the show that followed. However, many people had been listening to the *Chase and Sanborn Hour* at 8 p.m. and did not switch over to Welles's show until around 8:10. Not only had they missed the introduction but they tuned in just in time to hear fictional newscaster Carl Phillips, played by actor Frank Readick, reporting from a farm in Grover's Mill, New Jersey. He reported that a huge flaming object falling on a farm there was believed to be a meteorite.

Draw a box around the information in paragraph 4 that is from a primary source. What information does this source offer? Record your answer on the **Sources Chart**.

How did the news report format used by Welles likely play a role in convincing some people that the Martian invasion was real?

In the 1930s, the radio was a source of family entertainment in the home.

Why did so many people call the offices of *The New York Times* newspaper?

Draw a box around the primary source quoted in paragraph 8. What does the author of the text know that the witness in 1938 did not? Write your answers on the **Sources Chart**.

5   Then he announced that alien creatures were emerging from the flames: "A humped shape is rising out of the pit," Phillips gasped. "I can make out a small beam of light against a mirror. What's that? There's a jet of flame springing from the mirror, and it leaps right at the advancing men. It strikes them head on! Good Lord, THEY'RE TURNING INTO FLAME!" His words were interrupted by screams and shrieks. What were late-tuning listeners to think?

6   The airwaves went momentarily silent. Then an announcer broke in with news of difficulty transmitting the signal from Grover's Mill. He introduced Brigadier General Montgomery Smith, commander of the state militia, who said that two New Jersey counties were being placed under martial law. He told listeners that state militia would be evacuating homes in the area. The announcer returned, explaining that the charred body of Carl Phillips had been identified in a Trenton hospital. Then listeners were led to believe they were hearing the secretary of the interior speak from Washington, D.C., urging citizens to remain calm.

Out on the Streets

7   But many did not remain calm. In fact, they panicked. *The New York Times* newspaper's operators received 875 phone calls, including one from a man who asked, "What time will be the end of the world?" The city manager of Trenton, New Jersey, reported that police received two thousand panicked phone calls over the course of two hours. At a hospital in Newark, New Jersey, more than a dozen people were treated for shock and hysteria.

8   Once people began to panic, news of the invasion spread to people who weren't even listening to their radios. A man in Manhattan was one of hundreds fleeing from their homes in fear that New York City was being bombed. Samuel Tishman told reporters from *The New York Times*, "I came home at 9:15 p.m. just in time to receive a telephone call from my nephew who was frantic with fear. He told me the city was about to be bombed from the air and advised me to get out of the building at once. I turned on the radio and heard the broadcast, which **corroborated** what my nephew had said, grabbed my hat and coat and a few personal belongings, and ran to the elevator. When I got to the street there were hundreds of people milling around in panic. Most of us ran toward Broadway, and it was not until we stopped taxi drivers who had heard the entire broadcast on their radios that we knew what it was all about."

Newspapers clamored to tell the story of the panic caused by Welles's broadcast of *The War of the Worlds*.

9   The truth about the broadcast, however, did not spread as quickly or as forcefully as the fear it had inspired. New York police sent out a message stating, "To all receivers: Station WABC informs us that the broadcast just concluded over that station was a dramatization of a play. No cause for alarm." Also, at the end of the broadcast, Welles reminded listeners of its fictional content: "This is Orson Welles, ladies and gentlemen, out of character to assure you that *The War of the Worlds* has no further significance than as the holiday offering it was intended to be. The Mercury Theatre's own radio version of dressing up in a sheet and jumping out of a bush and saying 'Boo!'" But the damage had already been done. People were shocked and outraged when they understood the truth about the broadcast.

On the Defense

10   The Columbia Broadcasting System (CBS) issued a statement saying, "Naturally, it was neither Columbia's nor the Mercury Theatre's intention to mislead anyone, and when it became evident that a part of the audience had been disturbed by the performance, five announcements were read over the network later in the evening to reassure those listeners."

Why were people "shocked and outraged" when they discovered the truth?

Draw a box around the primary sources quoted in paragraphs 9 and 10. What does the author tell you using these primary sources? Record your answers on the **Sources Chart**.

How does the author use information from primary sources in paragraphs 11 and 12? What information do these quotations convey to readers? Record your answers on the **Sources Chart**.

11   In addition, Orson Welles offered his words: "Orson Welles, on behalf of the *Mercury Theatre on the Air*, is deeply regretful to learn that the H. G. Wells fantasy, *The War of the Worlds*, which was designed as entertainment, has caused some **apprehension** among Columbia network listeners. . . . We feared that the classic H. G. Wells story, which has served as inspiration for so many moving pictures, radio serials, and even comic strips might appear too old-fashioned for modern consumption. We can only suppose that the special nature of radio, which is often heard in fragments, or in parts disconnected from the whole, has led to this misunderstanding."

12   Despite these comments, many citizens urged officials at the Federal Communications Commission (FCC) to investigate the broadcast. Frank P. McNinch, chairman of the commission said, "I withhold final judgment until later, but any broadcast that creates such general panic and fear as this one is reported to have done, is, to say the least, regrettable." Yet, after completing an investigation, the FCC ruled on the side of free speech and brought no charges against the broadcasters or Welles.

13   Out of the controversy came success for the creators of the radio program. The Mercury Theatre group received its first sponsor. Two years later, Orson Welles directed and starred in his first feature film, *Citizen Kane*, which won many awards and is considered one of the greatest stories ever told. There were no official reports of moviegoers running in panic from the theaters after watching it.

Defend

Some people thought the members of the Mercury Theatre should be arrested because of their broadcast. Would the chairman of the FCC have agreed? Why or why not?

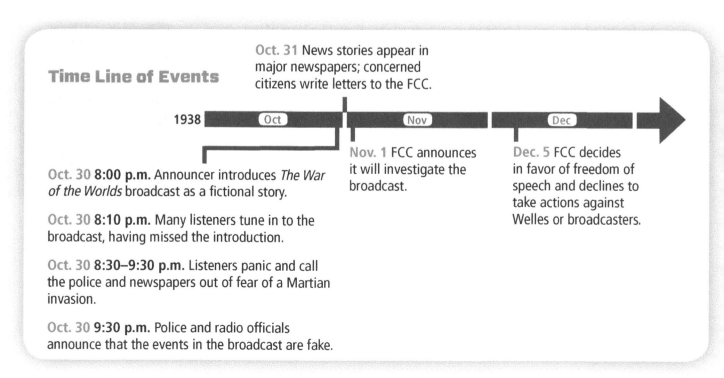

Time Line of Events

Oct. 31 News stories appear in major newspapers; concerned citizens write letters to the FCC.

1938 | Oct | Nov | Dec

Oct. 30 **8:00 p.m.** Announcer introduces *The War of the Worlds* broadcast as a fictional story.

Oct. 30 **8:10 p.m.** Many listeners tune in to the broadcast, having missed the introduction.

Oct. 30 **8:30–9:30 p.m.** Listeners panic and call the police and newspapers out of fear of a Martian invasion.

Oct. 30 **9:30 p.m.** Police and radio officials announce that the events in the broadcast are fake.

Nov. 1 FCC announces it will investigate the broadcast.

Dec. 5 FCC decides in favor of freedom of speech and declines to take actions against Welles or broadcasters.

Vocabulary: Synonyms and Antonyms

The English language often has two or more words that express the same idea. **Synonyms** are words that have almost the same meaning. For example, you can express the idea that you *like* something in a number of ways: you might prefer, enjoy, appreciate, feel attached to, be keen on, or be crazy about it. **Antonyms** have opposite meanings. Here are some antonyms of *like*: *dislike, hate, abhor, detest, loathe,* and *despise.* As you read, notice words that have synonyms or antonyms. Think about how the use of a different word would affect the meaning or tone of the sentence.

Try It Read this sentence from the selection.

> His plan was to update H. G. Wells's classic novel *The War of the Worlds* in a way that would **transfix** his listeners.

One synonym for the word *transfix* is *fascinate*. An antonym is *repel*.

> Discuss   **What are other synonyms for the word *transfix*? Does *transfix* have another antonym?**

The words in the first column appear in "Panic on the Airwaves." Use a dictionary to write the definition of each word. Then use a thesaurus to write a synonym and an antonym for each word.

Word	Definition	Synonym	Antonym
inventive, p. 259			
corroborated, p. 260			
apprehension, p. 262			

Respond to Text: Analyze Primary and Secondary Sources

Think about the letters and article you read. They all refer to the 1938 radio broadcast of *The War of the Worlds*. The letters are primary sources that were written at the time of the event by people who witnessed it. The article is a secondary source written by an author looking back at the broadcast and analyzing its effects on listeners at the time.

Try It Think about what kinds of details each source gives about *The War of the Worlds* broadcast and its effects. Why is it important to read both primary and secondary sources when learning about an event?

 Discuss **Imagine that you have to write a report on *The War of the Worlds*. What information can you gather from each source?**

On Your Own Think about the information provided by the letters and the article. Then consider the differences between them as sources. Write a paragraph in which you analyze the relationship between the primary and secondary sources. Use the guide on the following page to plan your response. Then write your response on a separate sheet of paper.

Checklist for a Good Response

A good paragraph

✔ compares and contrasts the types of information in each source.

✔ considers the author of each source and why the source was written.

✔ analyzes the relationship between a primary source and a secondary source.

✔ includes a topic sentence, supporting details, and a concluding statement.

My Analysis of the Sources

1. **Topic Sentence** Include this information in your topic sentence:

   As primary sources, the letters provide information about _____

   _____ .

   As a secondary source, the article provides information about _____

   _____ .

2. **Detail Sentences** Compare the details in the primary and secondary sources. Use this chart to organize your ideas.

	Primary Source	**Secondary Source**
Dates, Facts, and Quotes		
Authors		
Evidence		

3. **Concluding Sentence** Your concluding sentence should state your analysis of the relationship between the primary and the secondary sources.

   _____

   _____

On a separate sheet of paper, write your analysis.

Mars Attacks / Panic on the Airwaves 265

Read on Your Own

Read the selections independently three times, using the skills you have learned. Then answer the Comprehension Check questions.

(**First Read**) Practice the first-read skills you learned in this lesson.

(**Second Read**) Practice the second-read skills you learned in this lesson.

(**Third Read**) Think critically about the selections.

A Walk on the Moon

Draw Inferences Think about how the people at MCC probably felt as they heard Neil Armstrong come down the ladder and step onto the moon's surface.

Primary Sources (Circle) the names of the people who participated in the event. One has been circled for you. Think about why it is important to know who was involved.

Critical Thinking Think about why Armstrong said, "That's one small step for man; one giant leap for mankind" as he stepped onto the moon's surface.

1   On July 20, 1969, two American astronauts from the Apollo 11 mission became the first men to land and walk on the moon. The following excerpts contain dialogue from the transmissions between the astronauts—Neil Armstrong and Edwin (Buzz) Aldrin, Jr.—and Bruce McCandless at NASA's Mission Control Center (MCC) in Houston, Texas. Excerpt 1 begins as the astronauts maneuver the ladder that will allow them to step from the lunar module onto the moon. Excerpt 2 begins after Armstrong and Aldrin have taken some pictures and samples of the moon's surface.

EXCERPT 1

2   (MCC:) OK. Neil, we can see you coming down the ladder now.

3   ARMSTRONG: OK. I just checked getting back up to that first step, Buzz. It's—not even collapsed too far, but it's adequate to get back up.

4   MCC: Roger. We copy.

5   ARMSTRONG: It takes a pretty good little jump.

6   MCC: Buzz, this is Houston. F/2—1/16th second for shadow photography on the sequence camera.[1]

7   ALDRIN: OK.

8   ARMSTRONG: I'm at the foot of the ladder. . . . I'm going to step off the LM[2] now. That's one small step for man; one giant leap for mankind.

[1]**F/2 ... camera** Mission Control is providing specifications for the equipment Aldrin is setting up.
[2]**LM** Lunar module, the vessel that carried the astronauts and their equipment from the main rocket ship in orbit to the surface of the moon

And the surface is fine and powdery. I can—I can pick it up loosely with my toe. It does adhere in fine layers like powdered charcoal to the sole and sides of my boots. I only go in a small fraction of an inch, maybe an eighth of an inch, but I can see the footprints of my boots and the treads in the fine, sandy particles.

9   MCC: Neil, this is Houston. We're copying.

10 ARMSTRONG: There seems to be no difficulty in moving around . . . It's absolutely no trouble to walk around. OK. The descent engine did not leave a crater of any size. It has about one foot clearance on the ground. We're essentially on a very level place here. I can see some evidence of rays emanating from the descent engine, but a very insignificant amount. OK, Buzz, we ready to bring down the camera?

11 ALDRIN: I'm all ready. I think it's been all squared away and in good shape.

12 ARMSTRONG: OK.

13 ALDRIN: OK. You'll have to pay out all the LEC.[3] It looks like it's coming out nice and evenly.

14 ARMSTRONG: OK. It's quite dark here in the shadow and a little hard for me to see that I have good footing. I'll work my way over into the sunlight here without looking directly into the sun.

15 ALDRIN: OK. It's taut now.

16 ALDRIN: OK. I think you're pulling the wrong one.

17 ARMSTRONG: I'm just . . . OK. I'm ready to pull it down now. There was still a little bit left in the . . .

18 ALDRIN: OK. Don't hold it quite so tight. OK?

19 ARMSTRONG: Looking up at the LM. I'm standing directly in the shadow now, looking up at Buzz in the window. And I can see everything quite clearly. The light is sufficiently bright, backlighted into the front of the LM, that everything is very clearly visible.

[3]**LEC** Lunar equipment conveyer, a ropelike device the astronauts used to transfer equipment from the Lunar Module to the moon's surface; *to pay out* is to unravel or let down

Draw Inferences
What problem are the astronauts dealing with in paragraphs 12–17? Underline the details that tell you.

Primary Sources Think about why these recorded transmissions might be valuable sources for people who are writing a history of the American space program.

EXCERPT 2

20 ALDRIN: Looks like it's a little difficult to dig through the initial crust.

21 ARMSTRONG: This is very interesting. It's a very soft surface, but here and there where I plug with the contingency sample collector, I run into a very hard surface. But it appears to be a very cohesive material of the same sort. I'll try to get a rock in here. Just a couple.

22 ALDRIN: That looks beautiful from here, Neil.

23 ARMSTRONG: It has a stark beauty all its own. It's like much of the high desert of the United States. It's different, but it's very pretty out here. Be advised that a lot of the rock samples out here, the hard rock samples, have what appear to be vesicles[4] in the surface. . . .

24 ALDRIN: OK. The handle is off the . . . in about six or eight inches into the surface. I could . . . easy . . .

25 ARMSTRONG: Yes, it is. I'm sure I could push it in farther, but it's hard for me to bend down farther than that.

26 ALDRIN: Now, you can throw so far.

27 ARMSTRONG: You can really throw things a long way up here.

[4]**vesicles** small cavities or sacs filled with air; Armstrong appears to be warning Aldrin that the rocks might be fragile

Apollo Has Landed

1   On July 20, 1969, two American astronauts who were part of the Apollo 11 mission walked on the moon. The historic touchdown of the *Eagle* landing craft occurred at 4:17:40 p.m. EST and provided the people of Earth with the first personal account of conditions on the moon's surface.

2   Neil Armstrong, mission commander; Edwin E. Aldrin, Jr., lunar module pilot; and Michael Collins, command module pilot, participated in the Apollo 11 mission. Aldrin, known as Buzz, accompanied Armstrong to the surface of the moon, while Collins stayed behind in the command module, *Columbia*.

3   President Nixon congratulated the astronauts as they orbited in space, saying, "Because of what you have done, the heavens have become a part of man's world. And as you talk to us from the Sea of Tranquility[5] it required us to redouble our efforts to bring peace and tranquility to Earth."

4   It was a previous U.S. president who had **initiated** the race to the moon. In 1961, President John F. Kennedy challenged a new federal agency, the National Aeronautics and Space Administration (NASA), to transport a man to the moon before the end of the decade. Soon the United States was in a fierce competition with the Soviet Union to land an astronaut on the moon's surface. Four prior Apollo missions had **paved** the way for Apollo 11's success.

[5]**Sea of Tranquility** a large crater on the surface; the landing site of the Apollo 11 lunar module

> **Draw Inferences** What effect did the astronauts' landing on the moon have on people on Earth? Underline details that help you make this inference.

Secondary Sources
Think about what questions this secondary source answers that the primary source does not.

Critical Thinking
Why was the Apollo 11 mission important? Why do people keep reading and writing about it?

5   The trio of astronauts was launched from the Kennedy Space Center, located outside Orlando, Florida, on July 16. They arrived in lunar orbit three days later, after traversing more than 200,000 miles. While traveling at a speed of 3,660 miles per hour, they completed a full orbit around the moon in approximately two hours.

6   Aldrin and Armstrong then put on special pressurized spacesuits and crawled into the lunar module called *Eagle*. Collins released the hatches connecting the *Eagle* to the main ship, and the two vessels separated. Then Aldrin and Armstrong piloted the lunar module to the far side of the moon and navigated it toward the surface. After landing, they worked to get the ladder in place that would allow them to exit the lunar module. Armstrong climbed down the ladder. As the mission commander, Armstrong had the honor of setting foot on the powdery surface first. It was after he set foot on the moon that he made his now-famous statement: "That's one small step for man; one giant leap for mankind."

7   The Apollo 11 mission to the moon was an American success story, and news of the astronauts' achievements was broadcast in newspapers and on radio and television programs around the world. People everywhere in the world marveled at the accomplishment of safely transporting a human being to the moon and back. For the first time ever, they saw images of Earth as it appears from outer space.

✅ Comprehension Check

1. What is the main idea of the article "Apollo Has Landed"?

   _____

   _____

   _____

2. Why might the transcripts be considered important primary source documents? Who might use them and why?

   _____

   _____

   _____

3. What inference can you make about how the astronauts felt about being the first human beings to land on the moon? Cite textual evidence to support your inference.

   _____

   _____

   _____

4. What information in "Apollo Has Landed" was likely based on primary sources?

   _____

   _____

   _____

5. How do the two texts—the excerpts from the transmissions and the article—complement each other? What did you learn from reading both?

6. Suppose the Apollo 11 mission had been a failure, and Armstrong never walked on the moon. Would people still be interested in reading and writing about it? Explain.

7. The word *initiated* is used in paragraph 4 of "Apollo Has Landed." Write a dictionary entry that includes the part of speech of the word and a definition. Then, use the word in a sentence.

8. Read this sentence from the article.

   Four prior Apollo missions had paved the way for Apollo 11's success.

   Think of a synonym and an antonym for the word *paved*. How does each change the meaning of the sentence?

Glossary

academic vocabulary the words used in schools or informative texts that describe the thinking skills people use when they read about a subject, such as *analyze* or *evaluate*, or words used to connect ideas, such as *moreover* or *nevertheless* (Lesson 7)

act a large section of a long drama, made up of more than one scene (Lesson 3)

affix a word part that comes either before or after a root word and changes the root word's meaning; often derived from Greek or Latin (Lesson 2)

allusion a reference to a commonly known character or situation, often to a myth or to figures from literature or popular culture (Lesson 9)

analogy a type of figurative language; an extended comparison in which one situation or idea is used to reveal information about a similar situation or idea (Lessons 5, 6, 9)

anecdotes short, personal stories that illustrate an idea (Lesson 7)

antonyms words that have opposite meanings, such as *like/dislike* (Lesson 10)

appeal to reason a persuasive appeal that uses logical arguments based on facts, evidence, and expert testimony (Lesson 9)

argument a form of nonfiction writing in which an author seeks to change your mind or influence your opinion using reasons supported by logic, facts, and emotional appeals (Lesson 9)

aside in a drama, when a character speaks dialogue that he or she wants the audience or one character, but not the other characters onstage, to hear (Lesson 3)

ask and answer questions a reading strategy in which you ask yourself *who*, *what*, *when*, *where*, *why*, and *how* questions to help you understand what is going on in a text; the questions can be literal, interpretive, or evaluative (Lessons 2, 8)

author's point of view the author's opinion about a topic, influenced by his or her experiences, cultural background, age, or personal taste (Lesson 5)

author's purpose the author's reason for writing, such as to inform, persuade, explain, or entertain (Lessons 8, 9)

bias the attitudes or beliefs that influence a person's argument despite contrary facts or evidence (Lesson 9)

case studies long-term studies of a single person, thing, group, or event (Lesson 7)

categorization a text structure that orders ideas, events, or people into separate categories to highlight their distinctions (Lesson 6)

cause and effect a text structure that tells the reason for something happening (the cause) and the results of that cause (the effect) (Lesson 6)

characterization the way an author reveals a character's personality—through the character's words, behavior, thoughts, or feelings, as well as through comments made about the character by others in the story (Lesson 3)

chronology a text structure that tells a sequence of events in the order in which they occurred (Lesson 6)

climax the turning point of a story that may involve great physical danger or strong emotions for the main characters (Lesson 1)

compare to identify how two or more things are alike, often signaled by a clue word such as *like*, *similar*, or *same* (Lessons 3, 6)

comparison and contrast a text structure that tells the similarities and differences between ideas, events, or people (Lesson 6)

concluding sentence a sentence that restates the main idea of a paragraph or text (Lesson 7)

connotation the emotion or idea that a word expresses, either negative, positive, or neutral (Lessons 1, 5)

context clues words or phrases near an unknown word that give clues to its meaning (Lessons 1, 5)

contrast to identify how two or more things are different; in a text, signaled by clue words such as *unlike*, *rather than*, *as opposed to*, and *but* (Lessons 3, 6)

counterargument an argument of the opposing side that a good persuasive writer refutes (Lesson 9)

denotation the literal dictionary meaning of a word (Lessons 1, 5)

details information that supports a selection's main idea (Lessons 5, 10)

diagram a drawing with labels that shows technical information, such as the names and locations of specific parts, how the parts might work together, or the steps in a process (Lesson 8)

dialogue words spoken by characters in a text that sometimes reveal their thoughts and reactions to plot events (Lesson 1)

dictionary an alphabetical reference source listing words with their pronunciations, syllabications, parts of speech, and meanings (Lessons 3, 6, 10)

direct quotation the exact words someone has said, enclosed in quotation marks (Lesson 7)

domain-specific vocabulary professional and technical terminology whose use is limited to a particular subject area, kind of work, field of study, activity, or profession (Lessons 6, 8)

drama a play; a story meant to be performed onstage, made up of acts and scenes, and told mainly through the characters' dialogue (Lesson 3)

dramatic irony the tension that exists when the reader knows something that the characters in a text do not know (Lesson 1)

dramatic structure the way in which a play is organized, including acts, scenes, and stage directions (Lesson 3)

draw inferences to decide what the author implies but does not state directly by using the facts and details in the text and your prior knowledge and experience (Lessons 2, 6, 10)

emotional appeal a persuasive appeal that uses strong language to make you angry or excited (Lesson 9)

evaluate to decide whether evidence is reliable, credible, and sufficient, and whether it successfully supports the author's ideas (Lesson 7)

evaluative questions questions that ask you to make a judgment about a text (Lesson 8)

evidence information that supports ideas and opinions, including examples, research and survey results, statistics, case studies, expert opinions, anecdotes, and direct quotations (Lesson 7)

examples specific instances that illustrate a general idea (Lesson 7)

expert opinion a judgment by someone who has researched the specific topic being discussed and is considered to be an authority on the subject (Lesson 7)

exposition a story's beginning, in which the characters and setting are introduced (Lesson 1)

fact a piece of information that can be proved true (Lesson 6)

falling action the point after the climax during which a story begins to wind down (Lesson 1)

fiction a story made up from an author's imagination; forms include short stories, novels, and plays (Lesson 1)

figurative language a word or phrase that means something other than its literal dictionary definition (Lesson 4)

glossary an alphabetized collection of the specialized, unusual, or domain-specific words in a text, usually found at the end of a nonfiction book (Lesson 6)

historical texts a genre of factual writing on historical subjects dependent on the author's effective use of details and specific examples (Lesson 6)

interpretive questions questions that ask about details that the author does not state explicitly in a text (Lesson 8)

literal questions questions that ask for specific details from a text (Lesson 8)

literary nonfiction a genre of writing often called creative nonfiction because it uses the techniques of fiction writing to tell factual stories; includes memoirs, biographies, speeches, and autobiographies (Lesson 5)

main idea the most important concept an author wants to convey, sometimes stated directly in a topic sentence or in the selection title (Lessons 5, 10)

make predictions to consider what has happened so far in a story or in a persuasive argument and to make a forecast about what might happen or be said next, based on what you know about life in general and on what you are reading (Lessons 1, 9)

metaphor a direct comparison between two unlike things that does not use the word *like* or *as* (Lesson 4)

multiple-meaning word a word with more than one meaning; these words may have different pronunciations and might be different parts of speech (Lesson 3)

narrative poem a poem that tells a story with a beginning, middle, and end and has a setting and characters; the lines do not have to rhyme, and the poem may be short or long (Lesson 4)

nuance a small but important shade of meaning in a word (Lesson 7)

opinion a statement of belief or personal feeling that cannot be proved true (Lesson 6)

paragraph structure the organization of a paragraph; traditionally, a topic sentence followed by supporting sentences and a concluding sentence (Lesson 7)

paraphrase to restate a text in your own words (Lesson 4)

personification figurative language that gives human qualities to something that is not human (Lesson 4)

persuasive nonfiction a text, such as a newspaper editorial, political pamphlet, or online blog, that seeks to convince the reader of a particular point of view (Lesson 9)

plot the series of events in a story that includes the characters' actions, a conflict, and a resolution (Lesson 1)

poetry a genre of writing that is separated into lines and often stanzas in which a poet uses descriptive language and sometimes sound devices, such as rhyme and rhythm, to create meaning and produce emotion in the reader (Lesson 4)

point of view the perspective from which a story is told (Lesson 1)

prefix a word part added to the beginning of a word that changes the meaning of the root word (Lesson 2)

primary source a document, speech, image, memoir, or other piece of evidence created by someone who was present when an event happened (Lesson 10)

pun a verbal joke; a play on the multiple meanings of a word or on two words that sound alike but have different meanings (Lesson 9)

reasoned judgment a conclusion based on facts and opinions, supported by relevant and sufficient evidence (Lesson 6)

research and survey results information gathered through scientific investigation (Lesson 7)

resolution a story's end, where conflicts are resolved and loose ends are tied up (Lesson 1)

rhyme scheme the pattern of words that rhyme at the end of each line of poetry (Lesson 4)

rising action the point at which a story's main problem or conflict is introduced and starts to build (Lesson 1)

root the main part of a word that carries its core meaning (Lesson 2)

scene a small unit of a play, sometimes found within an act; the scene often changes when the setting or characters onstage change (Lesson 3)

scientific text a text that provides factual information about a topic that is related to science (Lesson 7)

secondary source writing that depends on information gleaned from primary sources to describe an event and has a broad view of the subject; written after the fact (Lesson 10)

sequence the order in which events in a story take place; in a technical text, the order of steps to follow to complete a process; clue words for determining sequence are *before, after*, *next*, *then*, *last*, and *finally* (Lessons 1, 8)

setting where and when the action of a story takes place, including the geographic location, the physical scenery, the historical time period, and the cultural and social environment (Lesson 2)

simile a comparison between two unlike things that uses the word *like* or *as* (Lesson 4)

sonnet a poem with fourteen lines, usually with an eight-line section that describes a situation or problem and a six-line section that presents a new idea or solution to that problem (Lesson 4)

stage directions in a play, information about setting and about the manner in which characters are to move or speak (Lesson 3)

statistics information in number form (Lesson 7)

suffix a word part added to the end of a word that changes the meaning of the root word (Lesson 2)

summarize to capture and restate the main and essential ideas of a selection while omitting your opinion (Lessons 3, 5, 7)

supporting sentences sentences that contain specific details that support, or explain, the main idea of a paragraph or text; they usually follow the topic sentence (Lesson 7)

synonyms words that have similar meanings (Lessons 4, 10)

technical text a text that explains how things work or how to do things (Lesson 8)

technical vocabulary words and phrases you need to know to understand a specific concept; language that is used in a technical field (Lesson 8)

text structure the way text is organized, such as cause and effect, chronological order, comparison and contrast, analogy, and categorization (Lesson 6)

theme the central message an author wants to convey; either a lesson the author wants to teach or a general observation about life (Lesson 2)

thesaurus a reference source that lists words and their synonyms and antonyms (Lesson 7)

tone an author's attitude or feelings toward the subject of a text, such as humorous, angry, bitter, sad, or joyful (Lessons 4, 5)

topic sentence a statement of the main idea of a paragraph, usually the first sentence of the paragraph (Lesson 7)

traditional literature the myths, folktales, fairy tales, fables, and legends that originated long ago as oral tales and were passed down and later written down (Lesson 2)

verbal irony a literary technique in which what is said contrasts with the literal or usual meaning of the words (Lesson 9)

visualize to use images in a text and prior experience to picture a scene or action (Lesson 4)

word choice the careful selection of words or phrases for sound, meaning, rhythm, or repetition (Lessons 4, 5)

Acknowledgments

Photo Credits 232, 235–236 Department of Defense imagery; 243 Getty Images; 143 History of Medicine (IHM); 98, 137, 141–142, 144, 151–152, 241, 250 Library of Congress; 180, 267, 269–270 NASA; 168–170 National Marine Sanctuaries Media Library; 111 NOAA Photo Library; 31, 59, 85, 92, 123, 125, 131–134, 150, 157, 247 Shutterstock; 97 The Boys of '76; 5, 89–91, 97–99, 101–102, 106, 148–149, 151, 159–160, 163, 175–178, 191, 194–197, 203, 206–208, 219, 223–226, 231, 244, 250–254, 268 Thinkstock; 187 usa.gov; 251–254 U.S. National Archives and Records Administration; 259 Wikimedia Commons.

Illustrations 9–12, 16–17, 19, 20 Christine Chang; 25, 26–28, 42–44 Akbar Ali; 35–38 Piotr Parda; 45–47 Christine Kornacki; 53–56 Craig Orback; 63–65, 71–74 Penny Weber; 79–82 Jeremy Tugeau; 107–108 Fabio Leone; 114–118 Q2A; 126, 167, 185, 213, 216, 261 Peter Bull; 179, 186, 195–198, 201, 204–206 XNR Productions.

Name: _____

Sequence Chart

Page 8   **Page 9**   **Page 11**

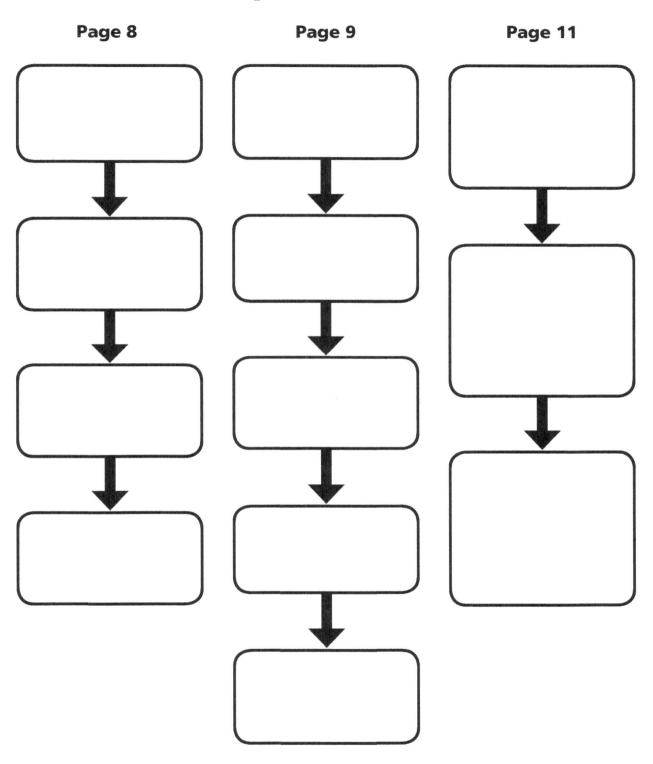

Name: _____

✏️ Close Reading Worksheet

Second Read: Plot Elements (green boxes)

Page 8: The actions that Captain Diaz performs drive the plot by _____

_____

_____.

Page 9: The dialogue sets up the rest of the story by _____

_____

_____.

Page 12: Victor noticing that the boulders are not natural _____

_____

_____.

Third Read: Critical Thinking (blue boxes)

Page 9: Diaz makes the point about the importance of their mission _____

_____.

Page 10: Raquel Shapira's role is to _____

_____.

Page 11: Artie can see ahead because _____

_____.

Synthesize—Page 12: Based on the plot so far and the talents of the characters, the

stone blocks will almost definitely _____

_____

_____.

Name: _____

Make Predictions Chart

My Prediction	Supporting Details	Revised Prediction

Page 16

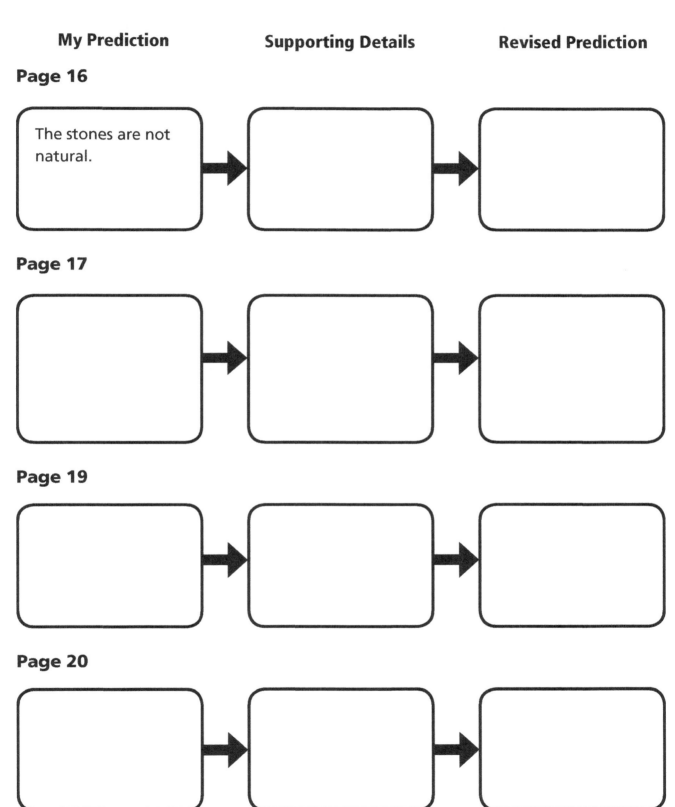

The stones are not natural.

Page 17

Page 19

Page 20

Name: _____

✏️ Close Reading Worksheet

Second Read: Differences in Points of View (green boxes)

Page 17: Most crew members feel _____.

My point of view so far is _____.

Page 18: An example of dramatic irony here is _____

_____

_____.

Page 19: Victor's excitement affects the story by _____

_____.

Third Read: Critical Thinking (blue boxes)

Page 18: Diaz and Paulus are planning for the long term because they realize _____

_____

_____.

Page 20: The narrator never specifies the danger because _____

_____.

Connect—Page 20: The mission succeeds because _____

_____

_____

_____.

Inference Chart

Inference	Support
Page 35: The farmer refuses help because	
Page 35: The farmer feels he has no use for the gold because	
Page 36: The merchant plots revenge against his brother because	
Page 38: The farmer considers the servant worthy of gold because	

Name: _____

✏️ Close Reading Worksheet

Second Read: Analyze Theme (green boxes)

Page 34: Some qualities of the two main characters are _____

_____ and _____.

The theme might be about _____.

Page 36: The theme the author is developing is that _____

_____.

Page 38: The theme of the story is _____

_____.

Third Read: Critical Thinking (blue boxes)

Page 34: The merchant _____

_____.

Page 35: The king considers gold and land a fitting reward for the farmer because

_____

_____.

Page 37: The merchant doesn't order the thieves to kill his brother because _____

_____.

Interpret—Page 38: The purpose of the farmer's telling the servant about the bag of

wisdom is _____

_____.

Name: _____

✏️ Close Reading Worksheet

First Read: Ask and Answer Questions (orange boxes)

Page 44: The elderly gentleman explains to the boy that _____

_____

_____.

Page 46: Savannah enjoys _____

_____.

Page 47: Abaju doesn't want to tell Savannah about Mudjadji because

_____.

Page 48: From the Lovedu rainmaking ceremony, Savannah learns _____

_____

_____.

Third Read: Critical Thinking (blue boxes)

Page 43: The mountain most likely represents _____

_____.

Page 45: Savannah is interested in attending the rainmaking ceremony because

_____.

Analyze—Page 48: The people believe in Mudjadji's power because _____

_____

_____.

Name: _____

Setting Chart

"Thunderbird"

The Brothers' Village and the Mountain	Other Side of the Mountain / Home of the Thunderbirds
Page 42:	Page 43:

"The Power of Rain"

Savannah's Village	Mudjadji's Home
Page 45: Page 46:	Page 47:

Summary Chart

Page 63: Summarize what you know about how Mrs. Twiller and her daughter ended up on the show.	
Page 64: Summarize the exchange between Mrs. Twiller and Dr. Loretta.	
Page 65: Summarize the exchange between the producer and Mrs. Twiller.	
Page 66: Summarize what Amber says about her experience trading places with her mother.	

Name: _____

✏️ Close Reading Worksheet

Second Read: Dramatic Structure (green boxes)

Page 62: The setting tells me _____

_____

_____.

Page 64: The producer speaks in an aside because _____

_____

_____.

Page 66: The turning point comes at the end of scene 1 because _____

_____.

Third Read: Critical Thinking (blue boxes)

Page 62: The producer and the assistant are different because _____

_____

_____.

Page 65: Dr. Loretta is different because _____

_____

_____.

Analyze—Page 66: The author is poking fun at reality shows by _____

_____

_____.

Compare and Contrast Web

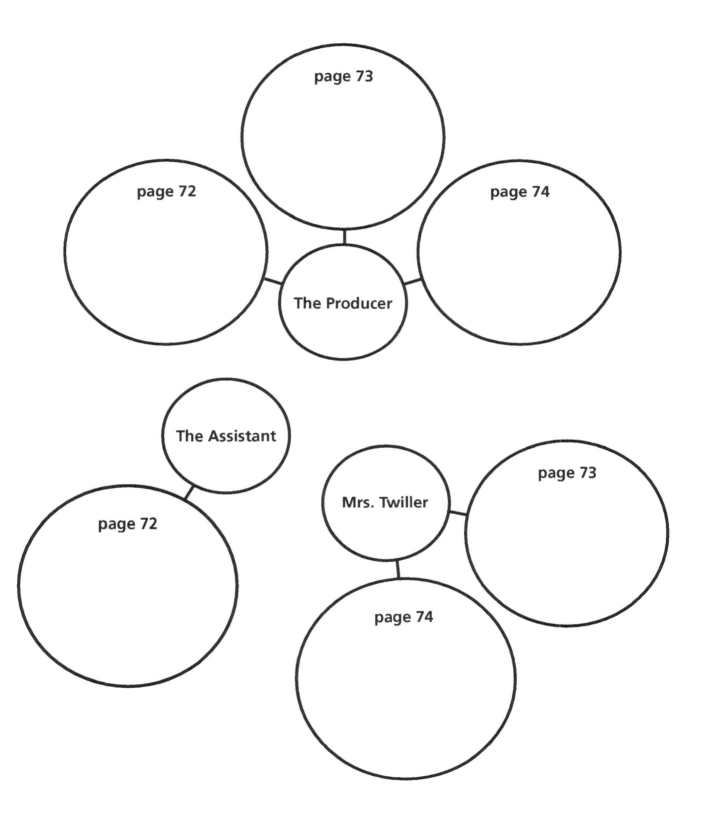

page 73

page 72

page 74

The Producer

The Assistant

page 72

Mrs. Twiller

page 73

page 74

The Setup, Scenes 2 and 3

Name: _____

✏️ Close Reading Worksheet

Second Read: Characterization (green boxes)

Page 70: The escalating conflicts are: _____

_____

_____.

Page 71: At the end of scene 2, the producer _____

_____.

Page 73: The playwright conveys that Mrs. Twiller is humble and caring by _____

_____.

Third Read: Critical Thinking (blue boxes)

Page 70: The girls' behavior contrasts with the producer's expectations because _____

_____.

Page 72: The producer seems to have changed because _____

_____

_____.

Analyze—Page 74: At the end of *The Setup*, the producer's interests seem different

because _____

_____

_____

_____.

Visualization Chart

The War God's Horse Song, p. 88

The War God's Horse Song, p. 89

The Tyger, p. 90

Sea Fever, p. 92

Name: _____

✏️ Close Reading Worksheet

Second Read: Word Choice and Tone (green boxes)

Page 88: The things the horse is compared to suggests a tone that is _____

_____ .

Page 91: The tone of the "The Tyger" is _____ .

The word *burning* makes the tiger seem _____

_____ .

Page 92: The descriptions in "Sea Fever" support the title because _____

_____

_____ .

Third Read: Critical Thinking (blue boxes)

Page 89: "The War God's Horse Song" suggests that traditional Navajo culture

emphasizes values like _____

_____ .

Page 91: The poet means _____

_____

_____ .

Judge—Page 92: The poem with the most powerful visual images is _____

_____ because _____

_____ .

The War God's Horse Song / The Tyger / Sea Fever

Name: _____

✏️ Close Reading Worksheet

Second Read: Paraphrase (orange boxes)

Page 96: Paraphrase "Paul Revere's Ride," lines 6–14. _____

_____

_____.

Page 99: Paraphrase "Paul Revere's Ride," lines 77–80. _____

_____.

These lines are important to the poem as a whole because _____

_____.

Page 100: Paraphrase "Paul Revere's Ride," lines 107–110. _____

_____.

Page 102: Paraphrase "Remember," lines 13–14. _____

_____.

Third Read: Critical Thinking (blue boxes)

Page 96: I could find out if the events of "Paul Revere's Ride" are accurate by

_____.

Page 97: The dead are described as "in their night-encampment" because

_____.

Argue—Page 102: The sonnet is the better poetic structure for this poem because

_____

_____.

Compare Poetic Structures Chart

Poem Feature	"Paul Revere's Ride"	"Remember"
Characters	p. 96: p. 97:	
Setting	p. 96: p. 99:	
Plot	p. 97: p. 98:	
Lines and stanzas	p. 101:	p. 102:
Rhyme scheme	p. 101:	p. 102:

Name: _____

✏️ Close Reading Worksheet

Page 114: The main idea of "Saving the Sun" is that _____

_____.

Page 115: The main ideas the author explains about the royal astronomers are that

_____

_____.

Page 116: The story of Hsi and Ho mainly shows that the ancient Chinese

_____

_____.

Third Read: Critical Thinking (blue boxes)

Page 115: The eclipse monsters in ancient myths took so many different forms because

_____

_____.

Page 116: Meteors and comets were viewed in the same way as eclipses because

_____

_____.

Analyze—Page 118: Scholars and scientists call the bones from ancient China *oracle*

bones because _____

_____

_____.

Word Choice Chart

Word Choice / Analogy	Meaning or Tone
Page 114: Word Choice	**Page 114:** The tone in paragraph 1 is
Page 115: The constellations are compared to The sun is compared to	**Page 115:**
Page 116: Word Choice: dates, sequence, and words such as	**Page 116:** These word choices contribute to a tone.
Page 117: The moon is compared to	**Page 117:**

Page 118: The overall tone of the selection created by the author's word choices is

Summary Chart

Page 122: The most important point in paragraph 1 is

Page 123: Details of how Rowling came up with her ideas

Page 124: Details from the time Rowling was writing her first novel

Page 125: How Rowling came up with her characters

Page 126: Important ideas about Rowling's personal story

Name: _____

✏️ Close Reading Worksheet

Second Read: Author's Point of View (green boxes)

Page 123: The author's point of view about Rowling is that _____

_____.

Page 124: The author seems to feel _____ toward Rowling during the years she struggled to support herself and her daughter.

Page 126: In the context of other classic children's books, the author feels that

Rowling's books _____

_____.

Third Read: Critical Thinking (blue boxes)

Page 122: The author italicizes the word *one* in paragraph 3 because _____

_____

_____.

Page 123: Rowling most likely felt lightheaded when Harry Potter appeared outside

the window of the train because _____

_____

_____.

Analyze—Page 126: The author implies that the genre of fantasy literature _____

_____

_____.

Name: _____

✏️ Close Reading Worksheet

First Read: Draw Inferences (orange boxes)

Page 140: The author probably begins with the scenario to _____

_____.

Page 141: The disease must have spread _____ because _____

_____.

Page 142: The disease was hard to track because _____

_____

_____.

Page 144: The statistics are probably different because _____

_____.

Third Read: Critical Thinking (blue boxes)

Page 140: Ways to find out if the statements are facts or opinions are _____

_____.

Page 143: States probably prohibited spitting because _____

_____.

Argue—Page 144: The disease could have been slowed by _____

_____

_____.

Fact and Opinion Chart

FACT	OPINION
Page 140:	Page 140:
	Page 142:
	Page 143:
Reasoned Judgment—Page 142:	

Name: _____

Compare and Contrast Chart

Compare and Contrast	Similarity	Difference
Page 149: Laymen of different ages		
Page 150: Women in fifteenth century Women in eighteenth century		
Page 151: Women in Victorian era Women in Roaring Twenties		
Page 152: Women in twentieth century Men in twentieth century		

Name: _____

✏️ Close Reading Worksheet

Second Read: Text Structures (green boxes)

Page 148: Paragraph 2 is organized by _____

_____.

Page 149: The information in "Medieval Europe" is organized by _____

_____.

Page 151: The invention of the _____ made styling hair easier. It changed how

people styled their hair because _____.

Third Read: Critical Thinking (blue boxes)

Page 148: The author's point of view is _____

_____.

Page 149: Medieval men's and women's hairstyles were determined by _____

_____.

Page 151: Hollywood was becoming a factor in the 1920s because _____

_____.

Page 152: The author's attitude is _____

_____.

Assess—Page 152: The author's point of view is _____ and the effect of

this is _____

_____.

Name: _____

✏️ Close Reading Worksheet

Page 166: A gyre is _____

_____.

Page 167: When plastic ends up in the ocean, it _____

_____.

Page 169: Scooping up the trash from the garbage patch wouldn't help because

_____

_____.

Page 170: Ways to keep the garbage patch from getting bigger are _____

_____

_____.

Third Read: Critical Thinking (blue boxes)

Page 166: I know the garbage patch is in the (Northern / Southern) Hemisphere

because _____

_____.

Page 168: One way the garbage patch will harm humans is _____

_____.

Connect—Page 170: The "3Rs" can help the local environment by _____

_____

_____.

Types of Evidence Chart

Examples	Research and Survey Results	Statistics
Page 168:		Page 167:
Case Studies	**Expert Opinions**	**Direct Quotations**
		Page 166:

Name: _____

✏️ Close Reading Worksheet

Page 174: The main idea of paragraph 3 is that _____

_____.

It develops the concept from the title by _____

_____.

Page 177: Paragraph 12 is structured _____

_____.

Page 179: The main idea is _____.

GOES and POES _____

_____.

Third Read: Critical Thinking (blue boxes)

Page 175: Fallen power lines contribute to creating fire _____

_____.

Page 176: Examples of human carelessness include _____

_____.

Page 178: The Forest Service used to put out all forest fires because _____

_____.

Evaluate—Page 180: It (is / is not) worth it to spend millions of dollars on high-tech

equipment because _____

_____.

Evaluating Evidence Chart

Piece of Evidence	Reliable	Credible	Sufficient
p. 174, Evidence that two different approaches are necessary			
p. 176, Evidence that humans cause nearly all wildland fires			
p. 177, Evidence that El Niño is responsible for forest fires			
p. 179, Evidence that fire tracking has become high tech			

Count each "yes" answer in each column to give the selection a score from zero to four for that criterion.

Reliable _____   **Credible** _____   **Sufficient** _____

How would you rate the evidence in this selection? What could be done to improve it?

_____

_____

Name: _____

Sequence Chart

Page 195:

Nail the wood together to build the box and use caulk to seal the interior and exterior seams.

Page 196:

Glue the cans into columns and paint them. Then make a header and footer.

Snap the can columns into the header and footer and then place the can columns into the box.

Page 197:

Make a stand that holds it at an angle so it can better collect the sunlight.

Name: _____

✏️ **Close Reading Worksheet**

Second Read : Author's Purpose (green boxes)

Page 197: The optional steps the author suggests are _____

_____.

The author's purpose in adding these steps is _____

_____.

Page 198: The three parts of the text are _____

_____.

Third Read: Critical Thinking (blue boxes)

Page 194: The author implies that _____

_____.

Page 195: The illustrations add to the text by _____

_____.

Page 197: The seal has to be tight so _____.

Evaluate—Page 198: It is worth the time and effort because _____

_____.

Canned Heat: How to Build a Solar Heater

Name: _____

✏️ Close Reading Worksheet

Page 202: A fossil fuel is _____.

Fossil fuels are bad because _____

_____.

Page 203: An electric car is not a good solution because _____

_____.

Page 208: Most future car designs _____

_____.

Third Read: Critical Thinking (blue boxes)

Page 203: Hybrid cars are better because _____

_____.

Page 205: A series hybrid would be useful for city buses because _____

_____

_____.

Page 207: Hybrid designers include these features because _____

_____.

Defend—Page 208: Hybrids are still a better choice because _____

_____

_____

_____.

Graphic Information Organizer

Title of Graphic	Description of Graphic	Information Learned
Page 204: Gas and Electric Car Diagrams		
Page 205: Series Hybrid Car Diagram		
Page 206: Parallel Hybrid Car Diagram		

Name: _____

✏️ Close Reading Worksheet

First Read: Make Predictions (orange boxes)

Page 222: Based on the title and opening quotation, the author will probably argue that

_____.

Page 223: In comparing journalists writing for the Internet versus newspapers, the

author will probably say _____

_____.

Page 224: The author will probably say that (print / the Internet) is more reliable and

true because _____

_____.

Third Read: Critical Thinking (blue boxes)

Page 222: The author might be biased because _____

_____.

Page 225: The values the author holds in highest esteem are _____.

I know because _____.

Analyze—Page 226: Having read the argument, I think the author's role as a newspaper

editor (influenced / did not influence) his point of view because _____

_____

_____

_____.

Argument Evaluation Chart

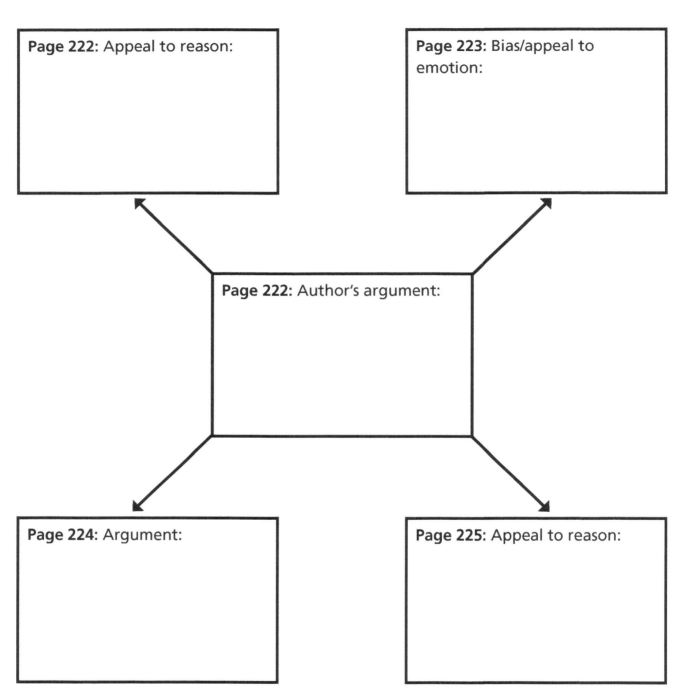

Page 222: Appeal to reason:

Page 223: Bias/appeal to emotion:

Page 222: Author's argument:

Page 224: Argument:

Page 225: Appeal to reason:

Page 226: The author's argument (is / is not) valid and reasonable because

Name: _____

✏️ Close Reading Worksheet

Page 230: The author's purpose in writing this article is that she _____

_____.

Page 232: The detail about Keiko's home in Iceland furthers the author's purpose by

_____.

Page 233: The author shows that her deepest concern is _____

_____.

Page 234: In "Freedom Isn't Free," the author's purpose is to _____

_____.

Page 235: The author's use of humor _____

_____.

Third Read: Critical Thinking (blue boxes)

Page 232: Keiko needed to learn to hunt _____

_____.

Page 235: The author compares Keiko to a king because _____

_____.

Evaluate—Page 236: The essay that does a better job of persuading me is ("Fighting

for Keiko" / "Freedom Isn't Free") because _____

_____.

Argument Chart

Page	Author's Argument	Counterargument	How Author Refutes Counterargument
Fighting for Keiko			
230			
231	Two more *Free Willy* films and at least one documentary followed.		
233		Was the job worth it? Was the whale worth it?	
Freedom Isn't Free			
234	There are worse problems we should solve instead of freeing whales.		
236			

Main Idea Chart

Main Ideas	
Letter from the city manager	**Letter from a listener in South Dakota**
Page 251:	Page 253:

Page 253:

_____

_____

_____

_____

_____

Name: _____

✏️ Close Reading Worksheet

Second Read: Primary Sources (green boxes)

Page 250: I can tell that these are primary sources because _____

_____.

Page 252: The letter answers the questions _____

_____.

Page 253: This letter answers the questions _____

_____.

Third Read: Critical Thinking (blue boxes)

Page 251: The letter writer's purpose was to _____

_____.

Page 251: The letter writer felt _____ because _____

_____.

Page 253: The letter writer thought that the people _____ because

_____

_____.

Argue—Page 254: I think the (first / second) letter writer made a better argument. If

I were a director at the FCC, I would _____

_____

_____.

Name: _____

✏️ Close Reading Worksheet

First Read: Draw Inferences (orange boxes)

Page 258: Based on what I have read, I can infer that Welles was _____

_____ because _____

_____.

Page 260: I think that people called the newspaper because _____

_____.

Page 261: People were probably "shocked and outraged" by the truth because

_____

_____.

Third Read: Critical Thinking (blue boxes)

Page 258: People's worries about a real war might have caused them to _____

_____

_____.

Page 259: The format Welles used probably caused people to think the invasion was real

because _____

_____.

Defend—Page 262: The chairman of the FCC (would / would not) have agreed that

Welles should be arrested because _____

_____.

Name: _____

Sources Chart

	Primary Source	Secondary Source
Page 258		
Page 259		
Page 260		
Page 261		
Page 262		